PORTABILITY
AND THE
C
LANGUAGE

HOWARD W. SAMS & COMPANY
HAYDEN BOOKS

Kochan & Wood's
Hayden Books C Library

Programming in C, Revised Edition
Stephen G. Kochan

Advanced C: Tips and Techniques
Paul Anderson and Gail Anderson

Programming in ANSI C
Stephen G. Kochan

Kochan & Wood's
Hayden Books UNIX® System Library

Topics in C Programming
Stephen G. Kochan, Patrick H. Wood

Related Titles

C Programmer's Guide to NetBIOS
W. David Schwaderer

C Programmer's Guide to Serial Communications
Joe Campbell

QuickC™ Programming for the IBM®
Carl Townsend

Turbo C® Developer's Library
Edward R. Rought and Thomas D. Hoops

C Programmer's Guide to Microsoft® Windows 2.0
Carl Townsend

The Waite Group's Advanced C Primer++
Stephen Prata

The Waite Group's Essential Guide to ANSI C
Naba Barkakati

The Waite Group's Microsoft® C Bible
Naba Barkakati

The Waite Group's Microsoft® C Programming for the IBM®
Robert Lafore

The Waite Group's QuickC™ Bible
Naba Barkakati

The Waite Group's Turbo C® Bible
Naba Barkakati

The Waite Group's Turbo C® Programming for the IBM®
Robert Lafore

For the retailer nearest you, or to order directly from the publisher, call 800-428-SAMS. In Indiana, Alaska, and Hawaii call 317-298-5699.

PORTABILITY AND THE C LANGUAGE

Rex Jaeschke

HAYDEN BOOKS

A Division of Howard W. Sams & Company
4300 West 62nd Street
Indianapolis, Indiana 46268 USA

International Standard Book Number: 0-672-48428-5
Library of Congress Catalog Card Number: 88-62230

Acquisitions Editor: *James S. Hill*
Cover Art: *Meridian Design Studio*
Typesetting: *Pipeline Associates, Inc.*

This entire text was edited and processed under UNIX. The text was formatted using `troff`, with the assistance of `tbl` for the tables. The `troff` output was converted to PostScript using `devps`. The camera ready copy was printed on an Apple LaserWriter Plus, with no pasteup required.

Printed in the United States of America

Hayden Books
C
Library

The C Library is an integrated series of books covering basic to advanced topics related to C programming. The books are written under the direction of Stephen G. Kochan and Patrick H. Wood, who worked for several years teaching introductory and advanced courses at Bell Laboratories, and who themselves have written many books on C programming and the UNIX system.

The first book in the series, *Programming in C*, teaches the fundamentals of C programming. All aspects of the language are covered in this text, and over 90 *complete* program examples are shown with their output.

Topics in C Programming takes up where *Programming in C* leaves off. In this advanced-level book you'll learn more about the subtleties of working with structures and pointers in C. The book also covers the functions provided in the Standard C and Standard I/O Libraries. Of special interest to UNIX programmers are the chapters on the UNIX System Interface Library and on the `curses` routines for writing terminal-independent programs. The `make` program is also covered in the text, and the book describes in detail how to debug programs using tools like `lint`, the preprocessor, `ctrace`, and `sdb`.

Advanced C: Tips and Techniques is an in-depth book on advanced C programming, with special emphasis on portability, execution efficiency, and application techniques. Among the things you'll learn about are: C's run-time environment, debugging techniques, fast array transfers, multidimensional arrays, and dynamic memory allocation. Practical examples are given to demonstrate these techniques.

Programming in ANSI C is for people who want to learn how to write programs in the new ANSI standard C. Using the same approach as *Programming in C*, the book covers all of the features of ANSI C. Over 90 program examples are presented with step-by-step explanations of all the procedures involved.

Contents

Preface

Early in 1986, I was invited to teach a 3-day seminar on portability as it pertained to the C language. The seminar was to be offered in several major cities around the U.S. As it happened, the series was cancelled, but by then I had put together a 70-page manuscript intended for use as class handouts.

Ever since I came to the C fold, I have been fascinated by the apparent contradiction of C being both a low-level systems implementation language yet, somehow, also being a portable one. And every time I heard someone speak, or write, enthusiastically about C's "inherent" portability, I became more uneasy with the fact that either I or a significant part of the C community was missing some major part of the "C picture." As it happens, I don't think it's me although it does seem that a surprising amount of well-written C code can be ported relatively easily.

Driven by the fact that I had a base portability document and an acute interest in the C phenomenon generally, and in the ANSI C Standard and portability in particular, I embarked on a formal and detailed look at C and portability. The fact that I also make a substantial living from consulting in C and teaching introductory and advanced seminars about it added more weight to my decision to develop a serious manuscript for a 3-day portability seminar. Along the way, I decided the end result was worthy of becoming a book, and as you can see, Howard W. Sams & Company agreed. Also, my investigation led to the design and implementation of the portability software suite discussed in Appendix C.

At first I expected to produce about 200 book pages. Then it became 300 and finally 400, but only after I decided to cut quite a few appendices, purely for space reasons. In fact, since the amount and utility of the material left "on the editing room floor" is substantial, I am looking at ways to distribute that as well, perhaps through a future revision, or a companion volume. In any case, this book does not contain *all* my findings.

This book attempts to document C-specific issues you may encounter when porting existing code, or when writing code that is to be ported to numerous target environments. I use the term *attempt* since I don't believe this book provides all the answers, and in many cases it does not even pretend to do so. For example, if you are porting from one flavor of UNIX to another, this book does not discuss all (or in fact any of) the dark corners of that operating system. Nonetheless, I do believe it to be a credible beginning on which future works can be based. It is, as far as I can tell, the first widely published work of more than 20-30 pages that specifically addresses portability as it pertains to C. Since I do not claim to be well-versed in more than 3-4 operating system and hardware environments, I have overlooked some relevant issues. Alternately, I may have overindulged in various esoteric aspects that may occur only in theory.

Whatever your interest in portability is, I hope this book provides some food for thought, even if only to help convince you that portability is not for you. If that is all this book achieves, it will have been wildly successful. If, on the other hand, it helps you define a port strategy, or saves you going down a few wrong roads, then, too, I am happy. Whatever your opinion of this text, let me know since only by getting constructive criticism, outside input, and more personal experience can I improve it in future revisions or in a companion volume. (Contact details are provided in Appendix C.)

Anyone who has ever written a lengthy document that is to be read by more than a few people knows that after the first 2-3 reads, you no longer actually read what is written. You simply read what *should be* there. Therefore, you need technically competent reviewers who can provide constructive criticism. In this regard, the following people made significant contributions by proofing all or major parts of the manuscript: Steve Bartels, Don Bixler, Don Courtney, Dennis Deloria, John Hausman, Bryan Higgs, Gary Jeter, Tom MacDonald, and Sue Meloy. While I implemented many of their suggestions, space and time constraints prohibited me from capitalizing fully on their organizational and other suggestions. But as software vendors say, "We have to leave something to put in the next release."

Others who have had more than a passing influence on my relatively short but intense C career are: P. J. Plauger, ANSI C Secretary, ISO C Convener and President of Whitesmiths Ltd, an international vendor of C and Pascal development tools; Tom Plum, ANSI C Vice-Chair, Chairman of Plum Hall, and leading C author; Larry Rosler, formerly the Editor of the Draft ANSI C Document, and AT&T's principal member on the ANSI C Committee (now of Hewlett-Packard); and Jim Brodie, an independent consultant (formerly of Motorola) who convened the ANSI C Standards Committee in mid-1983 and has so ably chaired it to its (hopefully) successful completion in late 1988 or thereabouts. Also, to my colleagues on the ANSI C X3J11 Standards Committee, I say thanks for the opportunity to work with you all—without your papers, presentations, and sometimes `volatile` (pun intended) discussions both in and out of committee, the quality and quantity of material in this book would have been significantly reduced, perhaps to the point of not being sufficient for publication.

REX JAESCHKE

Reader Assumptions and Advice

This book does not attempt to teach introductory, or even advanced, C constructs. (Nor is it a tutorial on ANSI C.) In fact, at times some paragraphs seem as terse as C itself. Yet while I have attempted to soften such passages, I make no apologies for those that remain. Portability is not something a first time or trainee C programmer embarks on—quite the opposite. Portability in C requires more than a passing background in C, and years of experience are not necessarily a good measure of C expertise. Many programmers with 5-7 years of C experience often know far less about the language than those with 1-2 years. A lot depends on your background and attitude.

The text is aimed specifically at those aspects directly related to porting a C language routine. However, it does not provide a "recipe" for successfully porting a system in any given set of target environments—it merely details many of the problems and situations you may encounter or may need to investigate. The book presumes that you are familiar with the basic constructs of the C language, such as all the operators, statements, and preprocessor directives and that you are fluent with data and function pointers and interfacing with the standard run-time library.

The organization of the text merits some comments. Part I attempts to get you into a portability mindset, addresses some of the misconceptions about C and portability, and helps put portability, as a discipline, in perspective. Part II covers language and preprocessor issues and closely follows the order of sections in the ANSI C Language Standard. In fact, almost all of the chapter, section, and subsection headings are taken directly from that document and are presented in the same order. Part III covers the standard run-time library. While this is one section in the Standard and Rationale, in this book, each header has its own chapter. Part IV provides some useful information, particularly in Appendix B where a detailed list of related reading material is provided as is information about obtaining a copy of the ANSI C Standard. Also, the optional portability software suite is briefly described.

You may notice a small amount of duplication. This is intentional since I decided to organize it that way rather than to have you chase down critical and related information via forward references.

Note also, that I have not always used the "new style" of declaring and defining functions, or other ANSI "goodies." This is not an oversight but, rather, a deliberate choice. The reason for this is simple. Since there is not yet an ANSI C Standard, no implementation yet conforms, and many C implementations support few (if any) of the additions and/or changes introduced by that Standard. Also, many people porting code may be doing so from one non-ANSI compiler to another.

Since the Standard, its accompanying Rationale document, and this text have the same basic organization, having a copy of each is advantageous, although not completely necessary since the Standard can be "heavy going." However, the Rationale is much more leisurely paced and readable by the non-linguist. Note though that, having participated in the deliberations of the ANSI committee for four years, my vocabulary reflects that of the C Standard. Therefore, a copy of that document will prove very useful.

Just for the record, all references (unless otherwise stated) to K&R refer to the first edition (1978) of Kernighan and Ritchie's book since, at the time of writing, that was THE K&R. Also, all references to ANSI C are actually references to the *Draft ANSI C Standard* dated May 13th, 1988. This is the version of the Standard made available for the third public comment period. It is expected there will be little (if any) difference between this document and the final Standard.

Numerous references to acronyms, abbreviations, and specialized terms are made throughout the book. Most are in common use in the C industry today; however, some are defined here (their definitions taken verbatim from the ANSI C Standard) in case they are new to you:

- *Unspecified behavior* - Behavior, for a correct program construct and correct data, for which the Standard imposes no requirements.

- *Undefined behavior* - Behavior, upon use of a nonportable or erroneous program construct, of erroneous data, or of indeterminately valued objects, for which the Standard imposes no requirements. Permissible undefined behavior ranges from ignoring the situation completely with unpredictable results to behaving during translation or program execution in a documented manner characteristic of the environment (with or without the issuance of a diagnostic message), to terminating a translation or execution (with the issuance of a diagnostic message).

    If a "shall" or "shall not" requirement that appears outside of a constraint is violated, the behavior is undefined. Undefined behavior is otherwise indicated in the Standard by the words "undefined behavior" or by the omission of any explicit definition of behavior. There is no difference in emphasis among these three; they all describe "behavior that is undefined."

- *Implementation-defined behavior* - Behavior, for a correct program construct and correct data, that depends on the characteristics of the implementation and that each implementation shall document.

- *Locale-specific behavior* - Behavior that depends on local conventions of nationality, culture, and language that each implementation shall document.

- *lvalue* - An expression (with an object type or an incomplete type other than `void`) that designates an object. When an object is said to have a particular type, the type is specified by the lvalue used to designate the object.

  (The name "lvalue" comes originally from the assignment expression `E1` = `E2`, in which the left operand `E1` must be a (modifiable) lvalue. It is perhaps better considered as representing an object "locator value." What is sometimes called "rvalue" is in the Standard described as the "value of an expression." An obvious example of an lvalue is an identifier of an object. As a further example, if `E` is a unary expression that is a pointer to an object, `*E` is an lvalue that designates the object to which `E` points.)

- *Modifiable lvalue* - An lvalue that does not have array type, does not have an incomplete type, does not have a `const`-qualified type, and, if it is a structure or union, does not have any member (including, recursively, any member of all contained structures or unions) with a `const`-qualified type.

- *Multibyte character* - A sequence of one or more bytes representing a single character in the extended character set of either the source or the execution environment. The extended character set is a superset of the basic character set.

- *Compiler* - This term is usually used to mean a C language translator and includes such tools as interpreters and incremental compilers as well. When some aspect is peculiar to one or more of these specific tools, this is so stated.

- *ANSI* - This organization is the American National Standards Institute. It is the focal point for standards for numerous industries including those related to data processing hardware and software. The ANSI X3 Secretariat oversees Data Processing with the X3J11 Committee being designated as the group standardizing the C language. X3J11 is the committee and ANSI C is their product.

- *POSIX* - Another ANSI standards group is IEEE, the Institute for Electrical and Electronic Engineers. One of their committees, P1003, is chartered with forming a standard for a portable operating system definition based on UNIX. This system is known as POSIX.

- *SVID* - The base documents used by X3J11 and P1003 came from AT&T who has developed its own *de facto* Standard. This standard is known as the System V Interface Definition (SVID).

- *X/OPEN* - This is a hardware and software consortium involved in operating system, language, and applications development tool standardization. It is building on existing *de facto* and official standards.

The ANSI C Standard contains a more complete list of definitions and, in particular, discusses the criteria for conformance of programs and implementations. It also introduces the term *obsolescent*, which identifies certain existing practices as "frowned upon" now that a (presumably) better alternative has been made available.

The various standards and documents mentioned above are discussed further in Appendix B.

Introduction and Overview

1

Introduction

✦ Defining Portability ✦

How many times have you heard the statement "C is a portable language"? Given the large number of meanings, such a claim might imply the statement is, at best, vacuous. That is, for such a claim to make sense, one must define what they mean by portability.

According to *The Prentice-Hall Standard Glossary of Computer Terminology* by Robert A. Edmunds, portability is defined as follows. *Portability: A term related to compatibility. Portability determines the degree to which a program or other software can be moved from one computer system to another.* The key phrase here is "the degree to which a program can be moved."

We can talk about portability from two points of view: generic and specific. Generically, portability simply means running a program in a host environment that is somehow different from the one for which it was designed. Since the cost of producing and maintaining software far outweighs that for producing hardware, we have a huge incentive to increase the shelf life of our software beyond the current incarnations of hardware. It simply makes economic sense to do so.

Specific portability involves identifying the individual target environments in which a given program must run and clearly stating how those environments differ. Some examples of port scenarios follow:

- Moving from one operating system to another on the same machine (VAX Ultrix or UNIX to VAX/VMS; IBM MVS to VM/CMS; DEC's RSTS to RSX)

- Moving from a version of an operating system on one machine to the same operating system on another machine (UNIX on an AT&T Bell 3B2 to a VAX)

- Moving between variants of the same operating system (BSD4.x UNIX to System III or System V UNIX or to XENIX; PC-DOS to MS-DOS)

- Moving between two entirely different hardware and software environments (Honeywell GCOS to Cray COS)

- Moving between different compilers on the same system (Lattice C to Microsoft C under MS-DOS)

- Moving from one version of a compiler to another version of the same compiler

The last scenario may seem out of place. However, it is common to encounter problems when taking existing code that compiles without error, runs, and does the job adequately and running it through a new version of the same compiler. The impact of the upgrade can vary from none to traumatic depending on how well the original code was written and the kinds of extra checking, new features, etc., that exist in the new compiler. While it can be argued that such upgrades are not typically traumatic, this situation is changing with the advent of the ANSI C Standard.

Perhaps the most noticeable aspect of such an upgrade is the ANSI C requirement that you be overt when mixing pointers of one type with another or with pointers and integer types or with pointers to data and pointers to functions.

Recommendation: Since ANSI C is a significantly different environment compared to all existing non-ANSI C environments, the task of upgrading to an ANSI C compiler (or one that has just implemented the bulk of ANSI C for the first time) should be considered as a port project, if you ever intend to recompile existing code with the new compiler in ANSI-mode.

There are even more subtle situations that really involve porting yet are not often recognized as such. One such example involves programming on MS-DOS systems that support various memory models. Consider the case where you develop an application in the small memory model, where all pointers are 16 bits. Eventually, adding extra code and/or data forces you to compile using another model. If data pointers now require 32 bits, you can no longer store such a pointer in an `int`, and `register` declarations of such pointers may be ignored since registers are only 16 bits long. Also, twice as much storage space is needed on the heap and the stack for data pointers that are automatically and dynamically allocated. And if you hard-coded the number of bytes to allocate as 20 instead of 10 times `sizeof(char *)`, your program will likely fail in mysterious ways.

Porting just doesn't involve getting a piece of software to work on multiple targets. It also involves doing so with a reasonable (and affordable) amount of resources, in a timely manner, and in such a way that the resulting code will perform adequately. There is little point in porting a system to a target such that when the port is complete, it runs so slowly or uses so many system resources, it is rendered unusable.

Important questions to ask yourself are:

- Am I porting to or from an ANSI C compiler? If so, are all targets ANSI-conforming?

- Am I porting code that was designed and written with portability in mind?

- Do I have the luxury of starting completely from scratch?

- Do I know what all the target environments will be up front and how many of them I will actually have available for testing?

- What are my performance requirements regarding speed, memory, and disk efficiency?

◆ Portability Is Not New ◆

C is a relatively new programming language and since it has spawned a whole generation of programmers, many of its advocates likely have spent little, if any, time working with many other languages. Along with the wide availability of good and cheap C compilers and development tools in the early 1980s, the idea of software portability has become popular. So much so that, to hear some people talk, portability became possible because of C.

The plain and simple facts are that the notion of portability is much older than C and that software was being successfully ported long before C (presumably) became an idea in Ritchie's head. In 1959, a small group defined a standard business language called COBOL, and in 1960, two vendors (Remington Rand and RCA) implemented compilers for that language. In December of that year, they conducted an experiment where they exchanged COBOL programs, and according to Jean E. Sammet, a member of the COBOL design team, "with only a minimum number of modifications primarily due to differences in implementation, the programs were run on both machines." Regarding COBOL's development of a description for data that is logically machine independent, Sammet wrote in 1969, "[COBOL] does not simultaneously preserve efficiency and compatibility across machines." It is the author's opinion that this statement holds true today for all languages commonly used as a portability vehicle.

The fact that a program was written in C provides no indication whatsoever as to the effort required to port it. The task may be trivial, difficult, impossible, or uneconomical. Given that a program was written in any language without regard to the possibility of its being ported to some different host environment, the ease with which it may actually be ported to that environment probably depends more on the discipline and idiosyncrasies of its author, than on the language itself. That is, porting an existing C program may inherently be no easier than porting any other language program. In fact, given C's strengths (and its initial purpose) in system programming, the idea of a low-level implementation language such as C being portable is inherently contradictory.

Designing a program to be portable over a range of environments, of which some may not yet be defined, may be difficult, but it is not impossible. It just requires considerable discipline and a good dose of common sense. The main aim in such a project is not to write a program that will run on any system without modification, but to isolate environment-specific functions so they may be rewritten for new systems. The major portability considerations are much the same for any language. Only the specific implementation details are determined by the actual language used.

♦ Who Needs Portability? ♦

There is no doubt that portability is a specialized topic and one that is not often implemented either because it is not deemed necessary or desirable or because the required resources are not available. In order to put the idea of portability in perspective, the author has developed a crude rule of thumb regarding its need and rate of success. The rule is, that perhaps no more than 5% of the programs being written are required to run in more than one environment, and of those 5%, only 5% are likely to be implemented successfully in more than one environment without a significant rewrite along the way. The intersection of these percentages is 0.25%, which indicates a fairly rarefied atmosphere. Even if the success rate were 100% of 5%, the requirement for portability is still very low.

Despite this, it has been this author's experience that perhaps seven (or more) out of ten people choosing C as the language for a given project, or as the strategic language for their company's future, cite portability as a major factor in arriving at that decision. Portability should become a factor only if it is, or is likely to be, required by the project being implemented. Unfortunately, this is not often the case. Not only is portability irrelevant for most C projects, it is also very likely that C itself is not the most appropriate language, but that topic is outside the scope of this book.

♦ The Economics of Portability ♦

Two main requirements for being successful at porting are: having the necessary technical expertise and tools for the job and having management support as well as approval.

Clearly, one needs to have, or be able to get and keep, good C programmers. The term *good* does not imply guru status alone or at all since such staff can often have egos that are difficult to manage. And perhaps the most important attribute required in a successful port project is discipline both at the individual and the group levels. So even if the technicians are not stellar, the project can succeed if the project manager is experienced and well disciplined.

The issue of management support is often more important, yet it is largely ignored both by the developers and by management itself. The following (not atypical) example should demonstrate the problem.

A software company decides to develop a commercial package in C that will run on both MS-DOS and UNIX systems. A main part of the rationale is that these systems represent a significant piece of the retail market permitting a potentially large number of units to be sold.

Now due to the relatively low cost of MS-DOS-class machines, system software, and tools, each programmer has his or her own DOS system. And expanding the team is as easy as getting another PC configuration. No developer impacts any other developer since each has his or her own development resource. Perhaps the systems are even linked using some form of local area network (LAN) so resources can be shared.

Regardless of good intent, an implied order of precedence almost always exists when it comes to selecting the target environments. And if such an order exists, either firmly stated or simply "understood," this should be made known and accepted. In this example, the company may well be "interested" in the UNIX market because it seems to be large and growing, yet this same company won't spend, for example, the $30,000 or so up front needed for a MicroVAX and UNIX System V license. That is, supporting UNIX "would be nice, but we're not quite sure, yet."

So, the developers implement XENIX (a UNIX derivative) on one of their 80x86 systems so they can test the C sources. Now while this permits the code to be run under XENIX, it by no means is tested against UNIX System V (given that XENIX is not currently System V-conformant). And since XENIX runs on the same processor as their DOS versions, the developers do not run into machine-specific issues. So even if the project is completed and runs on both DOS and XENIX, this is no guarantee it will run on another derivative of UNIX or, indeed, a version of XENIX running on another processor family.

A second possibility is that adequate hardware and software is provided for all (or a representative subset) of the specified target environments and the development group religiously runs all its code through all targets at least weekly. Often, it submits a test stream in batch every evening.

Six months into the project, management reviews progress and finds that the project is taking more resources than anticipated (doesn't it always?) and decides to narrow the set of targets, at least on a temporary basis. That is, "we have to have something tangible to demonstrate at tradeshows since we have already announced the product" or "the venture capitalists are expecting to see a prototype at the next board meeting." Whatever the reasons, testing on, and development specifically for, certain targets is suspended, often permanently.

From that point on, the development group must ignore the idiosyncrasies of the dropped machines since they are no longer part of the project and the company can't afford the extra resources to consider them seriously. Of course, management's suggestion is typically "while we don't want you to go out of your way to support the dropped environments, it would be nice if you don't do anything to make it impossible or inefficient for us to pick them up again at some later date." That is, "do what you can, but we're not going to give you the resources to do the job properly."

Of course, as the project slips even further, competitors announce and/or ship alternative products, or the company falls on hard economic times, other targets may also be dropped, possibly leaving only one since that is all that development and marketing can support. And each time it drops a target, the development group starts to "cut corners" since it no longer has to worry about "that particular piece of deficient" hardware and/or operating system. Ultimately, this decreases the chances of ever starting up on dropped targets at some later date as all code designed and written since support for those targets was dropped needs to be inspected (assuming, of course, that this code can even be identified) to ascertain the effort required and the impact on resuming that target. You may well find that certain design decisions that were made either prohibit or negatively impact reactivating the abandoned project(s).

The end result often is that the product is initially delivered for one target only and is never made available in any other environment. Another common situation is to deliver for one target and then go back and salvage "as much as possible" for one or more other targets. In such cases, the project may be no different than one in which you are porting code that was never designed with portability in mind.

A third situation occurs when you try to anticipate what a specific target (or family of targets) will require from a portability viewpoint. This can happen because either you have abandoned that target or it is perceived as being a long-term possibility. (For example, you might try to develop software that will run on any twos-complement, ASCII, byte architectures with word sizes of 16, 32, or 64 bits.) Whatever the reason, this is usually an untenable situation both because you can't know everything there is to know without actually experimenting, and because support for this "optional" target is not officially sanctioned.

♦ Measuring Portability ♦

How do you know when or if a system has been successfully ported? Is it when the code compiles and links without error? Is it when the same output is produced by all targets?

Certainly, the code must compile and link without error, but because of implementation-defined behavior it may be quite possible to get different results from different targets. The legitimate results may even be sufficiently different as to render them useless. For example, floating-point range and precision may vary considerably from one target to the next such that results produced by the most limited floating-point environment are not precise enough. Of course, this is a design consideration and should be considered before the system is ported.

A general misconception is that exactly the same source code files must be used on all targets such that the files are full of conditionally compiled lines. This need not be the case at all. Certainly, you may require custom headers for some targets. You may also require system-specific code written in C, and possibly in assembler or other languages. Provided such code is isolated in separate modules and the contents of, and the interfaces to, such modules is well documented, this approach need not be a problem—in fact, it may well be necessary.

If you are using the same data files across multiple targets, you will need to ensure that the data is ported correctly, particularly if it is stored in binary rather than text format. If you do not, you may waste considerable resources looking for code bugs that do not, in fact, exist.

The bottom line is that, unless you have adequately defined what your specific portability scenario is, you cannot tell when you have achieved it. And by definition, if you achieve it, you must be satisfied. If you are not, your requirements have either changed, or your design was flawed. And most importantly, successfully porting a program to some given number of environments is not necessarily a reliable indication of the work involved in porting it to yet another target.

♦ The Porting Toolbox ♦

A number of basic tools are necessary or desirable when porting code. Even though most of them may be obvious, they are listed nonetheless.

- A full-screen text editor and preferably with some knowledge about the C language. For example, when you enter a left brace, it can be programmed to insert a new-line and indent the next line by an extra horizontal tab.

- A code beautifier or reformatter is used to make code produced by different developers, or by the same developer on different occasions, look consistent and be easily recognized during maintenance.

- A source code pagination and listing utility preferably with a cross-reference capability that shows not only where each identifier is used and its type, class, and other declaration attributes but also whether it is used as a modifiable lvalue.

- A `lint`-like static analysis tool that performs code quality checking beyond that provided by most compilers.

- A C compiler that provides more than just fatal error messages. *Quality of implementation* is a term that was discussed often at ANSI C meetings as the reason for not putting something in the C Standard. So whether your compiler provides warning or informational messages is up to the implementer. Various other compile-time options are highly desirable. They include: the ability to extract function prototypes from source input files and the ability to view not only the final output produced from the preprocessor but also intermediate stages of macro expansion when macros are nested. The ability to save preprocessor output as a file suitable for input to the compiler (without modification) is useful as is the ability to have the preprocessor preserve all whitespace (including comments).

- A symbolic debugger that permits debugging at the C source level. This implies that it is case-sensitive and can handle the same length identifiers the compiler produces, as well as variables that happen to be optimized into registers.

- A make-like system build facility to ensure quality assurance when source modules and/or headers are changed.

- A source code control system to maintain sources, headers, and compilation and build procedures, in a project involving a large number of modules and/or programmers.

- A grep-like text search tool that can be used to search a file (or set of files) for a given text string or series of adjacent C tokens.

- Communications software (or other media) that permits reliable transmission and/or conversion of source and data from one target to another.

- Some type of list management tool that permits you to maintain an on-line data base of external identifiers currently in use by user-written source, or reserved by your compilers and third-party libraries and tools. Not only should a user be able to find if a particular name is in use or reserved, they should also be able to enquire about specific spelling patterns such as wnd*, for example, where * represents an unlimited length text string, possibly of length zero.

♦ Environmental Issues ♦

As pointed out elsewhere in this chapter, many portability issues have little or nothing to do with the implementation language. Rather, such issues are relevant to the hardware and operating system environments on which the program must execute. Many of these issues are hinted at in the main body of this book, but they are summarized here as follows:

- Mixed language environments. Certain requirements may be placed on C code that is to call, or be called by, some other language processor. For example, calling VAX C from VAX Fortran (or any other VAX language using the CALLG calling instruction) on VAX/VMS requires the called C function to treat its formal argument list as read-only. It cannot assume such arguments exist as copies on the stack, since this is not the case. Similarly, calling Microsoft Fortran, Pascal, or Quick Basic from Microsoft C requires the use of extended keywords and/or the use of special compile-time switches so the stack setup and cleanup mechanism used across function calls is compatible.

- Command-line processing. Not only do different command-line processors vary widely in their behavior, but the equivalent of a command-line processor may not even exist for some of your targets.

- Data representation. This is, of course, completely implementation-defined and may vary widely. Not only can the size of an `int` differ across your targets, but you are not even guaranteed that all bits allocated to an object are used to represent the value of that object. For example, on a Cray super-computer, `sizeof(short)` is 8 yet only 24 of the 64 bits allocated are used to represent the `short int` value. Another significant problem is the ordering of bytes within words and words within longwords. Such encoding schemes are often referred to as *big-endian* or *little-endian*. Also, this has been referred to as the NUXI problem, indicating the possible ordering of the letters when the word UNIX is stored in a 4-byte quantity. (Refer to Appendix B for references on this topic.)

- CPU speed. It is a common practice to "know" that executing an empty loop *n* times in a given environment causes a pause of 5 seconds, for example. However, running the same program on an Intel 80386 instead of an 8088 will invalidate this approach. (The same is true when running it on versions of the same processor having different clock speeds.) Or perhaps the timing is slightly different when more (or less) programs are running on the same system. Related issues include the frequency and efficiency of handling timer interrupts, both hardware and software.

- Operating system. The principal issues here are single- versus multi-tasking and fixed- versus virtual-memory organization. Other issues involve the ability to field synchronous and asynchronous interrupts, the existence of reentrant code, and shared memory. Seemingly simple tasks such as getting the system date and time may be impossible on some systems. Certainly, the granularity of system time measurement varies widely.

- File systems. Whether multiple versions of the same file can coexist or whether the date and time of creation or last modification are stored, is implementation-defined. Likewise for the character set permitted in file names and whether or not such names are case-sensitive. And as for device and directory-naming conventions, the variations are as broad as their inventor's imaginations. Consequently, the ANSI C Standard says nothing about file systems except for sequential files being accessed by a single user.

- Development support tools. These necessary tools may have a significant impact on the way you write, or are required to write, code for a given system. They include: C translator, linker, object and source librarian, assembler, source code management system, macro preprocessors, and utility libraries. Examples of restrictions include the casing, significance, and number of external identifiers; perhaps even the size of each object module or the number and size of source modules. Perhaps the overlay linker has significant restrictions on the complexity of the overlay scheme.

- Compiler optimization. Many C programmers "know," for example, that i++ is more efficient that i = i + 1 and that certain unreadable expressions involving numerous comma and conditional operators are "necessary" for efficiency reasons. While this can, in fact, be true, it is often not the case. Optimization technology is sufficiently advanced that what used to be the case on your old compiler 3-5 years ago is almost certainly no longer true. For example, as predicted by Ritchie in 1978, the register storage class is ignored by most compilers since they are better equipped than most programmers to decide just which variables are used more often than others.

  Not only can different code be generated when you upgrade your compiler (or simply use different optimization command-line switches), it may also result with the same compiler when a few lines of code and/or data are added or removed since, now, the optimizer views the code from a different perspective.

- Cross-compilation. In environments where the target is not the system on which the software is being developed, differences in character sets and arithmetic representations become important.

- Screen and keyboard devices. The protocols used by these vary widely. While many implement some or all of various ANSI standards, just as many do not or contain incompatible extensions. Getting a character from standard input without echoing it, or without needing to press the return or enter key as well, is not universally possible. The same is true for direct cursor addressing and graphics display and input devices such as light pens, track balls, and mice.

- Other peripheral interfaces. Your design may call for interactions with printers, plotters, scanners, and modems, among other pieces of equipment. While some *de facto* standards may exist for each, you may be forced, for one reason or another, to adopt "slightly" incompatible pieces. And beware of compatibility claims. For example, the Victor 9000 was a PC-compatible system except for the "minor" facts that it could neither read nor write PC-DOS-compatible diskettes and that its video interface was different. DEC's Rainbow was likewise "PC-compatible."

◆ Programmer Portability ◆

In all the discussions on portability, we continually refer to the aspect of moving code from one environment to another. And while this is an important consideration, it is more likely that C programmers will move to a different environment more often than the software they write. For this reason, the author has coined the term *programmer portability*.

Programmer portability can be defined as the ease with which a C programmer can move from one environment to another. This is an issue important to any C project, not just those involving code portability. If you adopt certain programming strategies and styles, you can make it much easier and quicker to integrate new team members into the project. Note though that, while you may have formulated a very powerful approach, if it is too far from the mainstream C practice, it will either be difficult and/or expensive to teach or to convince other C programmers of its merits. An example of this could be the use of mixed-case identifier names or the use of macro names spelled entirely in lower-case.

The C Language and Preprocessor

HOWARD W. SAMS & COMPANY

Bookmark

DEAR VALUED CUSTOMER:

Howard W. Sams & Company is dedicated to bringing you timely and authoritative books for your personal and professional library. Our goal is to provide you with excellent technical books written by the most qualified authors. You can assist us in this endeavor by checking the box next to your particular areas of interest.

We appreciate your comments and will use the information to provide you with a more comprehensive selection of titles.

Thank you,

Vice President, Book Publishing
Howard W. Sams & Company

COMPUTER TITLES:

Hardware
- ☐ Apple 140   ☐ Macintosh 101
- ☐ Commodore 110
- ☐ IBM & Compatibles 114

Business Applications
- ☐ Word Processing J01
- ☐ Data Base J04
- ☐ Spreadsheets J02

Operating Systems
- ☐ MS-DOS K05   ☐ OS/2 K10
- ☐ CP/M K01   ☐ UNIX K03

Programming Languages
- ☐ C L03   ☐ Pascal L05
- ☐ Prolog L12   ☐ Assembly L01
- ☐ BASIC L02   ☐ HyperTalk L14

Troubleshooting & Repair
- ☐ Computers S05
- ☐ Peripherals S10

Other
- ☐ Communications/Networking M03
- ☐ AI/Expert Systems T18

ELECTRONICS TITLES:
- ☐ Amateur Radio T01
- ☐ Audio T03
- ☐ Basic Electronics T20
- ☐ Basic Electricity T21
- ☐ Electronics Design T12
- ☐ Electronics Projects T04
- ☐ Satellites T09

- ☐ Instrumentation T05
- ☐ Digital Electronics T11

Troubleshooting & Repair
- ☐ Audio S11   ☐ Television S04
- ☐ VCR S01   ☐ Compact Disc S02
- ☐ Automotive S06
- ☐ Microwave Oven S03

Other interests or comments: _____
_____
_____

Name_____
Title _____
Company _____
Address _____
City _____
State/Zip _____
Daytime Telephone No. _____

A Division of Macmillan, Inc.

4300 West 62nd Street   Indianapolis, Indiana 46268   **48428**

Bookmark

*HOWARD W. SAMS
& COMPANY*

C Programmer's Guide to NetBIOS

W. David Schwaderer
ISBN: 0-672-22638-3, $24.95

C Programmer's Guide to Serial Communications

Joe Campbell
ISBN: 0-672-22584-0, $26.95

QuickC™ Programming for the IBM®

Carl Townsend
ISBN: 0-672-22622-7, $22.95

Turbo C® Developer's Library

Edward R. Rought and Thomas D. Hoops
ISBN: 0-672-22642-1, $24.95

C Programmer's Guide to Microsoft® Windows 2.0

Carl Townsend
ISBN: 0-672-22621-9, $24.95

The Waite Group's Advanced C Primer++

Stephen Prata
ISBN: 0-672-22486-0, $24.95

The Waite Group's Essential Guide to ANSI C

Naba Barkakati
ISBN: 0-672-22673-1, $6.95

The Waite Group's Microsoft® C Bible

Naba Barkakati
ISBN: 0-672-22620-0, $24.95

The Waite Group's Microsoft® C Programming for the IBM®

Robert Lafore
ISBN: 0-672-22515-8, $24.95

The Waite Group's QuickC™ Bible

Naba Barkakati
ISBN: 0-672-22632-4, $24.95

(more titles on the back)

To order, return the card below, or call 1-800-428-SAMS. In Indiana call (317) 298-5566.

Please send me the books listed below.

Title	Quant.	ISBN #	Price

☐ Please add my name to your mailing list to receive more information on related titles.

Name (please print) _____

Address _____

City _____

State/Zip _____

Signature _____
(required for credit card purchase)

Telephone # _____

Subtotal _____

Standard Postage and Handling __**$2.50**__

All States Add Appropriate Sales Tax _____

TOTAL _____

Enclosed is My Check or Money Order for $ _____

Charge my Credit Card: ☐ VISA   ☐ MC   ☐ AE

Account No. _____   Expiration Date _____

☐☐☐☐ ☐☐☐☐ ☐☐☐☐ ☐☐☐☐

48428

The Waite Group's Turbo C®
Bible
Naba Barkakati
ISBN: 0-672-22631-6, $24.95

The Waite Group's Turbo C®
Programming for the IBM®
Robert Lafore
ISBN: 0-672-22614-6, $22.95

Programming in C, Revised
Edition
Stephen G. Kochan
ISBN: 0-672-48420-X, $24.95

Programming in ANSI C
Stephen G. Kochan
ISBN: 0-672-48408-0, $24.95

Advanced C: Tips and
Techniques
Paul Anderson and Gail Anderson
ISBN: 0-672-48417-X, $24.95

Topics in C Programming
Stephen G. Kochan, Patrick H. Wood
ISBN: 0-672-46290-7, $24.95

Place
Postage
Here

HOWARD W. SAMS & COMPANY

Dept. DM
4300 West 62nd Street
Indianapolis, IN 46268-2589

C H A P T E R

◆ ◆ ◆ ◆ ◆ ◆

2

The Environment

When a C program is written, consider two primary environments—that in which it is compiled (or translated) and that in which it will be executed. For the vast majority of C programs, these two environments are one and the same. However, C is used in an increasing number of situations where the execution environment has properties different than that of the translation environment.

◆ Conceptual Models ◆

Translation Environment

Translation Phases.   In the past, C compilers have varied widely in the way in which, they recognize and process tokens, particularly with regard to the timing of, and order in which preprocessing directives are processed. For example,

```
#ifdef DEBUG
#define DBG
#else
#define DBG /\
*
#endif
DBG          printf(...); /*...*/
```

The idea here is to fool the preprocessor into defining a macro DBG that is equated to /* without its recognizing this as the token that begins a comment. This works only if the #define directive is processed before the backslash continuation character is processed. If this is indeed the case, the macro call expands to either

```
/*          printf(...); /*...*/
```

or

```
        printf(...); /*...*/
```

the first of which makes the whole line a comment, thus deactivating the debug trace, while the second causes `printf` to be called.

In order to nail down the order in which source tokens should be processed, ANSI C explicitly identifies a set of rules collectively known as *the phases of translation*. Since this information is critical and must not leave room for ambiguity, it is reprinted here verbatim from the ANSI Standard.

> The precedence among the syntax rules of translation is specified by the following phases. (Implementations must behave as if these separate phases occur, even though many are typically folded together in practice.)
>
> 1. Physical source file characters are mapped to the source character set (introducing new-line characters for end-of-line indicators) if necessary. Trigraph sequences are replaced by corresponding single-character internal representations. [A trigraph is a three-character sequence of the form `??x` where x is one of a set of nine printable characters.]
>
> 2. Each instance of a new-line character and an immediately preceding backslash character is deleted, splicing physical source lines to form logical source lines. A source file that is not empty shall end in a new-line character, which shall not be immediately preceded by a backslash character.
>
> 3. The source file is decomposed into preprocessing tokens and sequences of white space characters (including comments). A source file shall not end in a partial preprocessing token or comment. Each comment is replaced by one space character. New-line characters are retained. Whether each sequence of other white space characters is retained or replaced by one space character is implementation-defined. (The process of dividing a source file's characters into preprocessing tokens is context-dependent. For example, see the handling of `<` on a `#include` preprocessing directive line.)
>
> 4. Preprocessing directives are executed and macro invocations are expanded. A `#include` preprocessing directive causes the named header or source file to be processed from phase 1 through phase 4, recursively.
>
> 5. Escape sequences in character constants and string literals are converted to single characters in the execution character set.
>
> 6. Adjacent character string literal tokens are concatenated and adjacent wide string literal tokens are concatenated. [A wide string literal is used with multi-byte character processing.]

7. White space characters separating tokens are no longer significant. Preprocessing tokens are converted into (normal) tokens. Unsuccessful conversion of a preprocessing token is equivalent to a violation of a syntax rule. The resulting tokens are syntactically and semantically analyzed and translated.

8. All external object and function references are resolved. Library components are linked to satisfy external references to functions and objects not defined in the current translation. All such translator output is collected into a program image which contains information needed for execution in its execution environment.

These rules break programs that previously relied on a different order of translation. The preprocessor example shown earlier is invalidated since continuation lines (phase 2) are handled before tokens and comments are recognized (phase 3), resulting in the / and * being recognized as a start comment token. The end result will be a syntax error since the #endif directive will not be recognized inside the comment.

Phase 1 requires that trigraphs be complete tokens in the source file—they cannot be split on consecutive lines using the backslash notation discussed in phase 2.

The recognition and processing of continuation backslash/new-line sequences is defined in phase 2. Since this phase appears very early in translation it permits ANY token (except trigraphs, as noted above) to be continued across input lines.

Recommendation: Do not gratuitously break tokens across multiple lines—be overt. This capability is primarily intended for C source generated under program control. Prior to ANSI C, the only token that most implementations allowed to be continued using the backslash new-line convention was a string literal. Most implementations also permitted a macro definition line to be continued in this manner.

Phase 3 disallows incomplete tokens (including comments) at the end of a source file so it is not possible to paste tokens across multiple source files. Some implementations allow such pasting across two consecutive header files or a header and a source file. Phase 3 also requires that comments be replaced by a space character, which outlaws the practice of pasting tokens in the preprocessor using a/**/b. (This approach assumes that comments are replaced by nothing such that a token ab is seen. This capability is supported by ANSI C via the ## preprocessor token-pasting operator.)

ANSI C does not require a conforming implementation's preprocessor to save its output for inspection by the programmer. However, most implementations do so since it is desirable to see intermediate and/or final macro expansion when debugging complex and nested macros.

ANSI C does not require the preprocessor to be a separate or stand-alone program, although it permits it. The preprocessor is permitted to work without knowing the specific properties of the target implementation. (Thus ANSI C does not require that `sizeof` be permitted in preprocessor `#if` directives since `sizeof` and types are part of the C language and involve implementation-dependent sizes and representations.)

Diagnostics. ANSI C defines the circumstances in which a conforming implementation is required to issue a diagnostic. The form of the diagnostic is implementation-defined. The Standard makes no statement about information or warning messages such as "Variable a used before being initialized" and "Unreachable code." These are considered to be *quality of implementation issues* best left for the marketplace to decide.

ANSI C allows extensions provided they do not render a strictly conforming program invalid. A conforming compiler must be able to disable (or diagnose) extensions. Extensions to a conforming compiler are limited to assigning meaning to syntax not given semantics by ANSI C (such as `register struct tag s`), or defining the meaning of otherwise undefined behaviors (the order of evaluation of function argument lists, for example).

Execution Environments

The manner and timing of static initialization is unspecified. However, all objects in static storage must be initialized before *program startup*, which occurs when a designated C function is invoked by the execution environment. For hosted environments, the designated C function is typically called `main`, although it need not be. (VAX C permits any function to be the program's entry point.) With ANSI C, function `main` is called at program startup. A program is not strictly conforming if an entry point other than `main` is used. Note that static objects are those of class `extern` and `static`.

Recommendation: For hosted implementations, always use `main` as the program's entry point unless you have a very good reason for not doing so, and you make sure you adequately document it.

In the following example,

```
int i = 123;
static int j = 876;

f()
{
        static int k = 345;
        ...
}
```

there is no guarantee that `i`, `j`, and `k` are initialized at compile-time; they may be initialized at run-time before control is passed to `main`. This is particularly so (and necessary) in memory-resident systems where the executable image cannot be reinitialized to compile-time values from disk each time the program is executed.

Although it is generally not a portability consideration as to when the initialization takes place, the timing may impact performance. For example, if your compiler produces code to initialize statics at run-time then you pay that price each time the program is run. If you are in a real-time process-control environment or you invoke a program from another program many times, the initialization overhead may become significant.

Freestanding Environment.   A *freestanding environment* runs without the benefit of an operating system, and, thus, program execution can begin in any manner desired. Although such application environments are somewhat nonportable by definition, much of their code can often be ported (to an upwards-compatible series of device controllers, for example) if designed properly. Even writers of embedded systems need to port to new and different environments.

The name and type of the function called at program startup is implementation-defined as is the method of program termination.

The library facilities (if any) available to a freestanding program are implementation-defined. However, ANSI C requires the header `stddef.h` in conforming free-standing environments.

Hosted Environment.   ANSI C permits `main` to have either none or two arguments. If present, they must be of type `int` and `char *[]` (or `char **`), respectively.

A common extension (particularly in UNIX-like and MS-DOS environments) is that the function `main` receives a third argument, `char *envp[]`. `envp` points to a NULL-terminated array of pointers to `char`, each of which points to a string that provides certain information about the environment for this execution of the process. Any program that defines more than two arguments is not strictly conforming. That is, it is not maximally portable.

Recommendation: Use the library function `getenv` instead of the `envp` argument in `main` to access environment variables. Note, however, that the format of the string returned by `getenv`, and the set of environment variables, is implementation-defined. Therefore, neither `envp` nor `getenv` may help when porting to dissimilar environments.

Some user manuals and books erroneously suggest `main` be defined as having type `void` (or some other type) instead of `int` since you rarely, if ever, explicitly `return` from `main` (with or without a return value).

> **Recommendation:** Always define function `main` as having `int` type.

ANSI C requires that `argc` always be nonnegative. Traditionally, `argc` has been at least one even if `argv[0]` was set to point to an empty string.

> **Recommendation:** Do not assume that `argc` is always greater than zero since ANSI C permits it to be zero.

ANSI C requires that `argv[argc]` contain the `NULL` pointer (not to be confused with a pointer to a null string). This means that the `argv` array contains `argc + 1` elements, not `argc` as before. This allows the `argv` pointer array to be processed without regard to the value of `argc`.

> **Recommendation:** Do not assume that `argv[argc]` exists or that it contains the `NULL` pointer value.

ANSI C makes no comment about the handling of quoted literals in command lines. Therefore the ability to handle quoted strings at all, or those containing embedded white space, is implementation-defined. If the host environment cannot handle command-line arguments containing both alphabetic cases, it must supply text arguments in lower-case.

> **Recommendation:** Make no assumptions about special handling of quoted literals in command-line processing. Such quotes may delimit strings or they may be considered part of the string in which case `"abc def"` would produce two arguments `"abc and def"`. The casing of letters might not be preserved, even in the presence of quotes. (Use `tolower` (or `toupper`) with command-line arguments before comparing them against a list of valid strings.) Even if quotes are recognized, the method of escaping a quote (so it can be passed in an argument) may vary. ANSI C doesn't even require that a command-line environment exist.

A primary use of command-line arguments is to specify switches that determine the kind of processing to be done by the program being invoked. In a text-processing utility, for example, you may wish to use multi-word switches. In this case, connect the words using an underscore as follows:

```
textpro /left_margin=10 /page_length=55
```

and ignore case during switch processing. With care you can design a command-line argument syntax that is extremely portable. Take care though that you don't need a larger command-line buffer than a system can support. (MS-DOS permits only 128 bytes.) If a program can potentially have many and/or long arguments you should enable the program to be passed the name of a file containing command-line options as sequential records. For example,

```
textpro /command_file=commands.txt
```

allows an unlimited number of arguments to be processed regardless of command-line buffer size.

According to ANSI C, `argv[0]` represents the "program name" (whatever that may translate to for a given implementation.) If this is not available, `argv[0]` must point to a null string. (Some systems that cannot determine the program's name have `argv[0]` point to a string such as `"c"` or `"C"`.) In MS-DOS versions 1.x and 2.x, the loader and Program Segment Prefix (PSP) do not store `argv[0]` so it is not available to C programs. MS-DOS 3.x, however, does store the complete filename and path used to invoke a program. For example, if a program `TEST.EXE` resided in the root directory of drive `B:`, then if `TEST` were run under DOS 3.x using the command-line

```
TEST
```

the string pointed to by `argv[0]` would be `"B:\TEST.EXE"`.

Recommendation: Don't assume the program's name is available. (In the case of MS-DOS, you may wish to conditionally compile code based on the version of DOS being used.) Even if `argv[0]` points to the program's name, the name may be as it was specified on the command-line (possibly with case conversion) or it may be the translated name the operating system used to actually locate and load the program. (Full name translation is often useful if you wish to parse the string pointed to by `argv[0]` to determine certain disk and directory information.)

ANSI C requires that the parameters `argc` and `argv`, and the strings pointed to by `argv`, be modifiable by the user program and that these may not be changed by the implementation while the user program is executing.

Recommendation: Do not assume that the strings pointed to by `argv` can be modified. Since `argc` and `argv` are formal parameters in `main` and arguments are passed in by value, these variables can be modified reliably as can formals in any C function that is called from another C function. (You might not be able to modify formals if the caller is written in some other language. For example, the VAX calling standard requires that formal arguments be treated as read-only so when calling VAX C from VAX Fortran or VAX Lisp [or other language using CALLG linkage], you must not modify formal arguments.)

Numerous environments, such as UNIX and MS-DOS, support the command-line operators <, >, and >>. In such systems these characters (and the filenames they refer to) are processed by the command-line processor (and removed) before it passes off the remaining command-line to the execution environment. Systems that do not handle these operators in such a manner pass them through to the execution environment as part of the command-line where they can be handled or passed through to the application program. ANSI C makes no comment about these operators.

The above-mentioned operators typically allow redirection of stdin and stdout. Some systems, notably UNIX, also allow stderr to be redirected. Some systems consider stderr to be the same as stdout.

Recommendation: Don't assume universal support for the UNIX-like command-line redirection operators <, >, and >>. Redirection of the standard files may be possible from within a program via the freopen library function.

Recommendation: Write error messages to stderr rather than stdout even if both file pointers are treated as the same. This way, you can take advantage of systems that do allow stdout and stderr to be independently redirected.

Since the command-line is passed to the program's startup code (after <, >, and >> have possibly been recognized and removed by the operating system/loader), implementations may allow special arguments that are intended for the startup code only. That is, they are not passed on to main or included in argc. For example,

```
prog =10000
```

may result in argc being 1 and the argument =10000 being used to specify the size of the run-time stack to be allocated at program startup. The mechanism may also allow a heap size to be given.

The support for, and syntax and semantics of, special command-line arguments, such as =xxx and =xxx/yyy, is implementation-defined. An implementation may require a program to be relinked before stack or heap size can be changed.

Recommendation: Since wild-card processing of command-line arguments is implementation-defined, do not rely on its existence. For example, an implementation's startup code might translate an argument of `*.dat` into a list of arguments corresponding to file names in the current directory having that name format.

Some implementations, particularly those that support free-standing code generation, supply source to the program startup code, enabling the user to modify it as necessary. An implementation may also allow some parts of program startup to be bypassed, resulting in a faster startup and a smaller program. (It is often desirable to remove `stdin`, `stdout`, and `stderr` and heap processing if these facilities aren't needed. Environment table processing of `envp` might also be optional.)

Recommendation: Don't assume that program startup source code is available. It may not be possible to bypass parts of program startup. As a measure of startup overhead, build a program that contains an empty `main` function only and look at the size of the resulting executable program for each of your implementations.

The method used to invoke `main` during program startup can vary. ANSI C requires that it be done as if the following code were used:

```
exit(main(argc, argv));
```

in which case, any value returned explicitly or implicitly from `main` will be passed on as the program's exit code.

It is a common misconception that dropping through the closing `}` of `main` is the same as leaving via `exit(0)`; this is not true, although a number of implementations have made it so. Such implementations invoke `main` as follows:

```
main(argc,argv);
exit(0);
```

in which case any value returned by `return;` or by falling through the closing `}` will be ignored, and an exit code of zero will be used instead. This is generally acceptable unless `return (n);` is used to terminate `main`. In this case, the explicit return value is discarded, and zero is used instead, which is not what the programmer appears to have intended. While it is very rare that anyone terminates `main` using `return` with a value, it is permitted since `main` has type `int`.

Recommendation: If you require a predictable exit code from a program, terminate `main` using `exit`(*expression*) rather than `return` *expression*.

Some implementations may restrict exit codes to unsigned integral values or to those values that fit into a byte. Refer to the library function `exit` for more details. Also, although UNIX and numerous other systems interpret an exit code of 0 as success, others may not. (VAX/VMS, for example, uses 1.) ANSI C requires that 0 mean "success." It also provides the implementation-defined macros `EXIT_SUCCESS` and `EXIT_FAILURE` in `stdlib.h`.

Recommendation: The range of values, meaning, and format of exit codes is implementation-defined. Even though `exit` returns an `int` argument, that argument may be modified, truncated, etc., by the termination code before being handed to the host system. Use `EXIT_SUCCESS` rather than 0 to indicate a success exit code.

If you are using exit codes to return information from one user program to its parent user program, you are typically free to adopt your own value conventions since the host environment probably won't be processing the code directly.

Program Execution.   ANSI C goes to some lengths to define an abstract machine and to give meaning to sequence points as follows:

"Evaluation of an expression (specifically, one that involves calling a function, incrementing or decrementing, assignment, or accessing a `volatile` object) may produce side effects, which are changes in the state of the execution environment incidental to the evaluation. At certain specified points in the execution sequence called sequence points, all side effects of previous evaluations must be complete and no side effect of a subsequent evaluation may have taken place."

While the notion of sequence points has always existed in implementations, the times and places at which they occur have been implementation-defined. One particular problem has been the handling of terminal input and output where some implementations have used buffered I/O while others used unbuffered I/O.

ANSI C specifies the following sequence points:

- Immediately prior to each function call, after all arguments to that function have been evaluated.

- After the first operand of the following operators has been evaluated: `&& || ?: ,`

- At the end of an initializer, after the expression is evaluated in an expression statement (such as `i++;`), after the controlling expression in an `if`, `while`, `do`, or `switch` statement, after the expression in a `return` statement, and after all three expressions in a `for` statement.

An optimizing compiler is permitted to optimize across sequence points provided it can guarantee the same result as if it had followed them rigorously.

♦ Environmental Considerations ♦

Character Sets

A C program is concerned with two possible character sets: source and execution. The source character set is that used to represent the source code program, and the execution character set is that available at run-time. Most programs execute on the same machine on which they are translated, in which case their source and execution sets are identical. Cross-compiled programs generally run on a different machine than that used for their development, in which case the source and execution sets may be different.

The characters in the source character set, except as explicitly specified by ANSI C, are implementation-defined. The characters in the execution character set (except for the `'\0'` character) and their values are implementation-defined. The execution character `'\0'` must be represented by all-bits zero.

The meaning of an unspecified character in the source text, except in a character constant, a string literal, or a comment, is implementation-defined. (A program with identifier names that include non-Roman characters [such as Ä] is not conforming.)

While the vast majority of C programs are translated and execute in an ASCII environment, other character sets are commonly in use. As the set of upper- and/or lower-case letters may not be contiguous (such as in the EBCDIC set), care must be taken when writing routines that are to handle multiple character sets. It is also possible when dealing with non-English characters that they do not have a corresponding upper- or lower-case equivalent. The collating sequence of character sets is also important when using the library function `qsort`.

Recommendation: If you write code that is specific to a particular character set, either conditionally compile it based on the host character set or document it as being an implementation-specific module. Use the `ctype.h` functions rather than testing characters against a specific set or range of integers.

Trigraph Sequences.   Sometimes, certain of the required source characters are not available to the programmer. This is typically because they are using a machine with a character set that does not include all the necessary punctuation characters. (It may also be because they are using a terminal that does not have keys for all the necessary punctuation characters.)

To enable the input of characters that are not defined in the ISO 646-1983 Invariant Code Set (which is a subset of the seven-bit ASCII code set), the following trigraph sequences have been made available in ANSI C.

Trigraph	*Meaning*
??=	#
??(	[
??/	\
??)	]
??'	^
??<	{
??!	|
??>	}
??-	~

A trigraph is a token consisting of three characters, the first two of which are ??. The three characters collectively are taken to represent the corresponding character in the table above.

The addition of support for trigraphs in a compiler may change the way existing character constants or string literals are interpreted. For example,

```
printf("??(error at line %d)\n", msgno);
```

will be treated as if it had been written as

```
printf("[error at line %d)\n", msgno);
```

and `sizeof("??(")` will be two, not four.

If such literal strings are intended to be displayed, then the impact of moving to a system supporting trigraphs from one that doesn't will be minimal and overt—the user will see a slightly different output. However, if the program parses a string expecting to find a specific character, such as ?, it will no longer find it if it has been interpreted as part of a trigraph sequence.

Even though the vast majority of C programmers will have absolutely no use for trigraphs, an ANSI-conforming implementation is required to support them. Therefore, you need to be aware of their existence so you can understand why seemingly innocent strings are being "misinterpreted."

If you can't quite imagine what a program with trigraphs would look like, here's a simple example.

```
#include <stdio.h>

int i[10][5];

main()
{
        printf("i[2][4] = %d\n",
                i[2][4]);
}
```

The trigraph version follows:

```
??=include <stdio.h>

int i??(10??)??(5??);

main()
??<
        printf("i??(2??)??(4??) = %d??/n",
                i??(2??)??(4??));
??>
```

Recommendation: Unless you are a masochist, don't use trigraphs when you don't have to.

Recommendation: Use a search program to check if sequences of `??` occur in existing source. If they do occur in more than a few places, you may wish to search specifically for the trigraph sequences.

Recommendation: To preserve sequences that look like trigraphs but are not intended to be, use the new ANSI C escape sequence `\?` to force a literal `?` character in a literal string or single-character constant. For example, `sizeof("\??(")` is four as is `sizeof("\?\?(")`.

Recommendation: If your implementation doesn't support trigraphs, you can protect against them in the future by using the `\?` sequence now since the backslash is supposed to be ignored if it does not begin a recognized escape sequence.

Character Display Semantics

ANSI C defines the term *active position*. This is the location on an output display device where the next output character will appear.

If a printable character is written when the active position is at the final position of a line, the behavior is unspecified.

If a backspace character is written when the active position is at the initial position of a line, the behavior is unspecified.

If a horizontal tab character is written when the active position is at or past the last defined horizontal tabulation position, the behavior is unspecified.

If a vertical tab character is written when the active position is at or past the last defined vertical tabulation position, the behavior is unspecified.

All lower-case letter escape sequences not defined by the Standard are reserved for future use. This may eventually conflict with existing extensions as might the addition of ' \a' (alert) and ' \v' (vertical tab).

Recommendation: The sequences ' \a' and ' \v' are ANSI C inventions. If an implementation does not recognize these sequences, it will ignore the backslash and treat the next character as a literal. Perhaps the easiest workaround is to use an octal or hexadecimal sequence to produce the same effect. For example on ASCII systems, ' \a' is equivalent to ' \007' (and ' \x07') and ' \v' is equivalent to ' \013' (and ' \x0B'). If string concatenation is supported, you could use

```
#define VT "\013"

printf("Title\n" VT "next line\n");
```

and if the internal representation of VT changed from one system to another, you could conditionally compile the #define directive accordingly.

Recommendation: Take care to deal with C's alphabetic escape sequences by name rather than by internal representation. That is, in an ASCII environment, use ' \n' rather than ' \012' . In any case, ANSI C does not define the mapping of these logical sequences—it simply requires that each have a unique representation and that it be representable in a char.

The alphabetic escape sequences may behave differently when written to an output device that is not a display. Such devices, and many displays as well, often provide a setup mode such that they can be programmed to interpret various control characters in different ways. In this case, it may be possible to drive different equipment with the same program by changing the hardware setup rather than the program itself.

On various operating systems, devices are managed by software device drivers. These programs often translate, or can be programmed to translate, data sent to the devices they control. For example, ' \f ' may be translated into multiple new-lines or vertical tabs. So if you are writing escape sequences to a file and you intend to read them back in, you may encounter problems. Not only won't the character you wrote be in the file, it may have been translated into multiple characters. The function printf returns the number of characters written out; however, this a logical count not a physical count. For example, fprintf(fp, "\tabd\f") may return a value of 5, yet because of translation by the device driver, many more characters could have been written. The numbers logically and physically written will agree only if translation is disabled.

Signals and Interrupts

ANSI C places certain restrictions on the kinds of objects that can be modified by signal handlers. With the exception of the signal function, the ANSI C library functions are not guaranteed to be reentrant and they are permitted to modify static data objects.

Environmental Limits

There are a number of environmental constraints on a conforming implementation as follows:

Translation Limits. A conforming implementation must be able to handle a program that contains at least one occurrence of the following:

- 15 nesting levels of compound statements, iteration control structures, and selection control structures

- 8 nesting levels in conditional compilation

- 12 pointer, array, and function declarators modifying a basic type in a declaration

- 31 declarators nested by parentheses within a full declarator

- 32 expressions nested by parentheses

- 31 significant characters in an internal identifier or a macro name

- 6 significant characters in an external identifier

- 511 external identifiers in one source file (This may be restricted by your linker, librarian or other development tools.)

- 127 identifiers with block scope in one block
- 1024 macro identifiers simultaneously defined in one source file (Watch out when including headers that nest.)
- 31 parameters in a function definition or call
- 31 parameters in a macro definition or invocation
- 509 characters in a logical source line
- 509 characters in a string literal (after concatenation)
- 32,767 bytes in an object (in a hosted environment only)
- 8 nesting levels for headers
- 257 case labels in a switch statement
- 127 members in a single structure or union
- 127 enumeration constants in a single enumeration
- 15 levels of nested structure or union definitions in a single struct-declaration-list.

Even in a conforming implementation, these numbers are somewhat misleading. For example, you can have 1024 currently defined macro identifiers and source lines may be 509 characters long, yet this does not mean you can have 1024 macros each with definitions of 509 characters. The Standard carefully states that the implementer must be able to demonstrate they can handle each of these limits in at least one program to claim conformance. That is, they get to supply the demo program. Therefore, they could show they can handle lines of 509 characters and also 1024 concurrent macros, etc., yet they may not be able to handle every possible combination of the minimum limits. In effect, ANSI C does not guarantee any specific support for combinations of limits.

Numerical Limits.   A conforming implementation must document all these items, which are specified in the headers `<limits.h>` and `<float.h>`. The values given below are replaced by implementation-defined values that must be equal or greater in magnitude (absolute value).

Sizes of integral types `<limits.h>`

- `CHAR_BIT` 8, maximum number of bits for smallest object (byte)
- `CHAR_MAX` ??[†] , maximum value for an object of type `char`
- `CHAR_MIN` ??[†] , minimum value for an object of type `char`

---

† The values for `CHAR_MIN` and `CHAR_MAX` depend on whether or not plain `char`s are signed. If they are, these macros are the same as `SCHAR_MIN` and `SCHAR_MAX`. If plain `char`s are unsigned, `CHAR_MIN` is 0 and `CHAR_MAX` is the same as `UCHAR_MAX`.

- `SCHAR_MAX` +127, maximum value for an object of type `signed char`
- `SCHAR_MIN` -127, minimum value for an object of type `signed char`
- `UCHAR_MAX` 255, maximum value for an object of type `unsigned char`
- `SHRT_MAX` +32767, maximum value for an object of type `short int`
- `SHRT_MIN` -32767, minimum value for an object of type `short int`
- `USHRT_MAX` 65535, maximum value for an object of type `unsigned short int`
- `INT_MAX` +32767, maximum value for an object of type `int`
- `INT_MIN` -32767, minimum value for an object of type `int`
- `UINT_MAX` 65535, maximum value for an object of type `unsigned int`
- `LONG_MAX` +2147483647, maximum value for an object of type `long int`
- `LONG_MIN` -2147483647, minimum value for an object of type `long int`
- `ULONG_MAX` 4294967295, maximum value for an object of type `unsigned long int`

ANSI C requires an `int` to be at least 16-bits and a `long int` to be at least 32-bits.

ANSI C does not require that `sizeof` be permitted in preprocessor `#if` arithmetic expressions. Therefore, the following construct is non-portable.

```
#if sizeof(int) == 2
long total;
#else
int total;
#endif
```

Conditionally compiling based on machine word-size is common. Here, the example assumes, perhaps, that if it isn't running on a 16-bit system, it's on a 32-bit machine. To achieve the same result, you must now use something like

```
#include <limits.h>

#if INT_MAX < LONG_MAX
long total;
#else
int total;
#endif
```

Characteristics of floating types <float.h>

This header has much the same purpose as limits.h except that it defines the floating-point characteristics of the target system. The meaning and formulas applied to each of these can be complex, and you are referred to your compiler manual or a copy of the ANSI Standard for specific details. (The FLT, DBL, and LDBL prefixes designate the types float, double, and long double, respectively. Note that several generic floating-point attributes have the prefix FLT, even though they are not float-specific.)

FLT_RADIX	2
FLT_ROUNDS	
FLT_MANT_DIG	
DBL_MANT_DIG	
LDBL_MANT_DIG	
FLT_EPSILON	1E-5
DBL_EPSILON	1E-9
LDBL_EPSILON	1E-9
FLT_DIG	6
DBL_DIG	10
LDBL_DIG	10
FLT_MIN_EXP	
DBL_MIN_EXP	
LDBL_MIN_EXP	
FLT_MIN	1E-37
DBL_MIN	1E-37
LDBL_MIN	1E-37
FLT_MIN_10_EXP	-37
DBL_MIN_10_EXP	-37
LDBL_MIN_10_EXP	-37
FLT_MAX_EXP	
DBL_MAX_EXP	
LDBL_MAX_EXP	
FLT_MAX	1E+37
DBL_MAX	1E+37
LDBL_MAX	1E+37
FLT_MAX_10_EXP	+37
DBL_MAX_10_EXP	+37
LDBL_MAX_10_EXP	+37

Recommendation: Most of the float.h macros are ANSI C inventions (based on the proposed ANSI Fortran 8X Standard), and others, previously in existence, may not be in wide spread use. Check with your target environments.

CHAPTER

3

Lexical Elements

◆ Tokens ◆

ANSI C defines a C source module to be made up of a series of tokens. A token is the smallest lexical element in the language. The various categories of tokens are: keywords, identifiers, constants, string literals, operators, and punctuators (called separators in K&R). Various characters are collectively known as white space. These are: blanks, horizontal and vertical tabs, new-lines, form feeds, and comments. (K&R includes tabs which are presumed to be horizontal tabs. It does not include form feeds.) Except for the fact that they separate tokens, white space characters are ignored. White space may only appear within a token if that token is a character constant or a string literal.

By definition, when source input is parsed into tokens, the longest possible valid token sequence must be formed. There must be no ambiguity as to what a particular construct means. For example, the expression a+++++b should generate a syntax error because the tokens found are a++, ++, +, and b, and the second ++ operator has an operand that is not an lvalue. Note that a++ + ++b is valid since the white space causes the tokens to be parsed as a++, +, ++, and b. Likewise for a+++ ++b.

Other language translators are permitted to try to work out what the programmer meant. For example, Fortran interprets DO10I = 1,10,1 as a DO loop, not as an assignment to the variable called DO10I. This kind of programming is largely avoided by C since the if, while, for, and switch constructs require their condition expressions to be enclosed in parentheses. So the worst you can write is while(i==4), for(i=1;i>5;i++), etc.

Recommendation: Use white space between binary operators and their operands. Not only does this greatly assist maintenance, it also explicitly defines the tokens. There is then no room for any substandard implementation to misinterpret the token sequence.

Many of the operators and punctuators are represented by two, and in some cases three, characters (e.g., ++, --, /*, */, >>, ==, >>=). To be considered a valid token, each of these sequences must be written without embedded white space. That is, you should use a >> b instead of a > > b. Some compilers allow these tokens to be other than a contiguous character sequence.

Recommendation: Always write multi-character tokens as contiguous character sequences without intervening white space.

Consider the following program:

```
#define OP *

main()
{
        int i, j, k;

        k = iOPj;
}
```

If the preprocessor substitutes a * for the macro name OP, the assignment is syntactically valid. Even though the (ANSI C) preprocessor is essentially a string substitution facility, it uses the same definition of a token as does the C language. Therefore, iOPj is a token and does not match any existing macro name. An error should be generated since iOPj has not been declared. Beware of preprocessors that do otherwise. (A similar situation exists with the token 1E1. No match should be attempted for a macro named E—the token should be interpreted as a valid floating-point constant.)

Recommendation: Avoid idiosyncrasies of preprocessors that follow tokenizing rules different from their corresponding C compilers.

Some preprocessors allow tokens to be created from other tokens. For example:

```
#define PASTE(a,b) a/**/b

main()
{
        int ij;

        f(PASTE(i, j));
}
```

The intent here is to call function `f` with one argument, `ij`. The preprocessor must replace the comment in the macro definition with nothing, rather than a space. See the section on preprocessing for a discussion on preprocessor token pasting using the `##` operator.

Recommendation: If you wish to paste tokens together, use the token-pasting operator `##` provided by ANSI C.

♦ Keywords ♦

The following tokens (with the exception of `entry`) are defined as keywords by ANSI C.

auto	enum	signed
break	extern	sizeof
case	float	static
char	for	struct
const	goto	switch
continue	if	typedef
default	int	union
do	long	unsigned
double	register	void
else	return	volatile
entry	short	while

The keywords `const`, `volatile`, and `signed` were not defined in K&R and were inventions of ANSI C. `enum` and `void` also were not defined in K&R but have been used in UNIX compilers since the early 1980s.

ANSI C does not contain the `entry` keyword previously reserved in K&R and most C compilers. Very few, if any, commercial compilers provide semantics for this keyword.

It is possible that existing code uses identifiers that have been added by ANSI C as keywords. However, if you compile such code with an ANSI C compiler, the code should break in an obvious manner, although this may not necessarily be the case. Such an implementation is not ANSI-conforming unless the keyword begins with an underscore.

Recommendation: Before you attempt to port a system use `grep` (or another pattern recognition tool) to search for all the extended (and new ANSI C) keywords in the source. It is better to know about potential conflicts beforehand rather than find them on a case-by-case basis each time the compiler complains. Never use identifiers that could potentially conflict with the name space reserved for implementers.

If you have code that uses an identifier called `const`, for example, you have two choices. You can either change all occurrences of that identifier name to something else that is not a keyword (the best long-term solution), or you could redefine it as follows:

```
#define const constant

f()
{
        int const;
}
```

This solution is messy and should be considered as a temporary fix only. To use it you must place the `#define` directive in all appropriate source files or put it into a header. Since it is extremely unlikely that the same header is already included in all affected source files, you would need to add `#includes` as necessary. Finally, this approach is misleading to programmers, particularly if they use a symbolic debugger. The debugger will know the identifier as `constant`, whereas programmers know it as `const`. And, of course, it would be messy, if not impossible, to start using the `const` keyword in the code as well. (Having the name `const` recognized in some source files and not others would be a maintenance nightmare.)

Recommendation: Unless you can justify otherwise, change all occurrences of an identifier if it conflicts with a keyword added by ANSI C, since, in the future, these keywords will be increasingly accepted by implementations. If an identifier name conflicts with an extended keyword you may be able to disable extended keyword recognition using a compiler switch. (This is commonly done by requesting "ANSI" or "Standard" compilation mode.) Failing that, you may need to change its name. Beware of using the ANSI C

#pragma preprocessor directive to disable/enable extended keyword recognition on a line-by-line basis. (This capability need not be provided since the semantics of pragmas is implementation-defined.)

Many implementations support extended keywords; asm is a common one as is fortran. Numerous MS-DOS compilers support the keywords near, far, huge, cdecl, fortran, and pascal. Some implementations have extended keywords whose names begin with an underscore (as required by ANSI C).

Recommendation: When porting code between implementations that support the same extended keyword, be sure the semantics in each implementation are identical or are, at least, compatible.

Any non-standard keyword can be caused to be ignored by equating it to nothing as follows:

```
#define then

f()
{
        ...
        if (cond) then
                ...
}
```

This approach may, however, cause other problems depending on the semantics of the code remaining after the keyword is "removed." For example,

```
#define const

f()
{
        const ci;
}
```

now generates a syntax error since ci has no type. If the const keyword were recognized, the type int would be assumed.

Recommendation: When confronted with porting code containing extended keywords, do not simply #define them to nothing (or int, in the case of void) until you have studied the repercussions of doing so.

Using the preprocessor #define directive, you can redefine a keyword.

Recommendation: Do not redefine keywords. For example, you may be tempted to #define int as long int (or using the corresponding typedef) to save changing declarations when moving from a 32-bit machine to one with 16-bit ints. This would be a "quick and dirty" solution.

♦ Identifiers ♦

K&R and ANSI C allow underscores, letters, and digits only to appear in an identifier. Identifiers may not begin with a decimal digit. Some implementations permit characters other than these in identifiers. They may even allow characters that are not defined in the required source character set. A number of popular operating systems (including VAX/VMS) use system library entry point names containing the ' $ ' symbol. To access these routines, a C program must be able to specify function names containing this character.

Recommendation: Do not use non-standard characters in identifier names unless you need to access a library function or global variable with a non-standard name. Many assemblers allow non-C characters (such as ' $ ' and ' . ') in global names and function entry point names. Avoid using these characters in such names when writing routines (in other languages) that are to be called from C.

K&R declared that only the first eight characters of an internal identifier were significant. (An internal identifier is one not known outside of its parent source file.) Therefore, the identifiers totalpay and totalpayment were considered to be the same. ANSI C provides for 31 character significance on internal identifiers.

Recommendation: Most modern compilers acknowledge long identifier names. You should be restricted only to eight character significance on very old compilers or those that must run with less than optimum resources (typically memory).

ANSI C states that if identifiers that are intended to denote the same entity differ in any character, the behavior is undefined.

Since external identifiers are subject to other system limitations, the nature of their names may be far more restrictive. For example, DEC's RSX operating system requires that external names be six characters or less, that there be no case distinction, and that the underscore is not a valid character. (Of course, a compiler running on such a machine is free to map "unsupported" characters into something that is. For example, the '_' could be mapped to a '.' or '$'.) ANSI C requires externals be significant to at least six characters but does not require case sensitivity.

Depending on an implementation's external linkage model, different identifiers with the same leading significant characters may cause a diagnostic. For example, some implementations are very loose about requiring the keyword `extern` in front of external references. In fact, they may allow all references and the definition to have `extern`, or they might allow all of them to omit it. This is possible if the linker allocates the space rather than the compiler. (This approach is used on DEC PDP-11 and VAX systems where program sections with the overlay attribute are handed to the linker.)

On such systems, you might have a problem if you have two externals such as `total_time_used` and `total_time_taken`. If only the first eight characters are significant, all references to these variables now refer to the same variable, and only one lot of space is allocated. The linker will probably not complain, and the bug may take a while to manifest itself.

Recommendation: When choosing external identifier names, find the lowest common denominator of allowed length of significance, characters, and casing. If you use names that are longer than the significance for a particular implementation, be careful to make them unique within the length of significance. Check all the tools you will be using to see if they have external name limitations. These include assemblers, compilers, source and object librarians, debuggers, and linkers.

Recommendation: Regardless of target machine requirements, do not use identifiers whose spelling differs only in the casing of letters. This is simply a style issue—porting considerations just add more weight to the argument. Although the K&R style of upper-case names for macros and lower-case names for all other identifiers is common, there need be no restriction on mixed-case identifiers, provided each spelling is unique (ignoring case).

It may be necessary to port code containing long identifiers from an implementation with greater identifier significance to to one with lesser significance. In this case, the `#define` directive may be used as follows:

```
#define number_of_days_absent numdayab
#define number_of_days_sick numdaysk
```

This allows the code to compile without requiring the variable names to be changed. One problem with this approach is that such a variable will be known

by its shorter name within a symbolic debugger. As such, it must be manipulated by that short name even though the programmer still chooses to think of it
as having a long name. Adding the macro definitions to all the right places is also
error prone and potentially arduous as discussed with keyword redefinition
above.

Recommendation: Using the preprocessor to assign shorter names to
long identifiers should be viewed as a stop-gap measure.

Some implementations use identifiers (as library entry points and macros) whose
names begin with one or more underscores.

Recommendation: The user-defined names of identifiers with external linkage should not begin with an underscore unless you must do
so to map into existing libraries and/or headers. The name space of
identifiers whose names begin with an underscore is the domain of
implementers and future versions of the ANSI C Standard.

Recommendation: To avoid potential external naming conflicts
between your code and that provided in third-party libraries and
headers, add an application-specific prefix of the form XXX_, XX_,
or X_ (where the X prefixes represent a product code, abbreviation,
etc.) to all of your external identifiers and macros. Do likewise if you
are developing libraries and headers that are to be used by others.

Recommendation: Whenever you take delivery of a new compiler (or
version thereof), library, or header, create a list of all the identifiers
"reserved" by these products. Along with those identifiers reserved
by the ANSI C Standard, these comprise a list of identifiers to stay
away from when defining your own names. Create one list sorted
alphabetically by header and alphabetically across all headers. While
this task may be tedious, it is absolutely necessary if you are to avoid
unpleasant surprises once the port has begun. Try to gather as much
information about potential name conflicts before you start moving
the code. (Note that ANSI C reserved identifiers total approximately
200. Add those reserved by your specific compiler and layered products, and the number could easily approach more than 1000!)

It is possible to reduce the likelihood of external name conflicts by reducing the
number of external names while at the same time having the same number of

external "links." For example,

```
extern int value;
extern double measurements[100];
extern long int *link_pathname;
```

generates three external names while

```
struct group {
        int value;
        double measurements[100];
        long int *link_pathname;
};

extern struct group G;
```

generates only one. The second approach also removes any external name significance and casing restrictions from the three variables since they are now internal names. The main problem with this is that now all references to these variables must be prefixed with G. since they are part of a structure. This isn't necessarily bad since, as a by-product of this method, we can easily identify global identifiers by the format of their name. And we don't have to worry about local identifiers hiding globals we want to access since they cannot accidentally have the same names.

Some C translators generate assembler source (rather than object code), which must then be assembled. In these cases, all C external and static identifiers must be translated into labels acceptable to the assembler, possibly resulting in duplicate labels. Therefore, it is possible to write a syntactically correct C program that will generate errors when the code output from the compiler is ·assembled. Consider the following example used with one particular MS-DOS compiler:

```
int sub2_ssi = 10;

sub2 ()
{
        static int ssi = 75;
}
```

which generates the following code:

```
PUBLIC sub2_ssi_
sub2_ssi_ DW 10
...
PUBLIC sub2_
sub2_ssi_ DW 75
```

The `static` variable `ssi` has its parent function name and an "_" added as a prefix. In this case, both variables are assigned the same label in the generated code, and the assembler issues a "duplicate label" error message.

Recommendation: If your compiler generates assembler source only, make sure it doesn't fold otherwise unique C identifiers into the same name.

Scopes of Identifiers

An identifier is not in scope until it has been declared. (The only exception to this are function names. If a function is referenced and it has not been declared, it is assumed to have an `int` return type.)

If an identifier is declared outside of a function, it has file scope. If it is declared inside a function, it has block scope. That is, its scope is that block plus all subordinate blocks (unless it is hidden in a subordinate block by an identifier of the same name). Some implementations allow a little more latitude than this. Consider the following functions that both reside in the same source file:

```
f()
{
        extern int *check();
        int *pi = check();
}

g()
{
        int *pi = check();
}
```

In function `f`, function `check` is declared to be an external identifier. However, since the declaration is inside the function, the scope of `check`, strictly speaking, is limited to that block. Within function `g`, `check` is implicitly declared to be a function returning an `int` since the identifier `check` is currently not in scope. Some implementations will retain the first declaration of check across to the compilation of function `g`. When you compile this code on a compiler that has strict scope checking the return type of `check` in `g` will be interpreted (incorrectly) as an `int`. We can hope that the compiler would warn about assigning an `int` into a pointer, but that in itself is another "loose" area. On many implementations you will "accidentally" get the correct result if an `int` is the same size as a pointer to `int`. However, on those machines where these sizes differ (e.g., Intel large memory models), you will not.

To get the desired behavior write the code as follows:

```
extern int *check();

f()
{
        int *pi = check();
}

g()
{
        int *pi = check();
}
```

Ideally, the function declaration would reside in a header that would then be #included. Alternatively, check could be explicitly declared within each of the functions.

Recommendation: Follow the strict scope model for placement of external declarations. Better still, place external declarations in headers and #include them as appropriate.

It is possible to hide an outer identifier by one of the same name in subordinate blocks as in

```
int i = 100;

f()
{
        int i = 200;

        if (...) {
                int i = 300;

        }
}
```

Each i designates a different object. Another (perhaps) confusing example is

```
int x = 100;

main()
{
        int y = x;
        int x = 200;

        printf("y = %d, x = %d\n", y, x);
}
```

Here, the outermost identifier called x is used (legitimately) in the same block as another identifier of the same name. An acid test of a compiler's scope rules is

```
int x = 100;

main()
{
        int x = x;

        printf("x = %d\n", x);
}
```

The automatic variable x is initialized with itself, not with the value of the external int x.

Recommendation: Do not intentionally hide external (or other) identifiers within subordinate blocks. While this has no real impact on porting code, its style merits alone make it worth mentioning.

Linkages of Identifiers

While K&R defined a model to define and reference externals, numerous other models have been employed, and this has lead to some confusion. The models follow:

```
/* Strict REF/DEF Model */

/* source file 1          source file 2 */

int i;                     extern int i;
main()                     sub()
{                          {
        i = 10;                    int j = i;
}                          }
```

With this model, the variable declaration may occur once and only once without the keyword `extern`. All other references to that external must have the keyword `extern`. This is the model specified by K&R.

```
/* Relaxed REF/DEF Model */

/* source file 1          source file 2 */

int i;                    int i;
main()                    sub()
{                         {
        i = 10;                   int j = i;
}                         }
```

In this case, neither declaration includes the `extern` keyword. If the identifier is declared (somewhere) with the `extern` class, a defining instance must occur elsewhere in the program. If the identifier is declared with an initializer, one and only one declaration must occur with an initializer in the program. This model is widely used in UNIX-like environments. Programs that adopt this model conform to the ANSI Standard but are not maximally portable.

```
/* Common Model */

/* source file 1          source file 2 */

extern int i;             extern int i;

main()                    sub()
{                         {
        i = 10;                   int j = i;
}                         }
```

In this model, all declarations of the external variable `i` may optionally contain the keyword `extern`. This model is intended to mimic that of Fortran's COMMON blocks.

```
/* Initializer Model */

/* source file 1          source file 2 */

int i = 0;                int i;

main()                    sub()
{                         {
        i = 10;                   int j = i;
}                         }
```

Here, the defining instance is that containing an explicit initializer (even if that initializer is the default value).

ANSI C adopted a model which is a combination of the strict ref/def and initialization models. This approach was taken to accommodate as wide a range of environments and existing implemntations as possible.

ANSI C states that if an identifier with external linkage has incompatible declarations in two source files, the behavior is undefined.

Recommendation: Use the Strict REF/DEF external linkage model.

Some implementations cause object modules to be loaded into an executable image simply if one or more of the external identifiers defined in them are declared in user code yet are not actually used. ANSI C states that if an identifier with external linkage is not used in an expression, then there need be no external definition for it. You can't force an object to be loaded simply by declaring it.

The `static` class also poses some problems, particularly with forward references. For example,

```
extern double average();
extern double table[10];

f()
{
        average();
        table[1] = 1.2345;
}


static double table[10];

static double average()
{
}
```

Do the initial references to `average` and `table` refer to the `static` objects defined later, or are they mapped into external objects of the same name? The answer could be "yes" or "no" depending on the architecture of your compiler. Multi-pass compilers can fix up such forward references, but a single-pass compiler may have difficulty. In this simple example, the intent could be made unambiguous by using

```
static double table[10];

static double average()
{
}
```

```
f ()
{
        average ();
        table[1] = 1.2345;
}
```

However, this will not suffice if two `static` functions of non-int type call each other—they can't both be defined first.

ANSI C makes the following statement: "If the first declaration of an identifier having file scope contains the keyword `static`, the identifier has internal linkage. Otherwise, the identifier has external linkage. If a declaration contains the `extern` keyword, the identifier has the same linkage as any previous declaration of that identifier with file scope. If no such previous declaration exists, the identifier has external linkage."

Then by ANSI rules, in the first example above, we have undefined behavior since the same identifier is declared twice, with different linkage. To correct the code we could write

```
static double average ();
static double table[10];

f ()
{
        average ();
        table[1] = 1.2345;
}

static double average ()
{
}
```

To resolve the problem of two `static` functions calling each other, we could write

```
static int g ();

static int f ()
{
        if (...)
                g ();
}

static int g ()
{
        if (...)
                f ();
}
```

Recommendation: Where possible, define static external objects at the start of the source file so you need not forward reference them in declarations. (This is always possible with static data objects unless you have something strange like two static pointers that contain each other's address.) For static functions, use a forward reference with the `static` keyword rather than `extern`.

Name Spaces of Identifiers

K&R defined two disjoint classes of identifiers: namely, identifiers associated with ordinary variables and structure and union members and tags. ANSI C adds several new categories of identifier name space. The ANSI C groups are labels; structure, union, and enumeration tags; the members of structures and unions (with each structure and union having its own name space); and all other identifiers, called ordinary identifiers. This last group includes variables, `typedef` names, function names, and enumeration constants. The identifiers optionally allowed in function prototypes have their own name space. Their scope is from their name through the end of that prototype declaration. Therefore, the same identifier can be used in different prototypes, but it cannot be used twice in the same prototype.

The ANSI C position is just consolidating what has been the case in recent years anyway so it should be fairly safe to assume you have these four categories. In any case, having a label with the same name as a variable is considered bad programming practice. The same is true for `struct`, `union`, and `enum` tags, and variables.

K&R contains the statement, "Two structures may share a common initial sequence of members; that is, the same member may appear in two different structures if it has the same type in both and if all previous members are the same in both. (Actually, the compiler checks only that a name in two different structures has the same type and offset in both, but if preceding members differ the construction is nonportable.)" ANSI C eliminates this restriction by endorsing the separate member per structure name space.

A number of implementations support "anonymous" structures and unions. These aggregates permit nameless structures and unions to be nested yet the members of these nested objects belong to the parent structure or union's name space. For example,

```
struct s1 {
        union un1 {
                int _sname[5];
                char *_lname;
        } _un1_;
        /* ... */
};
```

```
    #define sname  _un1_._sname
    #define lname  _un1_._lname
```

requires the union's members to be fully qualified when referenced, either directly or via the use of macros as shown. With an anonymous union this would be written like

```
    struct s1 {
            union {
                    int sname[5];
                    char *lname;
            };
            /* ... */
    };
```

The union members sname and lname would behave as if they were members of struct s1 but would overlay each other as expected.

Recommendation: Do not use anonymous structures and unions since they are not part of K&R or ANSI C.

Storage Durations of Objects

There is a popular misconception that static variables are initialized at compile-time. While this is often the case, an implementation is free to do this at program startup (as in common and necessary for free-standing C environments such as ROMable applications). In extreme cases, this could become a performance consideration. For example, if your program invokes another C program continually many times in a loop, you could be paying the price of startup initialization every time the child program is started.

Conceptually, space for automatic variables is created when their parent block is entered at run-time and released when that block is terminated. Some implementations actually do this while others allocate all automatic space needed in a function at the time that function is entered.

While the timing of such space allocation has no affect on portability *per se*, it does affect the amount of temporary space required at any time. For example, if auto variables are stored on the stack and autos from all blocks within a function are allocated together, considerably more stack space may be needed than if they were allocated at the start of their respective blocks. If you are porting to an environment where stack space is at a premium, you may need to rearrange such functions to have fewer auto variables.

Recommendation: If stack space is limited, find out how your compiler allocates space for automatic variables in nested blocks.

In any event, you are guaranteed that the space is actually allocated. What you are not guaranteed, though, is the initial value of automatic variables if the block is entered in any way other than by falling into it (for example, by jumping to a label in that block).

```
#include <stdio.h>

main()
{
        int j = 3;

        goto label1;

        while (--j) {
                int i = 100;

label1:         printf("i = %d\n", i);
        }
}

i = -3577
i = 100
i = 100
```

Here we see that `i` has an "undefined" value in the first iteration of the loop since control was passed into the loop via a label. Subsequent iterations of the loop cause `i`'s parent block to be entered normally, and as we can see, the initializer list is honored.

A similar problem can occur when defining automatic variables within a `switch`'s main block as follows:

```
#include <stdio.h>

main()
{
        int i = 10;

        switch (i) {
                int j = 100; /* ?? */

        case 10:
                printf(" j = %d\n", j);
                break;
        }
}

  j = 232
```

While the space for j is allocated, it is not initialized to 100 since there is no way to execute the code at the beginning of the block. (Note that the initializer list of an automatic object is really executable code since it can be any arbitrary run-time expression.)

When a user program terminates, the execution environment (or user-supplied functions registered via the library function atexit) has access to all external variables. It can also reliably access any static objects for which it has an address.

Care should be taken when dealing with the addresses of automatic variables in certain cases. For example

```
#include <stdio.h>

main()
{
        int i = 50;
        int *pi;
        int *f();

        pi = f(&i);
        printf("*pi = %d\n", *pi);
}


int *f(ptr)
int *ptr;
{
        int k = 1000;

        printf("*ptr = %d\n", *ptr);
        return (&k);            /* ??? */
}

*ptr = 50
*pi = 1000  /* undefined behavior */
```

Since i exists when f executes, its address can be meaningfully used by f. However, f returns the address of k. Since k is an automatic variable which no longer exists when f returns, the address returned is where k used to be located. While main can copy that address to pi without error, it cannot meaningfully dereference the location pointed to by pi. Doing so could produce either the "correct" answer as shown above, some garbage value if the address has since been used for something else, or possibly even a run-time error since you are accessing a memory location you no longer control. (The same situation occurs if you dereference a pointer that points to space that has been released by the library routine free.)

Recommendation: On no account should pointers to `auto` variables be passed back to parent functions. There is no guarantee that these locations will contain predictable data when later accessed via those addresses. In fact, such locations might not even be accessible.

Identifier Types

ANSI C includes a number of types not present in K&R. They are:

```
signed char
unsigned char
signed short int
unsigned short int
signed int
signed long int
unsigned long int
long double
void
void *
enum
```

Also, all types derived from these types are permitted except that you cannot have an array of `void`. However, `void *` is permitted.

The representations and sets of values of the various types of pointers, integers and floating-point values is implementation-defined. (Note the ANSI C headers `limits.h` and `float.h` are intended to define the maximum and minimum values permissible for a conforming implementation.) C implementations exist for both ones- and twos-complement and sign-magnitude machines. Also, some machines (e.g., the VAX) have three or more floating-point representations; programmers may choose floating-point type mapping via a compile-time switch.

On Harris H-series machines, `long int` has a non-obvious representation; 48 bits with a hole at bit 23. The 47 bits that participate in the `long int`'s value are logically (although not physically) contiguous. Therefore, they obey the ANSI C rule that integral values be represented in a binary positional notation system.

An implementation may require certain types to have a specific alignment in memory either because of hardware limitations or for performance reasons. For example, the DEC PDP-11 requires that all types, other than `char`, begin on a word boundary (even address). On machines such as the Intel 8086 and the DEC VAX, certain benefits of decreased bus/memory cycles may be obtained by aligning certain types even though this is not required by the architecture. For example, storing a longword on a word boundary may be better than on a byte boundary, but not as efficient as on a longword boundary. For this reason, optimizing compilers on such systems may use padding to achieve better alignment. The net result is that programs may take significantly more data space in such an environment than they did in some other.

Recommendation: Determine the alignment criteria of your implementation. For structures, group members by type and in descending order of alignment requirements so that excessive padding can be avoided (or possibly eliminated altogether). Since structures may contain unused padding, use `sizeof` (rather than a hard-coded number) when referring to their size, as the size may change across implementations. Never assume the size of a structure is the sum of the sizes of each of its members—it may be larger.

By definition, a `char` is large enough to store any character in the implementation's basic execution character set. (For an ASCII machine, this means the characters 0-127, not 0-255.) Also, each character in that set is guaranteed to use a non-negative representation. If any other quantity (e.g., 128 in ASCII) is stored in a `char`, the behavior is implementation-defined. That is, it is implementation-defined whether a plain `char` is signed or unsigned. By definition, `sizeof(char) == 1`.

Recommendation: If you need signed and unsigned `char`s, make sure your implementation supports them directly, either by using plain `char` and the `unsigned` keyword or via a compile-time switch that makes plain `char`s unsigned. In the latter case, you could not have both signed and unsigned `char`s in the same program. The `signed` keyword forces signed values. However, this is an ANSI C invention and may not be available in all your implementations.

ANSI C added the `signed` keyword and permits it to be used with all of the integral types (including `char`). If a variable is `signed`, the keyword `int` is implied, so `signed i;` is equivalent to `signed int i;`.

Recommendation: If some of your implementations don't support the `signed` keyword, you have two choices: `#define` it to be nothing such that it is ignored and plain integral types are used (for this to work you must make sure `signed int` is used instead of just `signed` otherwise a syntax error will result) or use conditional compilation to include one declaration using `signed` or another without. Note that with the exception of `char`, plain integral types are signed so for these types, the `signed` keyword is superfluous.

The type `long double` is an ANSI C invention. It is defined to have a range and precision equal to or greater than that of a `double`. An implementation is at liberty to map `float`, `double`, and `long double` to the same size and representation. While the mapping of `float` to single-precision and `double` to double-precision representation is a common one, this is not guaranteed. All the three types could be mapped to single-precision, for example, as long as single-precision has the minimum precision required for `double` and `long double` as required by ANSI's `float.h`.

Recommendation: If floating-point operations are important to your application, find out the range and precision that you require and that are available in your target implementations. Some compilers provide compile-time options to change floating-point object mapping.

Recommendation: Since ANSI C does not permit `long float` to be a synonym for `double` (as allowed for in K&R) you should not use it—use `double` instead.

Since `long double` may not universally be supported you may need to have this declaration interpreted as `double`. This cannot be done using `#define` of `long` since that might affect `long int` declarations as well and you cannot `#define long double` to be `double`.

Recommendation: To use the type `long double` across implementations that do and do not support it, use something like

```
typedef long double LDOUBLE;
```

or

```
typedef double LDOUBLE;
```

as appropriate. That is, don't use the type `long double` directly in your code.

If you have source that uses the keyword `void` to designate a function with no return value, you can cause this to be accepted by a compiler that does not recognize this keyword by adding the following macro definition in the appropriate place:

```
#define void int
```

Note, however, that this will not provide the error checking possible if `void` were really supported. Alternatively, you could use `typedef` as follows:

```
typedef int void;
```

Recommendation: Even if your implementation does not support `void` functions, use the `void` keyword (`#defined` such that it is ignored as discussed above) as appropriate. If nothing else, it documents the programmer's intention. Then when you move this code to a compiler that does recognize `void`, simply remove the `#define` and recompile to get `void` checking performed. By using a vacuous name `void` (`#defined` to be `int`), you are no worse off than if you used nothing since the default type is `int` anyway. This approach should not cause `void *` to be interpreted as simply `*` since any compiler that supports `void *` obviously recognizes the keyword `void` and should, therefore, support `void` function types.

A pointer to `void` (written as `void *`) is an ANSI C invention. A `void` pointer is large enough to hold any other type's address such that a pointer to type *T* can be assigned into a `void *` object and back again without loss of information (or the need for a cast). Pointers to `void` are designed to allow the use of generic pointers, such as the types returned by the dynamic memory allocation functions. Having them return `char` pointers is no better than `int` or `double` pointers since these functions have no way of knowing the type of data to be stored in the allocated space anyway. You cannot dereference a `void` pointer (or perform arithmetic on it) since it has no attributes attached to it—it can be used only as a constant-width "temporary" storage area for some other pointer-type value.

Pointers to `void` are likely to be very useful on word architectures where pointers to `char` may be a different size than pointers to `int`, for example. On most (if not all) byte architectures, `void *` will likely be equivalent to `char *`. If you move code that includes calls to library functions, such as `malloc`, to an ANSI C environment and you have `#included` the appropriate header, the function prototype for `malloc` will declare that its return type is `void *`. If your code currently expects a `char *` value, this is OK since `void *` is compatible with all pointer types.

Recommendation: If your implementation used different sizes and/or representations for different pointer types, identify the differences and see if `void *` is supported. If you need to write special code for such implementations, isolate and document it.

Whether or not `int` and `long`, and `float` and `double`, (and `long` double) have the same respective sizes and representations is implementation-defined. Therefore you should avoid code such as

```
int i;
long l;
float f;
double d;

i = l;
f = d;
```

since it may cause truncation on some systems. Note that by explicitly casting the right-hand expression, you have the same situation since this is equivalent to the implicit conversion used above.

```
i = (int) l;
f = (float) d;
```

In the following example, the semantics of the conversion are well defined:

```
i = (int)(unsigned int)
        (unsigned long int) l;
```

Recommendation: Don't make assumptions about the size of any type. In particular, don't freely interchange between int and long, and never assign an int to or from a pointer without an explicit cast. Making the assumption that pointers and ints are the same size is one of the most common sources of error in C programs.

A common technique is to conditionally compile declarations based on the size of a particular type as follows:

```
#if sizeof(int) == 4
        int total;
#else
        long total;
#endif
```

However, this will not work in many implementations and is not permitted by ANSI C since sizeof is not allowed in preprocessor arithmetic constant expressions.

Recommendation: The `sizeof` operator is part of the C language and is evaluated at compile-time—it is not a preprocessor operator. Since the preprocessor, in the strictest sense, need know nothing about the C language and data types, sizes, etc., and it can be a stand-alone program quite separate from the compiler proper, ANSI C does not require that `sizeof` be permitted in `#if` expressions. To solve this problem, you can test one or more macros in the headers `limits.h` and `float.h` to determine object sizes or hard-code a macro definition in a `local.h` header indicating the characteristics of the target implementation.

ANSI C implements enumerations as definitions of integer constants. The ANSI C committee chose not to adopt the weakly typed form of enumerations as defined by the UNIX C compiler.

Recommendation: Don't expect a compiler to diagnose attempts to play "fast and loose" with enumerated types. For example, assigning an arbitrary integral expression to an `enum` need not be diagnosed.

◆ Constants ◆

ANSI C requires that an implementation use at least as much precision as is available in the target execution environment when handling constant expressions. It may use more precision.

Floating Constants

The default type of a floating-point constant is `double` (as defined by both K&R and ANSI C). ANSI C further permits constants to be declared type `float` or `long double` explicitly by using a suffix of F (or f) or L (or l), respectively.

Recommendation: For `long double` constants, use the suffix `L` rather than `l` as the latter can easily be confused with the digit `1`, particularly to someone porting code who is not used to `long double` constants.

```
long double ld = 12.3456789012345678901L;
long double ld = 12.3456789012345678901;
long double ld = 12.3456789012345678901;
```

The third example has an initializer of type `double` while the first two initializers have type `long double`.

A compiler may have a command-line switch that enables the default floating-point constant type to be `float` rather than `double`. (If this is the case, this rule is usually applied to all floating-point objects and operations.)

With implementations that support `float` and `long double` constants, make sure that floating-point constants used as function arguments have the correct type. For example,

```
f(1.234F, 1.234, 1.234L);
```

may produce a quite different argument list mapping than

```
f(1.234, 1.234, 1.234);
```

particularly if the function prototype for `f` inhibits widening of `float` to `double`. If `float` is widened to `double` and `long double` is mapped into the same type as `double`, the two calls will produce the same result. In other cases, they may not.

Recommendation: Explicitly type floating-point constants (or cast them) when their size is important (e.g., as function call arguments and with the `sizeof` operator).

Some implementations are liberal in the format of floating-point constants they accept as valid. Both K&R and ANSI C require that either the whole-number part or the fractional part (or both) be present and that either the decimal point or the exponent (or both) also be present.

Recommendation: Do not use non-standard format floating-point constants.

The minimum values or range of values required for floating-point types by ANSI C is defined by macros in the header `float.h`. Since larger ranges and precisions can exist, ANSI C does not specify the number of digits permitted in the whole and the exponent parts.

Integer Constants

ANSI C includes the suffix `U` (and `u`) to support unsigned constants. These suffixes can be used with decimal, octal, and hexadecimal constants. `long int` constants may be suffixed with `L` (or `l`).

Recommendation: For `long int` constants, use the suffix `L` rather than `l` as the latter can easily be confused with the digit `1`. For example,

```
long l = 1234567890L;
long l = 12345678901;
long l = 12345678901;
```

The last two examples use quite different values.

Since ANSI C supports the unsigned suffixes `U` and `u`, the following integral constant suffixes are permitted: `UL`, `Ul`, `ul`, `uL`, `LU`, `lU`, `Lu`, and `lu`. The recommended suffix is `UL` since it is easier to distinguish from the digits preceding it, even more so than `LU`.

K&R permitted octal constants to contain the digits 8 and 9 (which have octal value 10 and 11, respectively). ANSI C does not allow these digits in octal constants.

Recommendation: Don't use the digits 8 and 9 in octal constants.

The type of an integral constant depends on its magnitude, its radix, and the presence of optional suffix characters. This can cause problems when integral constants are used as function arguments. For example, the following function calls may produce a quite different argument list mapping:

```
f(64000);
f(64000U);
f(64000L);
f(64000UL);
```

On a 16-bit machine, 64000 might be interpreted as a `long int` and passed as four bytes while 64000U would be an `unsigned int` and passed as two bytes. On a 32-bit machine, all four might be passed as four byte `int`s.

Recommendation: Explicitly type integral constants (or cast them) when their size is important (e.g., as function call arguments and with the `sizeof` operator).

If your compiler does not support the `U` (or `u`) unsigned suffix and you need to pass a large unsigned value (such as 65535 on a 16-bit system) to a function, you can do so by using an explicit cast or a hexadecimal (or octal) constant as follows:

```
#include <stdio.h>

main()
{
        f(65535);
        f((unsigned) 65535);
        f(0xFFFF);
}

f(i)
unsigned int i;
{
        printf("i = %u\n", i);
}
```

The first call will not produce the expected result if a `long` is passed and `long`s are longer than `int`s.

A similar problem exists on such machines when dealing with NULL. For example,

```
#define NULL 0

f(NULL)
```

may behave differently than

```
#define NULL 0L

f(NULL)
```

This kind of problem is common when using the large memory model on Intel 8088-class CPUs. The code behaves correctly for the small model but does not when it is recompiled (without changes) using the large model.

Yet another problem can occur with constants that represent the largest negative number on a twos-complement system. For example,

```
#include <stdio.h>

main()
{
    printf("%lu\n", (unsigned long) sizeof(int));
    printf("%lu\n", (unsigned long) sizeof(long));
    printf("%lu\n", (unsigned long) sizeof(-32768));
    printf("%lu\n", (unsigned long) sizeof(0x8000));
    printf("%lu\n", (unsigned long) sizeof((int) -32768));
    printf("%d\n", (int) -32768);
    printf("%d\n", 0x8000);
}
```

```
2
4
4
2
2
-32768
-32768
```

On the 16-bit implementation used for this example, the size of an `int` is two bytes yet the size of the constant -32768, the smallest `int` value possible, is four bytes. This is because the type of the expression -32768 is `long`, NOT `int`. The reason for this is that in C there is no such thing as a negative constant (integral or floating point). Constant expressions such as -32768, are treated as expressions preceded by the unary minus operator. And since 32768 has type `long` on the 16-bit machine, -32768 also has type `long`. As shown by the example, if you need this expression to be interpreted as type `int` (so you can use it as an argument to a function expecting an `int`, for example), use a cast or represent it in hexadecimal notation.

Recommendation: When using the largest negative `int` on a 16-bit twos-complement system, make sure its type is consistent with its usage.

The reason for the above size problems is that different conversion rules have been used by various compilers. K&R required the following: "A decimal constant whose value exceeds the largest signed machine integer is taken to be `long`; an octal or hexadecimal constant which exceeds the largest unsigned machine integer is likewise taken to be `long`." That is, on a 16-bit machine such as the PDP-11, 65535 has type `long`.

ANSI C requires the following: "The type of an integer constant is the first of the corresponding list in which its value can be represented. Unsuffixed decimal: `int`, `long int`, `unsigned long int`; unsuffixed octal or hexadecimal: `int`, `unsigned int`, `long int`, `unsigned long int`; suffixed by the letter `U` (or `u`): `unsigned int`, `unsigned long int`; suffixed by the letter `L` (or `l`): `long int`, `unsigned long int`; suffixed by both `U` (or `u`) and `L` (or `l`): `unsigned long int`."

The ANSI C rules are a superset of those defined by K&R.

A problem common to many compilers is that they treat 65535 as an `unsigned int` rather than a `long`, thus causing the problems discussed above in function argument passing.

Recommendation: Hexadecimal and octal constants are likely to cause porting problems, especially when bit masks of machine integers are involved. Their use in code that is to be ported is generally discouraged.

Enumeration Constants

The names of the values defined for an enumeration variable are constants and ANSI C defines them to be `ints`. They cannot be declared to be `unsigned` or `long` (although they can be cast to those types). K&R did not include enumerations.

Character Constants

The mapping of characters in the source character set to characters in the execution character set is implementation-defined.

The value of a character constant that contains a character or escape sequence not represented in the execution character set is implementation-defined.

The meaning of an unspecified escape sequence (except for a backslash followed by a lower-case letter) in a character constant or string literal is implementation-defined. Note that unspecified sequences with a lower-case letter are reserved for future use by the ANSI C Standard. This means that a conforming-implementation is quite free to provide semantics for `'\E'` (for the ASCII Escape character, for example) but it should not do so for `'\e'`.

Recommendation: Do not use non-standard escape sequences in character constants. Do not assume that upper-case escape sequences have any meaning or the same meaning as their lower-case counterparts.

The value of a character constant that contains more than one character is implementation-defined. On a 32-bit machine, it may be possible to pack four characters into a word using `i = 'abcd';`. On a 16-bit machine, something like `int i = 'ab';` might be permitted.

Recommendation: Do not use multi-character constants since their internal representation is implementation-defined. It is determined by the packing of bytes within words and words within longwords and varies widely, for example, on IBM, DEC, and M68k systems.

ANSI C endorses the popular extension of a hexadecimal character constant. This commonly has the form `'\xh'` or `'\xhh'` where `h` is a hexadecimal digit. However, some implementations require that there always be two hex digits even if the first one is a zero. ANSI C permits an unlimited number of hex digits to allow for machines with `chars` larger than eight bits and to allow encoding of multi-byte characters such as those used by the Japanese kanji set.

> **Recommendation:** When using hexadecimal character constants (at least on an 8-bit byte machine), use the form `'\xhh'` rather than `'\xh'`.

K&R declared that if the character following the backslash is not one of those specified, the backslash is ignored. ANSI C says that the behavior is undefined. For example,

```
#include <stdio.h>

main()
{
        printf("'\q' = %d\n", '\q');
}
```

Therefore, an existing constant of the form `'\x'` will now have different meaning. The same is true for `'\a'` and `'\v'` since ANSI C has defined these to be the alarm and vertical tab characters, respectively.

Since ANSI C does not permit the digits 8 and 9 in octal constants, characters such as `'\078'` take on new meaning (it now becomes a two character, character constant).

To avoid confusion with trigraphs (which have the form `??x`), the character constant `'\?'` has been defined by ANSI C. An existing constant of the form `'\?'` will now have different meaning.

> **Recommendation:** Because of differing character sets, use graphic representations of a character instead of its internal representation. For example, use `'A'` instead of `'\101'` in ASCII environments.

Some implementations may allow `''` to represent the null character—ANSI C does not.

> **Recommendation:** Do not use `''` to represent the null character— use `'\0'` instead.

K&R did not define the constant `'\"'`, although it clearly is necessary inside of literal strings. In ANSI C, the characters `'"'` and `'\"'` are identical.

ANSI C invented the notion of a *wide character constant*, which is written just like a character constant with a leading `L` (e.g., `L'a'`.) The type of this constant is `wchar_t`, a type defined in `stddef.h` (among other places).

◆ String Literals ◆

ANSI C states that string literals need not be distinct and that if you attempt to modify a string literal, the behavior is undefined. K&R stated that all strings, even when written identically, are distinct. No statement was made about strings being modifiable.

One source of error can be met when using the `strcpy` library function as follows:

```
strcpy("this is a string", array);
```

Here, the programmer has erroneously swapped the order of the arguments causing `strcpy` to copy the array into the string. Since `strcpy` receives two pointers to `char` and that is what is being passed, it has no way of checking their "correctness."

Recommendation: Do not modify literal strings, even if your implementation allows it, since this is counterintuitive to the programmer. Also, do not rely on like strings being shared. If you have code that modifies string literals, change it to a `char` array initialized to that string and then modify that array. Not only does this not require literals to be modified, but it also allows you to share like strings explicitly by using the same array.

Recommendation: Do not write bizarre code such as `"abc"[1] = 'z';`. (This will actually work if strings are writable.)

The string `""` is legal and represents a string of length zero, containing only a `'\0'` terminator. This is different from the string `"\0"` which is represented as \0\0.

The strings `"'"` and `"\'"` are identical.

The maximum length of a literal string is implementation-defined, but ANSI C requires it to be at least 509 characters.

Since ANSI C does not permit the digits 8 and 9 in octal constants, strings such as `"\078"` take on new meaning. Such a string now becomes a two-character string instead of just one.

Since ANSI C supports the sequences `'\a'`, `'\v'` and `'\x'`, existing strings that contain these may have different meaning.

K&R and ANSI C permit a literal string to be continued across multiple source lines using the backslash/new-line convention as follows:

```
        static char *text = "a string \
of text";
```

However, this requires that the continuation line begin exactly in the first column. A better method is to use the string concatenation capability provided by ANSI C as follows:

```
static char *text = "a string "
                    "of text";
```

String concatenation was not invented by ANSI C; it was adopted from prior art and has existed in the UNIX C compiler for some time.

To avoid confusion with trigraphs (which have the form `??x`), ANSI C supports the character constant `'\?'`. An existing string of the form `"\?"` will now have different meaning. Existing strings that contain sequences, such as `"??x"` where `x` completes a valid trigraph, will now have different meaning. For example, a string that previously contained `"??="` must now be changed to `"\??="`, or `"\?\?="` if it is to retain its original meaning.

Recommendation: If you have literals containing sequences of the form `??x`, prefix the first `?` with a backslash to avoid potential conflict with trigraph sequence recognition. Trigraphs are an ANSI C invention to allow C source programs to be entered on terminals and machines with deficient character sets. (That is, they do not support all the punctuation characters needed to write C source programs.) Whether you need or use trigraphs, a conforming-compiler must recognize them and will convert any character sequence that looks like a trigraph.

ANSI C invented the notion of a *string of wide characters*, which is written just like a literal string with a leading `L` (e.g., `L"abcd".`) The type of this is *array of* `wchar_t`, a type defined in `stddef.h` (among other places).

♦ Operators ♦

ANSI C does not support UNIX Version 6-era assignment operators of the form =*op*. Even K&R hinted at this in the section entitled "17. Anachronisms." The assignment operators now have the form *op*= where *op*=, is a single token, and, therefore cannot contain embedded white space.

A common source of error on compilers that still recognize the =*op* form are `i=-10`, and `c=*pc`, where the intention is to initialize `i` with −10 and to initialize `c` with the contents of the location being pointed to by `pc`. While this type of error may generate a compiler message (in the second case the operands have incompatible types), in some cases you may just get the correct answer. For example,

```
f() {
        static i;

        i=-10;
        printf("i = %d\n", i);
}
```

Whether i=-10 is interpreted as i = i - 10 or as i = -10, the same answer occurs since i is static and has a guaranteed initial value of zero. And 0 - 10 is -10. However, if i had class auto, it may have an initial value of zero, and when that code was ported, different behavior would result.

Recommendation: Change all assignment operators of the form *=op* to *op=*. Make sure that *op=* is written as one token without embedded white space.

ANSI C includes two preprocessor-only operators, # and ##.

Although ANSI C includes the unary plus operator, this does not require a new lexical token since it overloads the existing binary plus operator token.

♦ Punctuators ♦

ANSI C has added the ellipsis punctuator. This has the form ... and has been added as part of the notation for prototype declarations and function definitions. (Function prototypes are an ANSI C invention adopted from C++.)

Recommendation: Use conditional compilation preprocessor directives to include/exclude function prototypes when porting to environments, some of which do not support prototypes. Prototypes are very useful quality assurance tools, so you should use them wherever possible. Just because one of your targets doesn't support prototypes, that is not good reason not to use them for other target implementations.

♦ Header Names ♦

ANSI C has provided a grammar for header names. If the characters ', \, ", or /* occur in an #include directive of the form <...>, the behavior is undefined. The same is true for ', \, and /* when using the "..." #include format.

◆ Comments ◆

Neither K&R nor ANSI C support nested comments, although a number of existing implementations do. Some allow this facility to be enabled/disabled via a compile-time switch. The worst problem with nested comments is when the final closing `*/` is omitted, and the compiler takes the rest of the source file as a comment and treats the end-of-file as an implied close comment, without complaining.

The need for nested comments is primarily to allow a block of code containing comments to be disabled as follows:

```
/*
        int i = 10; /* .... */
*/
```

The same affect can be achieved by using

```
#if 0
        int i = 10; /* .... */
#endif
```

Do not use the following approach since it will compile the code unnecessarily and might even generate code for it even though it can never be executed:

```
if (0) {
        int i = 10; /* .... */
}
```

Recommendation: Do not nest comments—use the conditional compilation approach shown above. If your compiler provides a compile-time switch to enable/disable nested comment recognition, make sure it is disabled.

ANSI C requires that during tokenization, a comment be replaced by one space. Some implementations replace them with nothing and, therefore, allow token pasting as follows:

```
#define PASTE(a,b) a/**/b
```

This causes `a` and `b` to be joined to form the token `ab`. ANSI C requires this to form two tokens, `a` and `b` since they are separated by a space.

Recommendation: Do not rely on comments being replaced by other than one space. If you embed a comment within an expression, put white space either side of the comment so it does not inadvertently cause token pasting.

4

Conversions

◆ Arithmetic Operands ◆

ANSI C states that if an arithmetic conversion produces a result that cannot be represented in the space provided the result, the result is undefined.

Characters and Integers

Whether a plain `char` is treated as signed or unsigned is implementation-defined.

Two different sets of arithmetic conversion rules are currently in use: unsigned preserving (UP) and value preserving (VP). With UP, if two smaller unsigned types (e.g., `unsigned char` or `unsigned short`) are present in an expression, they are widened to `unsigned int`. That is, the widened value is also unsigned. The VP approach widens such values to signed `int` (provided they will fit), else it widens them to `unsigned int`.

While the same result arises from both approaches almost all of the time, there can be a problem in the following situation. Here, we have a binary operator with one operand of type `unsigned short` (or `unsigned char`) and an operand of `int` (or some narrower type). Consider that the program is running on a 16-bit twos-complement machine.

```
#include <stdio.h>

main()
{
        unsigned char uc = 10;
        int i = 32767;
        int j;
        unsigned int uj;

        j = uc + i;
        uj = uc + i;
        printf("j = %d (%x), uj = %u (%x)\n",
                j, j, uj, uj);
        printf("expr shifted = %x\n",
                (uc + i) >> 4);
}
```

With UP, uc will be promoted to unsigned int as will i with the result of uc + i being an unsigned int. With VP, uc will be promoted to int, the type of i, and the two will be added to produce a result of type int. This in itself is not a problem, but if (uc + i) were used as the object of a right-shift (as shown), or as an operand to /, %, <, <=, >, or >=, different results are possible. For example:
UP rules produce:

```
j = -32759 (8009), uj = 32777 (8009)
expr shifted = 800
```

VP rules produce:

```
j = -32759 (8009), uj = 32777 (8009)
expr shifted = f800
```

UP rules cause zero bits to replace high-order bits if the expression has unsigned type, whereas the result is implementation-defined if the object is signed (due to arithmetic versus logical shift possibilities). In the second output example above, VP produced sign-bit propagation during the shift producing a quite different result.

Note that the above example only causes concern for certain values of uc and i, NOT in all cases. For example, if uc were 10 and i were 30,000, the output would be:
UP rules produce:

```
j = 30010 (753a), uj = 30010 (753a)
expr shifted = 753
```

VP rules produce:

```
j = 30010 (753a), uj = 30010 (753a)
expr shifted = 753
```

In this case, the high bit (sign bit) of `(uc + i)` is not set so both UP and VP produce the same result.

Casts should be used in such mixed-mode arithmetic to ensure that the desired results are achieved regardless of the rule used. For example,

```
#include <stdio.h>

main()
{
        unsigned char uc = 10;
        int i = 32767;
        int expr1, expr2, expr3;

        expr1 = ((int) uc + i) >> 4;
        expr2 = (uc + (unsigned) i) >> 4;
        expr3 = (uc + i) >> 4;
        printf("expr1 = %x\n", expr1);
        printf("expr2 = %x\n", expr2);
        printf("expr3 = %x\n", expr3);
}
```

UP rules produce:

```
expr1 = f800
expr2 = 800
expr3 = 800
```

VP rules produce:

```
expr1 = f800
expr2 = 800
expr3 = f800
```

As demonstrated, the results of the two expressions containing the explicit casts are the same, even though the results are different without them.

ANSI C uses VP rules despite the fact that the UNIX C compiler uses UP. This means that existing code that relies on UP rules may now give a different result. Specifically, a `char`, a `short` or an `int` bit field (all of them signed or unsigned) or an enumerated type may be used wherever an `int` may be used. If an `int` can represent all values of the original type, the value is converted to an `int`; otherwise, it is converted to an `unsigned int`.

Recommendation: Use a program similar to those above to determine whether your compiler uses UP or VP rules. Determine if your existing code performs the kinds of operations affected by UP/VP differences. Use casts as appropriate if you need to control the promotions directly.

Note that the "normal" integral widening rules also apply to bit fields and that bit fields can be signed as well as unsigned.

Floating and Integral

ANSI C dictates that floating-point values should truncate toward zero when converted to integers.

Floating Types.   ANSI C states that when a `double` is truncated to a `float` or a `long double` is truncated to a `double` or `float`, if the value being converted cannot be represented, the behavior is undefined. If the value is in the range but cannot be represented exactly, the truncated result is one of the two nearest representable values—it is implementation-defined as to which one of the two is chosen.

Note that by using function prototypes an implementation may allow a `float` to be passed by value to a function without its first being widened to a `double`. However, even though such narrow type preservation is permitted by ANSI C, it is not required.

On some implementations, a `float` representation is not a subset of a `double`. Therefore, it may require a subroutine call to convert from one to the other (and/or to/from `long double`). On other implementations, it is simply a matter of truncating the mantissa of a `double` to get a `float` and to add zero bits to the mantissa of a `float` to get a `double`.

Recommendation: If your implementation forces all floating-point operations to be done using `double` arithmetic, find out the real cost of using the `float` data type in arithmetic and as function arguments.

Usual Arithmetic Conversions.   These are changed by ANSI C to accommodate the VP rules adopted above. Expressions may also be evaluated in a "wider" mode than is actually necessary, to permit more efficient use of the hardware. Expressions may also be evaluated in a "narrower" type, provided they give the same result *as if* they were done in the "wide" mode. For example,

```
short s1, s2;

... = s1 + s2;
```

The `short` variables `s1` and `s2` need not be widened to `int` before the addition, provided the implementation can determine that the correct answer can be obtained by using `short` arithmetic only. The same is true for `char` expressions. Note that the ANSI C Standard does not require any specific approach; it does, however, require that the same answer must be obtained *as if* the "normal" widening were done. This is commonly referred to as the *as if* rule.

If an implementation allows narrower arithmetic, the resulting code may be smaller and/or faster. If an implementation uses wider arithmetic than necessary, the resulting code may also be smaller and/or faster since presumably this is the justification for taking that approach.

It is possible for the operands of a binary operator to have different arithmetic types, resulting in promotion of one or both operands.

The conversion rules defined by ANSI C follow:

- First, if either operand has type `long double`, the other is converted to `long double`.

- Otherwise, if either operand has type `double`, the other is converted to `double`.

- Otherwise, if either operand has type `float`, the other is converted to `float`.

- Otherwise, the integral promotions are performed on both operands. Then the following rules are applied:

- If either operand has type `unsigned long int`, the other is converted to `unsigned long int`.

- Otherwise, if one operand has type `long int` and the other has type `unsigned int`, if a `long int` can represent all values of an `unsigned int`, the operand of type `unsigned int` is converted to `long int`; if a `long int` cannot represent all the values of an `unsigned int`, both operands are converted to `unsigned long int`.

- Otherwise, if either operand has type `long int`, the other is converted to `long int`.

- Otherwise, if either operand has type `unsigned int`, the other is converted to `unsigned int`.

- Otherwise, both operands have type `int`.

These rules are very similar to those defined by K&R except that the VP rules are now accommodated, the new types `long double` and `unsigned long` have been added, and `float` arithmetic is allowed without widening.

♦ Other Operands ♦

Pointers

ANSI C introduced the concept of a pointer to void, written as void *. Such a pointer can be converted to a pointer to an object of any type without using a cast. An object pointer can be converted to a pointer to void and back again without loss of information.

Data object pointers need not all have the same size. For example, a pointer to char need not be the same size as a pointer to int. This is most likely true on word-oriented architectures where character addresses are really word addresses plus bit offsets.

In ANSI C, it is an error to convert a pointer to an object of one type to a pointer to an object of another type without an explicit cast. For example,

```
f()
{
        char *pc;
        int *pi;
        int i;

        pi = pc;                /* error */
        pi = (int *)pc;         /* OK */
        i = *pi;                /* possibly fatal */
}
```

While pc can actually be copied to pi, attempting to dereference pi may prove fatal. For example, on the PDP-11 all objects other than char must be aligned on word boundaries (even addresses). If pc contains an odd address (permissible since a char can be aligned on any byte boundary), then attempting to access that location with a "move word" operation would cause a fatal "Odd Address Trap."

Recommendation: Do not assume that pointers to data objects of different types have the same size and representation.

Recommendation: Always use a cast when you copy a data pointer of one type to a pointer of another data type.

Recommendation: Never dereference a pointer using a type with a less strict alignment requirement than that used to create the pointer value.

Recommendation: Whenever you think you need to copy a data pointer of one type to another pointer type, question the need to actually do so. Not only is it implementation-defined as to whether it will even work, but it is also generally illogical and a quick "fix" for a problem involving poor design.

While `ints` and data pointers often occupy the same size storage, the two types are quite distinct, and nothing portable can be said about interchanging the two except that zero may be assigned or compared to a pointer. Note that this null pointer concept does not require the null pointer value to be "all-bits-zero," although it may be implemented as such. All that C requires is that `(void *)` 0 represent an address at which no object or function will ever be stored. In the expression `p == 0`, zero is promoted to the type of `p` before being compared with it.

Recommendation: Do not assume that pointers and `ints` have the same size or that the null pointer (often called `NULL`) is represented by all-bits-zero.

A function pointer is quite distinct from a data pointer, and no assumptions should be made about the relative sizes of the two. The format and size of a function pointer may be quite different from that of a data pointer. For example, on one of the memory models on the Intel 8088, a data pointer can be 16-bits, while a function pointer is 32-bits. The opposite can be true in yet another memory model.

In ANSI C, even with an explicit cast, it is invalid to convert a function pointer to an object (data) pointer or to a pointer to `void`, or vice versa. For example,

```
f()
{
        char *pc;
        int (*pfi)();
        int (*pfj)();
        void *pv;

        pc = pfi;                   /* error */
        pc = (char *)pfi;           /* error */
        pv = pfi;                   /* error */
        pv = (void *) pfi;          /* error */
        pfi = pc;                   /* error */
        pfi = (int (*)())pc;        /* error */
        pfi = pv;                   /* error */
        pfi = (int (*)())pv;        /* error */

        pfi = pfj;                  /* OK */
        pfj = pfi;                  /* OK */
}
```

Recommendation: Do not assume that function pointers have the same size and representation as data pointers.

Recommendation: Do not copy a function pointer to an object pointer or a pointer to void, or vice versa, even with a cast since this violates ANSI C.

ANSI C requires an explicit cast when a pointer to a function returning one type is assigned to a pointer to a function returning a different type. For example,

```
f()
{
        int (*pfi)();
        char (*pfc)();

        pfi = pfc;                  /* error */
        pfi = (int (*)())pfc;       /* OK */
        pfc = pfi;                  /* error */
        pfc = (char (*)())pfi;      /* OK */
}
```

Recommendation: Do not copy a pointer to a function returning one type to a pointer to a function returning a different type without using an explicit cast.

ANSI C is even more restrictive when copying function pointers because of function prototypes. Now, the attributes of a pointer to a function not only involve that function's return type but also its argument list. For example,

```
f()
{
        int  (*pfi)();
        int  (*pfj)();
        int  (*pfk)(int, int);
        int  (*pfl)(int, int);
        int  (*pfm)(int, char);

        pfi = pfj;                          /* ?? */
        pfk = pfl;                          /* OK */
        pfk = pfm;                          /* error */
        pfk = (int (*)(int, int))pfm;       /* OK */
}
```

The pointers `pfk` and `pfm` are not of the same "type" since `pfk` is a pointer to a function returning an `int` and having two `int` arguments, while the function that `pfm` points to has an `int` and a `char` argument. This is subtle but true.

The pointers `pfi` and `pfj` both point to a function returning an `int` and having an unknown argument list. The question is, "Are these two unknown argument lists the same unknown?" That is, are these argument lists compatible? One could argue a case both for and against. However, since the vast majority of C code written does not use function prototypes, we must assume that compilers not supporting prototypes, consider `pfi` and `pfj` to be assignment-compatible. If, indeed, they were not, we could not make them compatible since it is impossible to write a cast to convert a pointer to a function having an unknown argument list to another pointer to a function that also has an unknown argument list. In fact, they are assignment-compatible.

Recommendation: If you use pointers to functions that have prototypes, then two pointers to functions returning the same type are not directly compatible if their functions have different prototypes. To make them compatible, use an explicit cast.

A common, but not so obvious, place where pointers are treated as integers occurs when pointer values are displayed with `printf`. For example

```
char c;
char *pc = &c;

printf("Address = %u\n",pc);
```

Here, the character pointer is treated as an unsigned int. (Pointers are unsigned quantities so they should not be displayed using %d.) This example relies on the size of a pointer being the same as that of an unsigned int. On the Intel 8088 large model, this is not the case, and a display mask of %lu is needed instead. To avoid this problem, ANSI C has added the display mask %p to printf. This is designed specifically for the purpose of displaying pointer values in an implementation-defined manner. Note, however, that %p expects a pointer to void, and so in the above example, the pointer argument would need to become ((void *)pc).

Recommendation: If you must display a pointer's value using printf, use %p if it is supported. Otherwise, use %u or %lu (or other edit mask) as appropriate since a pointer need not be the same size as an int.

Structures and Unions

ANSI C tightens up assignment-compatibility rules considerably and, in certain circumstances, requires an explicit cast when converting from one type to another. In the past, programmers have tended to be lazy about type compatibility, not only between pointers and ints but also with structures and unions. For example,

```
struct tag1 {
        int i;
        long l;
} st1a, st1b;


struct tag2 {
        int i;
        long l;
} st2a;


struct {
        int i;
        long l;
} st3a, st3b;
```

```
struct {
        int i;
        long l;
} st4a;


f()
{
        st1a = st1b;                    /* OK */
        st1a = st2a;                    /* error */
        st1a = (struct tag1) st2a;      /* error */
        st1a = st3a;                    /* error */
        st1a = (struct tag1) st3a;      /* error */

        st3a = st3b;                    /* OK */
        st3a = st4a;                    /* error */
}
```

All four structure types have the same member types and offsets, and even the same names, so it is difficult to see how an implementation could ever store them differently. However, they are four different types, and more importantly, these types are not assignment-compatible.

Since st1a and st1b both have the same type, struct tag1, they are compatible and can be copied to each other. The same is true for st3a and st3b. Even though st3a and st3b have some unknown struct type (there is no tag), they have the same unknown struct type since they were both declared using the same type declarator. And even though st4a also has an unknown struct type, this type is not the same as the unknown struct type of st3a and st3b, and so st3a and st4a are not compatible.

Note that all attempts at explicit casting fail since it is meaningless to cast an aggregate, generally. In the specific cases above, a cast may make sense, but what should happen if a structure having two members of type double is cast to one having a char * and an int as members?

The problem also will manifest itself when passing structures to functions in the presence of a prototype. Now, the structure passed must have the same type as that expected. Therefore, you could never use a structure of unknown type as an argument in the presence of a prototype since there is no way to declare a structure of unknown type in a prototype.

This sounds much nastier than it really is since, if you are running into this problem, you must ask yourself, "Why am I dealing with different structure types in the same expression?" If they really are the same thing then make them the same type—if they are not, then don't mix apples with oranges. The same applies when declaring a function that returns a structure by value. The structure returned can be assigned only to another structure of the same type; therefore, you cannot return a structure of an unknown type since not only is it not compatible with anything, but there is also no way to declare or define such a return type.

The whole of this section also applies to unions.

Recommendation: If you mean two structures (or unions) to have the same type, then make them have the same type. Don't define them to have types that "look identical" in terms of member numbers, types, and offsets. If they don't have the same tag name, they aren't the same types.

5

Expressions

Expressions are the fundamental building blocks of a C program, and as such, C programmers must understand them and how they interact.

ANSI C affects expressions in that it defines a new operator (unary plus), it specifically defines and identifies sequence points at which a subexpression must be completely evaluated, and it forces grouping parentheses to be honored in all cases.

◆ General Information ◆

The order in which subexpressions are evaluated is unspecified except for the function call operator `()`, the logical OR operator `||`, the logical AND operator `&&`, the comma operator and the conditional operator `?:`. While the precedence table defines certain operator precedences and associativity, these can be overridden by grouping parentheses. However, according to K&R, the commutative and associative binary operators (`*`, `+`, `&`, `|`, `^`) may be arbitrarily rearranged EVEN if grouping parentheses are present. (Note that for `&`, `|`, and `^`, the ordering is unimportant since the same result is always obtained.) However, an ANSI-conforming compiler MUST honor grouping parentheses in ALL expressions.

With the K&R rules (not ANSI), even though you may write

```
i = a + (b + c);
```

the expression may be evaluated as

```
i = (a + b) + c;
```

or even

```
i = (a + c) + b;
```

This can cause overflow on intermediate values if the expression is evaluated one way versus another. To force a specific order of evaluation, break up the expression into multiple statements and use temporary intermediate variables as follows:

```
i = (b + c);
i += a;
```

These examples cause a problem only in "boundary" conditions and even then only on some machines. For example, integer arithmetic on a two-complement machine is usually "well behaved." (However, some machines raise an interrupt when integer overflow occurs and presumably, this should be avoided.) In the following example (run on an Intel 8088 system), the same result is obtained regardless of the order of evaluation.

```
#include <stdio.h>

main()
{
        int i;
        int a = 32767;
        int b = 10;
        int c = -20;

        i = a + b + c;
        printf("i = %d\n", i);


        i = a + c + b;
        printf("i = %d\n", i);

        i = b + c + a;
        printf("i = %d\n", i);
}


i = 32757
i = 32757
i = 32757
```

(An inspection of the machine code generated for this example showed that the compiler evaluated the expressions in the same order in which they were written. In the above case, a + b overflows producing a value of -32759, which when added to c (-20), overflows again giving 32757, the correct answer.)

Recommendation: If you are concerned about the order of evaluation of expressions that associate and commute, break them into separate expressions such that you can control the order. Find out the properties of integer arithmetic overflow for your target systems and see if they affect such expressions.

The potential for overflow and loss of precision errors is much higher with floating-point operands where it is impossible to represent accurately certain real numbers in a finite space. Some mathematical laws that do not always hold true using finite representation are:

```
(x + y) + z == x + (y + z)
(x * y) * z == x * (y * z)
(x / y) * y == x    /* for non-zero y */
(x + y) - y == x
```

When a, b, and c are simple expressions involving constants or variables (as in the earlier example above), the order of evaluation is often irrelevant to the outcome as discussed above. However, if they are expressions that involve side effects, the order may be quite important. For example,

```
test()
{
        int i, f(), g();

        i = f() + g();
}
```

Here, f() may be evaluated before or after g(). While the value of i might be the same in either case, if f() and g() produce side affects, this may not be true. For example,

```
extern int j;

f()
{
        return (j += 5);
}


extern int j;

g()
{
        return (j -= 5);
}
```

If f is called before g, a different value will be assigned to i than if g had been called first. However, j will have the same final value either way. To force a specific order of evaluation, use something like

```
i = f();
i += g();
```

The order in which side effects take place is unspecified. For example, the following are unsafe expressions:

```
j = (i + 1)/i++;.
dest[i] = source[i++]
dest[i++] = source[i]
i & i++
i++ | i
i * --i
```

Which expression containing i is evaluated first in each line above is undefined.

Recommendation: Even if you can determine how your compiler evaluates expressions that contain side effects, don't rely on this being true for future releases of the same product. It may even vary for the same compiler given different circumstances. For example, by changing the source code in other, possibly unrelated, ways, you may change the optimizer's view of the world such that it generates different code for the same expression. The compiler writer is under no obligation whatsoever to support predictable behavior since the behavior is allowed to be undefined.

The results of bitwise operations (using ~, <<, >>, &, ^, and |) on signed types are inherently implementation-defined.

Recommendation: Since the outcome of bitwise operations depends on the representation of integral types you should determine the nature of shift and bit-masking operations, particularly for signed types.

The properties of floating-point arithmetic are implementation-defined. Bear in mind, too, that there may be differences between results obtained with software emulation and hardware execution. Also, a machine may have several different floating-point formats, any one of which might be able to be selected via a compile-time switch.

Recommendation: When using floating-point data types in expressions, identify the size, range, and representation of each such type. Also, determine if there are differences between floating-point emulation in software and the results produced by floating-point hardware. See if you can determine whether floating-point hardware is available at run-time.

If an arithmetic operation is invalid (e.g., division by zero) or produces a result that cannot be represented in the space provided (e.g., overflow or underflow), the result is undefined.

♦ Primary Expressions ♦

A primary expression consists of an identifier (that has been declared as an object), a constant, or a string literal. Note that the type of a constant depends on its form. For certain constants (e.g., -32768, 40000) their type may vary from one implementation to another. (Refer to "Lexical Elements" for details of identifiers, constants, and string literals and to "Constants" for a discussion of the typing rules for constants.)

♦ Postfix Operators ♦

Array Subscripting

The format of an array reference is `a[b]` where `a` and `b` are expressions. One of these expressions must have type pointer to some type (other than `void`), while the other expression must be of integral type. Neither K&R nor ANSI C require `a` to be the pointer expression and `b` to be the integer expression, even though that is normally the way a subscript is written. Specifically, `a[b]` can also be written as `b[a]`, which may be surprising to many people, including C veterans.

Recommendation: Do not write array references as *intexpr* [*ptrexpr*]. Apart from this being counterintuitive to users (even those experienced with C), numerous "full C" compilers won't recognize it as a valid construct.

For programmers who are new to C or frequently switch between C and other languages, it is easy to forget to start array subscripts at zero and/or to stop at n - 1 when looping through an array's elements as follows:

```
#include <stdio.h>

main()
{
        int i[5];

        for (j = 1; j <= 5; ++j)
                i[j] = j * j;

        /* ... */

        for (j = 1; j <= 5; ++j)
                printf("i[%d] = %2d\n",
                         j, i[j]);
}
```

```
i[1] =   1
i[2] =   4
i[3] =   9
i[4] = 16
i[5] = 25            /* undefined behavior */
```

Depending on the object being overwritten beyond the end of the array i, the intended result may be achieved. However, when the program is moved to another environment, it may break (possibly in strange ways) because the trashed area is now important. (Note that while i[5] can be computed, it is undefined as to whether it can be referenced. Attempting to do so may generate a fatal run-time error on some implementations.)

C does not require that the integral expression in an array reference have an unsigned value—it may be signed. For example,

```
#include <stdio.h>

int i[] = {0,1,2,3,4};

main()
{
        int *pi = &i[2];
        int j;

        for (j = -2; j <= 2; ++j)
                printf("x[%2d] = %d\n",
                         j, pi[j]);
}
```

```
x[-2] = 0
x[-1] = 1
x[ 0] = 2
x[ 1] = 3
x[ 2] = 4
```

C provides no array bounds checking so it is not a syntax error to have expressions such as i[5], i[234], or even i[-23] in the above program. However, whether such expressions have any useful value is another matter. If referenced, not only could they give useless results, but they might even cause a fatal run-time error.

Recommendation: For any given object *A* defined to be an array, never subscript *A* with a value other than 0 through n – 1, where n is the maximum number of elements defined to be in *A*.

Recommendation: It is OK to use a negative subscript with a pointer expression provided that the expression maps into a predictable place.

The following example demonstrates the technique of having arrays begin at any arbitrary subscript. (Note though that this technique is not supported by ANSI C and may not work on some implementations—those running on segmented memory architectures may cause it to fail since not all pointer arithmetic behaves in a "wraparound" manner.)

```
#include <stdio.h>

int k[] = {1, 2, 3, 4, 5};

main()
{
        int *p4 = &k[-1];
        int *yr = &k[-1983];

        printf("array p4 = %d %d %d %d %d\n",
                p4[1], p4[2], p4[3],
                p4[4], p4[5]);

        printf("array yr = %d %d %d %d %d\n",
                yr[1983], yr[1984],
                yr[1985], yr[1986],
                yr[1987]);
}
```

```
array p4 = 1 2 3 4 5
array yr = 1 2 3 4 5
```

By making `p4` point to `&k[-1]`, `p4` has subscripts 1 to 5. It is irrelevant that no space has been allocated for the element `k[-1]` since we never try to access that element. All we have done is invent a pointer expression that points to the location where `k[-1]` would be if it existed. Then when we have an expression `p4[1]`, which equals `*(p4 + 1)` or `*(&k[-1] + 1)`, it gives `*(&*(k - 1) + 1)`, `*(k - 1 + 1)`, and finally `*k`, which is the same as `k[0]`. That is, `p4[1]` and `k[0]` are interchangeable, and `p4[1]` through `p4[5]` map into the array `k`.

The use of the pointer `yr` takes the same idea further and allows `yr` to be used like an array with subscripts ranging from 1983 to 1987. The same idea would allow an array to have subscripts -1004 to -1000, simply by initializing a pointer to `&k[1004]`. The following example takes the idea to the extreme:

```
#include <stdio.h>

int k[] = {1, 2, 3, 4, 5};

main()
{
        int *p5 = &k[-1000000];


        printf("array p5   = %d %d %d %d %d\n",
               p5[1000000], p5[1000001],
               p5[1000002], p5[1000003],
               p5[1000004]);
}
```

```
array p5 = 1 2 3 4 5
```

The last two examples initialize pointers to addresses outside the range of actual elements. In the last example, we are one million elements outside the array `k`. Not only is this location outside our program's address space, it may well be outside the machine's address space.

Is this approach portable? Yes, at least for some "well-behaved" machines with a linear address space. Here, address arithmetic is unsigned so that subtracting 10 from address 6 gives, not -4, but a very large unsigned address. That is, the address arithmetic "wraps around" at both the high and the low end. In the case of `p5` in the previous example, we don't care what address `&k[-1000000]` corresponds to as long as when 1000000 is added to it, we get `&k[0]`. While this may not be the case on every conceivable machine (segmented architectures may cause problems), it certainly works well on many common ones.

It is possible to portably calculate the size of each dimension of an array by knowing only the number of dimensions.

```
#include <stdio.h>

main()
{
        int i[2][3][4];
        unsigned long dim1, dim2, dim3;

        dim3 =  sizeof(i[0][0])/
                sizeof(i[0][0][0]);
        printf("dim3 = %lu\n", dim3);


        dim2 =  sizeof(i[0])/(dim3 *
                sizeof(i[0][0][0]));
        printf("dim2 = %lu\n", dim2);

        dim1 =  sizeof(i)/(dim2 *
                dim3 * sizeof(i[0][0][0]));
        printf("dim1 = %lu\n", dim1);
}
```

```
dim3 = 4
dim2 = 3
dim1 = 2
```

`i[0][0]` is an array of four elements, so `sizeof(i[0][0])` divided by `sizeof(i[0][0][0])` is 4. Note that the type of `i[0][0]` is NOT `int *`, it is `int (*p)[4]`. That is, `p` is a pointer to an array of four `int`s and `sizeof(*p)` is `4 * sizeof(int)`.

Similarly, `i[0]` is an array of three elements each of which is an array of four `int`s. And finally, `i` is an array of two elements, each of which is an array of three elements, each of which is an array of four `int`s.

Function Calls

If a function call has no function prototype declarator in scope, and the number of arguments, or their types, after the default conversions do not match those of the formal parameters, the behavior is undefined.

If a function that accepts a variable number of arguments is called, and no prototype declarator with the ellipsis notation is in scope, the behavior is undefined.

Recommendation: Whenever you use variable length argument lists in functions, document it thoroughly and use the `stdarg` (or `varargs`) header as appropriate. Always declare such functions using a prototype with the appropriate ellipsis notation before you call them.

The order in which function arguments are evaluated is unspecified. For example,

```
f(i, i++);
```

contains an unsafe argument list; `i++` may be evaluated before `i`.

Recommendation: Never rely on the order of evaluation of arguments in a function call.

A function that has not been explicitly declared is treated as though it were declared with class `extern` and as returning type `int`. Apart from `stdio.h`, `ctype.h`, and `math.h`, implementations have varied widely in the names and nature of the "standard" headers they have supported. This problem has been compounded by the advent of ANSI C, which has caused some definitions and declarations to be moved to headers other than those where some users expect them.

Recommendation: When porting, take care that the headers in the target environment contain the necessary function declarations; otherwise, function calls will be interpreted as returning `int`s, whereas they would not be if a declaration was in scope. For example, ANSI C declares `atof` and `atoi` (and the `malloc` family) in `stdlib.h`, whereas many users expect them to be declared in `math.h`. (Refer to Appendix A for details of header contents.)

Problems can occur when porting code that uses integral constants as function arguments. For example,

```
f()
{
        g(60000);
}
```

```
g(i)
int i;
{
        /* ... */
}
```

This program works properly on a machine with 32-bit `ints`. But on a 16-bit machine, the actual argument to `g` will be a `long int`, while `g` will be expecting an `int`, two quite different types.

Recommendation: Take care when passing integral constants as function arguments since the type of such a constant depends on its magnitude and the limits of the current implementation. This kind of problem may be difficult to find if the constant is hidden in a macro (such as in `limits.h`). Use casts to make sure argument types match or call functions in the presence of a prototype.

ANSI C permits structures and unions to be passed by value as well as by address. Therefore, if `s1` is a structure (or union), the statements

```
f(s1);
f(&s1);
```

are quite different. By default, most modern compilers now pass by value instead of by address, so existing code that passes by address (by default) must have the address-of operator `&` added. The existing formal argument definitions will not change as they explicitly declare the argument as a pointer.

Recommendation: If your code passes structures (or unions) by address, make sure the expression is prefixed with the `&` unary operator. On older compilers where this is the default (and only) way of passing them, the `&` will be redundant. On compilers that support passing by value, the operator will be necessary.

The maximum size of a structure or union that may be passed by value is implementation-defined. For example, the VAX Calling Standard requires that an argument list be totally contained in 255 thirty-two-bit longwords (permitting, for example, one structure argument of size 1020 bytes only.)

Recommendation: If you pass large aggregates by value, make sure each implementation can pass objects of the required size. (For performance reasons, you should pass large aggregates by address, to avoid potentially time-consuming copies.)

ANSI C requires that an implementation allow at least 31 arguments in a function call. K&R placed no minimum limit.

Recommendation: If you use more than a few arguments in function calls, make sure your target environments support as many arguments as you need.

ANSI C permits pointers to functions to be used to invoke functions using either `(*pfunct)()` or `pfunct()`. The new latter format makes the call look like a normal function call, although presumably it will cause less sophisticated source cross-reference utilities to assume that `pfunct` is a function name rather than a function pointer.

Recommendation: When invoking a function via a pointer, use the format `(*fp)()` rather than `fp()` since the latter is an ANSI C invention.

Recommendation: A function prototype can be used to alter the argument widening and passing mechanisms used when a function is called. Make sure that the same prototype is in scope for all calls as well as the definition.

Recommendation: ANSI C requires that a strictly conforming program always have a prototype in scope (with a trailing ...) when calling a function with a variable number of arguments. Therefore, when using the `printf` and `scanf` family of routines, always `#include <stdio.h>`. If you don't, the behavior is undefined.

Structure and Union Members

Due to the addition of structure (and union) argument passing and returning by value and structure (and union) assignment, structure (and union) expressions can exist. For example,

```
extern struct s {
        int j;
        char *pc;
} s1, s2, s3;
```

```
extern int i;

f()
{
        struct s f1();

        s1 = f1();
        s1 = s2 = s3;
        s1 = i > 10 ? s2 : s3;
        s1 = (i++, s2);
        i = f1().j;
}
```

Note that the expressions used above,

```
f1()
s2 = s3
i > 10 ? s2 : s3
(i++, s2)
```

are not lvalues and, as such, cannot be assigned a value.

K&R states that in x->y, x may be either a pointer to a structure (or union) or an absolute machine address. ANSI C requires that each structure and union have its own member name space. This requires that the first operand of the . or -> operators must have type structure (or union) or pointer to structure (or union), respectively.

On some machines, such as the DEC PDP-11, the hardware I/O page is mapped into physical memory so that device registers look just like regular memory to any task that can map to this area. To access an offset (a structure member named status, for example) from a specific physical address, you previously could use an expression of the form

```
0xFF010->status
```

With each structure and union now having its own member name space, the status member being referenced is ambiguous. For example, three structures could be in scope, each having a member named status at different offsets within those structures. The members could also have different types. Therefore, the physical address must be converted to a structure pointer so the offset reference is unambiguous, as follows:

```
((struct tag1 *) 0xFF010)->status
((union tag2 *) 0xFF010)->status
```

Recommendation: Do not precede the -> operator with an integral constant expression—always cast that expression to the appropriate structure (or union) pointer type first. Don't forget to parenthesize the whole cast expression since the -> operator has precedence over casts.

Numerous compilers have been loose with expressions involving structure and member offsets. For example,

```
struct tag {
        int i;
        char *name;
};

f()
{
        int k;

        k.i = 26;
}
```

According to ANSI C, the expression k.i is erroneous—it should generate a constraint error since k is not a structure or union. However, some compilers happily accept this construct and interpret i as an offset of zero from object k. Therefore, k.i is synonymous with k, while k.name represents the "pointer" stored at location k + sizeof(int).

Recommendation: Do not attempt to use a member name to represent anything other than an offset from a structure or union of which it is a member. Members are not integral constants representing a generic offset from some base—they are specifically associated with a particular structure or union by the qualifier immediately preceding the . or -> operator.

When a union is accessed using a member other than that used to store the immediately previous value, the result is implementation-defined. No assumptions can be made about the degree of overlap of members in a union unless a union contains several structures, each of which has the same initial member sequence. In this special case, members in the common sequence of any of the structures can be inspected provided that the union currently contains one of those structures. For example,

```
struct rectype1 {
        int rectype;
        int var1a;
};


struct rectype2 {
        int rectype;
        float var2a;
};


union record {
        struct rectype1 rt1;
        struct rectype2 rt2;
} inrec;
```

If the union currently contains a structure of type `rectype1` or `rectype2`, the particular type being stored can reliably be determined by inspecting either `inrec.rt1.rectype` or `inrec.rt2.rectype`. Both members are guaranteed to map to the same area.

Postfix Increment and Decrement Operators

Some implementations consider post-increment and post-decrement operator expressions to be lvalues. This has not been adopted by ANSI C. Therefore, `(i++)++` generates an error since `i++` is not an lvalue and, therefore, cannot be incremented.

A pointer to `void` cannot be used as an operand to `++` and `--` since it does not point to an object of known type.

◆ Unary Operators ◆

Prefix Increment and Decrement Operators

Refer to "Postfix Increment and Decrement Operators."

Address and Indirection Operators

If an invalid array reference (one with a subscript "out of range"), null pointer reference, or reference to an object declared with automatic storage duration in a terminated block occurs or if allocated space that has been freed is accessed, the behavior is undefined. Note that depending on how the null pointer is implemented, dereferencing it may cause catastrophic results. For example, with VAX/VMS, an attempt to access a location within the first 512 bytes of an image generates a fatal "access violation."

```
main()
{
        int *pi, *f();

        pi = f();
        *pi = 10;
}


int *f()
{
        int i = 100;

        return (&i);            /* unsafe */
}
```

Recommendation: Do not return the address of an automatic variable since the pointer will point to a location that is no longer being used for that `auto` variable. Depending on the code generated and the program's logic, the previous example might work. However, there are plenty of cases where it won't and it isn't required to anyway. The same applies to the use of addresses of `auto` objects in inner-level blocks, after those blocks have been terminated. For example,

```
main()
{
        int *pi;

        {
                int i = 100;

                pi = &i;
        }

        *pi = 10;
}
```

While this program is not required to work reliably, it will work on many implementations since they don't deallocate the space allocated for the `auto` variable `i` until the parent function exits. Few implementations actually allocate and deallocate `auto` space at the block-level; however, they may reuse `auto` space in non-overlapping blocks. Note that a signal handler could be invoked in the meantime, which may cause the space to be overwritten.

ANSI C permits aggregates and functions to be used in conjunction with the address-of operator `&`. For example,

```
test()
{
        int i[10];
        void f();
        struct tag1 s;
        union tag2 u;

        f(i);           /* both cause    */
        f(&i);          /* &i[0] to be   */
                        /* passed to f   */

        g(f);           /* these two are */
        g(&f);          /* identical     */

        a(s);           /* these two are */
        a(&s);          /* not identical */

        b(u);           /* these two are */
        b(&u);          /* not identical */
}
```

In ANSI C, the use of the `&` operator is superfluous with function names. However, when the passing of structures and unions by value was added to the language, using `&` with a structure or union name was no longer superfluous—its absence means "value" and its presence means "pointer to."

Recommendation: Whenever you want the address of a structure or union, always use the unary `&` operator along with the structure or union name even if your compiler does not support passing structures and unions by value, or their assignment.

Some implementations accept *&bit-field* and return the address of the object in which the bit field is packed.

Recommendation: Do not attempt to take the address of a bit-field—it is not permitted by K&R or ANSI C.

Some implementations allow &*register-variable*, in which case the `register` class is ignored.

Recommendation: Do not attempt to take the address of a variable with class `register`—it is not permitted by K&R or ANSI C.

Some implementations allow you to take the address of a constant expression under special circumstances, such as in function argument lists.

Recommendation: Do not attempt to take the address of a constant—it is not permitted by K&R or ANSI C.

The address of a function may not in fact be the address at which that function's executable code begins. Consider the case of one compiler for the Intel 8086 family. For the P model it uses two-byte data pointers and four-byte code addresses. For efficiency, it is best if data and function pointers have the same size. But if all data pointers are extended to 32 bits, by adding a zero high-order word, this would defeat the purpose of using the P model instead of the L model. So rather than extend all data pointers (which are typically more common than function pointers), function pointers are forced to be accessed via 16 bits. This requires the use of a 16-bit "pseudo-function pointer." which points to a 32-bit address in the data segment, which in turn contains the real address of the function. Hence, for this model, the address contained by a function pointer is not the address of the function; it is a pointer to the address of the function.

Recommendation: Do not assume that the address of a function is the address of the first byte (or word) of that function's executable code.

A pointer to `void` cannot be dereferenced directly. It must first be cast to an object pointer type so that the attributes of the object pointed to become known.

A common use of space allocated on the heap is to build linked lists where each node contains a pointer to the next (and possibly the previous) node in the chain. The addresses of these nodes are absolute (physical or virtual) addresses, not relative to the start of the allocated space. If you use the library function `realloc` to expand or contract this allocated space, `realloc` is at liberty to move the list to a new allocated location. If this is done, the addresses stored in the nodes will point to the previously allocated space that was deallocated by `realloc`.

Recommendation: Never use `realloc` on heap space that contains pointers into itself (or if other pointers point there) since the space these pointers point to will be freed by `realloc` if it has to relocate that space.

Dereferencing a pointer may cause a fatal run-time error if the pointer was cast from some other pointer type and alignment criteria were violated. For example, the PDP-11 requires that all scalar objects other than `char` be aligned on word (`int`) boundaries. Therefore, if you cast a `char` pointer containing an odd address to an `int` pointer, and you dereference the `int` pointer, a fatal odd address trap error will result.

Recommendation: If you cast a pointer of one type to a pointer of another type, make sure alignment requirements are met before you dereference the resulting type.

Unary Arithmetic Operators

The unary plus operator is an ANSI C invention.

C does not support negative constant expressions. That is, in `-conexpr`, `conexpr` is a nonnegative constant expression used as an operand to the unary minus operator. This can cause a problem with the smallest negative integral value on twos-complement machines. On a 16-bit system, for example, -32768 is the smallest value that can be represented in an `int`. However, the type of the expression -32768 is `long`, not `int`, since the type of 32768 is `long`. This may cause a problem in `f(-32768)` where a `long` is passed but `f` expects an `int`, although it need not. For example, if -32768 is represented as two words containing 0xFFFF and 0x8000, it could be stored in memory in two ways, each with these words swapped. If the words are passed to function `f` in the order shown, `f` will map into the 0xFFFF and will give the wrong result. If the words are passed in reverse order, `f` will map into 0x8000, and the correct value will be used, although if `f` has arguments following the first, they will be misinterpreted.

Recommendation: Take care that the type of a negative decimal constant expression is what you want. If necessary, use a cast or represent the whole expression using octal or hexadecimal notation. For example, instead of `f(-32768)` use `f((int) -32768)`. Better still, use a prototype to force the argument to be `int` regardless of whether it is currently an `int`, `unsigned int`, or `long`. (Note that if `f` is called using `f(-32768)` and the prototype `int f(int);` is in scope, the argument passed will be an `int`, not a `long` since the prototype will implicitly cast the actual argument from `long` to `int`.)

The `sizeof` Operator

The `sizeof` operator returns the size, in bytes, of its operand. If the operand is a type name, it must be enclosed in parentheses; if it is an expression, the parentheses are not required although they are permissible since any expression can be enclosed in parentheses. That is, the parentheses are part of the expression, not part of the `sizeof` syntax in this case. For example, both `sizeof(i)` and `sizeof i` are permitted but `sizeof int` is not.

Since `sizeof` is a unary operator, a `sizeof` expression must have a type as well as a value. And this value should reflect the maximum array subscript possible for the implementation since, after all, you should be able to find the size of the largest possible `char` array that you can create. However, in many implementations the type of `sizeof` is a signed `int`. If this is the case on a 16-bit machine, the size of a 40,000 byte `char` array has a negative value—which is clearly an error, or at least, not intuitive.

ANSI C requires the derived type `size_t` to be defined in the library header `stddef.h` (among other places). `size_t` is the type of the value returned by the `sizeof` operator and must be an unsigned integral type. The choices an ANSI C implementation has for `size_t`, therefore, are `unsigned int` or `unsigned long int`.

Recommendation: If you care about the type of the `sizeof` operator, check each of your targets since it may be implemented as an `int` or a `long` and as signed or unsigned. (One case where you may be concerned about `sizeof`'s type is if you use it in an expression where a signed operand meets an unsigned operand.) The following program should allow you to determine these attributes:

```
#include <stdio.h>

main()
{
        printf("sizeof produces %s",
                sizeof(char) > -1 ?
                "a signed"
                : "an unsigned");

        printf(" %s value\n",
                sizeof(sizeof(char)) <
                sizeof(long) ? "int"
                : "long");
}
```

If `sizeof` is signed, it will compare greater than −1; otherwise, −1 should be promoted to `unsigned int` in which case the comparison should prove false.

Consider the case where `sizeof` gives a signed `int` and the following program is run on a twos-complement, 16-bit machine.

```
#include <stdio.h>

double d[5000];

main()
{
        printf("# elements in d = %d %d\n",
                sizeof(d)/sizeof(double),
                sizeof(d)/8);
}
```

```
# elements in d = -3192 -3192
```

If `sizeof` gave an `unsigned int`, the result would be

```
# elements in d = 5000 5000
```

The return type of the ANSI library function `strlen` is `size_t` since `strlen` can never legitimately return a negative size. However, many non-ANSI `strlen` versions return an `int`.

When an expression is used with `sizeof`, that expression is not evaluated, although its type must be found. For example, `sizeof(i++)` must not generate code to increment `i`. (Even if it did that would not affect the size produced.) Also, `sizeof(32767 + 10)` is not necessarily the same as `sizeof(32777)` since the first expression may have type `int` and the second type `long int`. The type of the operand in `sizeof(1 + 2L)` is `long` since the expression `1 + 2L` has type `long`. Note that when using `sizeof` with expressions such as `!t`, `-t`, and `t`, and `t` is one of the narrow types `char`, `short`, or `float`, type promotion is involved and the result may be different to that when the unary operators are omitted.

Recommendation: Do not rely on the expression used with `sizeof` to be evaluated—it shouldn't be, although on some implementations it is.

Some implementations accept `sizeof` (*bit-field*) and return the size of the object in which the bit field is packed.

Recommendation: Do not attempt to take the size of a bit-field—it is not permitted by K&R or ANSI C.

Numerous library routines require arguments and have return values of the type `size_t`. One example is `malloc`, which expects the size to be allocated to be an unsigned integral value. If you use `malloc(10)`, 10 is signed, not unsigned. In reality, this should not cause a problem since unsigned types are typically the same size as their signed counterparts—only the sign bit is interpreted differently. However, it is possible that this signed/unsigned mapping may not work for a particularly exotic implementation.

Recommendation: Always use a prototype when calling functions that expect `size_t` type arguments so that the arguments you supply can be implicitly cast by the prototype if necessary. Of course, you could always cast them to `size_t` yourself.

Even though `sizeof` indicates the number of "bytes" taken up by its operand, not all those bytes need be used to represent a value of that type. For example, a Cray is a 64-bit word computer, and on it, `sizeof(short)`, `sizeof(int)` and `sizeof(long)` all return eight. However, a `short` uses only three of those eight bytes. A similar case can exist on 36-bit word ASCII machines, which use nine bits for a `char` even though only eight of each are used.

Recommendation: Do not assume all bits allocated to an object are used to represent that object.

♦ Cast Operators ♦

ANSI C indicates that a cast expression is not an lvalue.

Some implementations allow a pointer to an object to be cast to a pointer to a function, allowing data to be invoked as a function. A pointer to a function may also be cast a pointer to an object, allowing a function to be inspected or modified (for example, by a debugger). These conversions are not endorsed by ANSI C.

Recommendation: Do not cast a pointer to data to a pointer to function or vice versa since they may not be compatible, either in size or representation.

The result of casting a pointer to an integer or vice versa (except for the value zero) is implementation-defined as is the result of casting one pointer type to a pointer type of more strict alignment.

Recommendation: Casting data pointers to and from integers is inherently nonportable. If you must do it, document it adequately and/or isolate the code appropriately. There is no guarantee that a data pointer can be represented in an `int` or even a `long int`.

For a detailed discussion on the conversions allowed between dissimilar data pointers and dissimilar function pointers, refer to the section on "Pointer Conversions."

You cannot cast a structure (or union) into any type nor can you cast into a structure (or union) type.

Explicit casting may be necessary to get the right answer because of "unsigned preserving" versus "value preserving" conversion rules.

```
/* mixed mode arithmetic and UP/VP */

f()
{
        unsigned short ui;
        int i;

        ... = ui + i;
}
```

It may be necessary to force type promotion to maintain accuracy.

```
#include <stdio.h>

main()
{
        int i1 = 10000;
        int i2 = 1234;
        double d1, d2;

        d1 = i1 * i2 * 10.0;
        printf("d1 = %f\n",d1);


        d2 = (double) i1 * i2 * 10.0;
        printf("d2 = %f\n",d2);
}

d1 = 192320.000000
d2 = 123400000.000000
```

On a 16-bit machine (as shown), d1 is incorrect. However, on a 32-bit machine, it should be correct since no overflow would occur.

A number of the ANSI C library functions return void * values, and this is reflected in their corresponding prototypes. Since void * is compatible with all other data pointer types, you will not need to explicitly cast the value returned. If your compiler does not support the strict assignment compatibility checking of ANSI C, then it will probably allow you to assign any data pointer type to any other such type without an explicit cast.

Using an elaborate series of casts, it is possible to write a "fairly" portable expression that will produce the offset (in bytes) of a specific member of a structure. (This was first proposed by Tom Plum.) However, this may not work on some implementations, particularly those running on word architectures.

```
#define OFFSET(struct_type, member) \
        ((size_t)(char *)\
        &((struct_type *)0)->member)
```

Recommendation: ANSI C provides the macro offsetof (in stddef.h) to portably find the offset of a member within a structure. This macro should be used instead of any "home-grown" mechanism, where possible.

Many implementations (and ANSI C) permit you to disregard the return value explicitly from a non-void function using a void cast as follows,

```
#include <stdio.h>

main()
{
        (void) printf("Hello\n");
}
```

The only value of this is to quieten lint or other such tools that complain about your not using return values. For many functions you don't want to—strcpy, strcmp, printf, for example, always return a value which can legitimately be ignored.

Recommendation: When assigning a long to int (or short or char) or a double to a float, use an explicit cast to indicate that the assignment is intentional. (This may stop your compiler or lint from warning you though.)

Recommendation: Do not assume that zero cast to a pointer type results in a value that has all-bits zero. However, a pointer with the value 0 (produced either by assigment or casting) must compare equal to zero.

Recommendation: Care should be taken when casting a pointer of one type to a pointer of another type with more strict alignment requirements. For example,

```
char c;
char *pc = &c;
int *pi;
int i;

pi = (int *)pc;
i = *pi;
```

On a PDP-11, for example, if `pc` contains an odd address, dereferencing `pi` will generate an odd address trap. On a Cray, the byte address will be truncated to a word address.

◆ Multiplicative Operators ◆

When negative operands are used in integer division, the sign of the remainder is implementation-defined.

Recommendation: The ANSI C library function `div` and `ldiv` produce integral quotient and remainder with well-defined sign semantics.

The multiplication operator is commutative and associative and (according to K&R) expressions involving several multiplications at the same level may be regrouped by the compiler without regard to grouping parentheses. The implications of this were discussed at the beginning of this chapter.

Recommendation: Do not use grouping parentheses in expressions containing multiple binary `*` operators at the same level since they can be ignored by the compiler. Note though that ANSI C requires grouping parentheses to be honored in ALL cases.

◆ Additive Operators ◆

The addition operator is commutative and associative and (according to K&R) expressions involving several additions at the same level may be regrouped by the compiler without regard to grouping parentheses.

Recommendation: Do not use grouping parentheses in expressions containing multiple binary + operators at the same level since they can be ignored by the compiler. Note though that ANSI C requires grouping parentheses to be honored in ALL cases.

If an integer is added to or subtracted from a pointer that is not pointing to a member of an array object, the result is undefined. ANSI C permits an integer to be subtracted from a pointer pointing to the element immediately beyond the last element in an array, provided the resultant address maps into the same array.

The length of the integer required to hold the difference between two pointers to members of the same array is implementation-defined. ANSI C provides the derived type `ptrdiff_t` to represent the type of such a value. This signed integral type is defined in `stddef.h`.

Recommendation: Since some implementations use an unsigned integer to represent the difference between two pointers, the results of subtracting a larger pointer from a smaller one may be surprising. In this case, you can ensure the right answer by using something like

```
int diff;

diff = (ptr1 > ptr2) ? ptr1 - ptr2
          : ptr2 - ptr1;
```

If two pointers that are not pointing into the same array object are subtracted, the result is undefined.

ANSI C endorses the widespread practice of allowing a pointer to be incremented one place beyond the end of an object. This does not require that the extra location exist since the pointer need not be dereferenced. For example,

```
char c[10];
char *pc1 = &c[0];
char *pc2 = &c[10];
```

Here, `pc2` points to a location just beyond the end of the array `c`. This allows `pc2 - pc1` to give the length of the object, exactly.

◆ Bitwise Shift Operators ◆

The result of a shift by a negative number or by an amount greater than or equal to the width in bits of the expression being shifted is implementation-defined.

Recommendation: Do not shift bits by a negative number or by a number greater than or equal to the number of bits in the expression being shifted.

Recommendation: Do not right-shift signed integral expressions having negative values since the result will be implementation-defined.

The widening rules of unsigned preserving and value preserving can cause different results with the `>>` operator. With UP rules, `(unsigned short + int) >> 1` is the same as dividing by 2, whereas with VP, it is not since the type of the expression to be shifted is signed.

In ANSI C the type of the shift count has no effect on the type of the result, although on some implementations it does.

Recommendation: Make sure the shift count has type `int` just in case your implementation uses its type to determine the final type of the expression being shifted. Specifically, don't use a shift variable of type `long`, an integral constant with suffix `L` (or `l`), or a cast to `long`.

Using the macro `CHAR_BIT` in `limits.h` and the `sizeof` operator, you can determine the number of bits in any type of object. However, not all bits allocated to an object need take part in that object's representation (as discussed earlier).

◆ Relational Operators ◆

If you compare pointers that are not pointing to the same aggregate, the result is undefined. "Same aggregate" means members of the same structure or elements in the same array. Notwithstanding this, ANSI C endorses the widespread practice of allowing a pointer to be incremented one place beyond an object. Therefore, if `p` points to the last element in an array object, `p + 1` is a legitimate reference and `(p + 1) > p`.

Recommendation: Comparison of two pointers that do not point into the same aggregate is, and always has been, nonportable since except for aggregates, you have no other control of the way in which objects are stored in memory.

The widening rules of unsigned preserving and value preserving can cause different results with the >, >=, < and <= operators.

♦ Equality Operators ♦

A pointer may be compared to 0. However, the behavior is implementation-defined when a nonzero integral value is compared to a pointer.

Structures and unions may not be compared except by member. Depending on the presence of, and contents of, holes, structures might be able to be compared for equality using the library function memcmp.

Take care when using these operators with floating-point operands since most floating-point values can be stored only approximately.

♦ Bitwise AND Operator ♦

According to K&R (but not ANSI C), expressions involving several binary & operations at the same level may be regrouped even in the presence of parentheses. As stated earlier, this will not affect the result of the expression.

Recommendation: Using constructs such as x & 0177700 may not be portable when specific bits are to be masked since this relies on knowing the number of bits in an int. Use x & ~077 instead.

♦ Bitwise Exclusive OR Operator ♦

Expressions involving several ^ operations at the same level may be regrouped even in the presence of parentheses. As stated earlier, this will not affect the result of the expression.

Recommendation: Using constructs such as x ^ 0177700 may not be portable when specific bits are to be masked since this relies on knowing the number of bits in an int. Use x ^ ~077 instead.

◆ Bitwise Inclusive OR Operator ◆

Expressions involving several | operations at the same level may be regrouped even in the presence of parentheses. As stated earlier, this will not affect the result of the expression.

Recommendation: Using constructs such as `x | 0177700` may not be portable when specific bits are to be masked since this relies on knowing the number of bits in an `int`. Use `x | ~077` instead.

◆ Logical AND Operator ◆

This operator is well defined and has no implementation-defined or undefined characteristics.

◆ Logical OR Operator ◆

This operator is well defined and has no implementation-defined or undefined characteristics.

◆ Conditional Operator ◆

Due to the addition of structure (and union) argument passing and returning by value and structure (and union) assignment, structure expressions can now exist.

```
struct s s1, s2, s3;
int i;

s1 = i > 10 ? s2 : s3;
```

Both K&R and ANSI C require that if either of the second or third operands to the conditional operator is a pointer, the other should be a pointer of the same type or the null pointer constant (or in the case of ANSI C, a pointer to `void`). Since ANSI C provides for much stricter type checking, expressions that were previously permitted by compilers (possibly with a warning being issued) may now be rejected. For example,

```
main()
{
        char *fpc();
        int fi();
        void fv();
        int i = 5;
        int f();
        int g(double);

        i > 10 ? fpc() : fi();          /* Error */
        i > 10 ? fpc() : 0;             /* OK */
        i > 10 ? fv()  : 0;             /* Error */
        i > 10 ? fv()  : 10;            /* Error */
        i > 10 ? f : g;                 /* OK */
}
```

Recommendation: Make sure that the second and third operands of the conditional operator have the same type, or can be promoted to the same type. While arithmetic operands can be implicitly promoted, pointers cannot be, in which case explicit casts should be used. ANSI C clearly defines the constraints on the operator types, and with the exception of things relating to new features of the language, these constraints are the same as specified by K&R.

◆ Assignment Operators ◆

Assigning a constant expressions whose value is 0 to any pointer is portable, but assigning any other arithmetic value is not. Assignment of a pointer to an `int` is not portable.

The effect of assigning one pointer type to a more strict pointer type is implementation-defined.

ANSI C requires an explicit cast to assign a pointer of one object type to a pointer of another object type. Note that a cast is not needed when assigning to or from a `void` pointer.

Recommendation: If you must assign a pointer of one object type to a pointer of another object type, use an explicit cast.

A structure or union can be assigned only to a like type structure or union. Structures and unions may not be cast (although pointers to such types, can be). Note that structure and union assignment has not always been part of the C language.

Simple Assignment

If an object is assigned to an overlapping object, the result is undefined. (This might be done with different members of a union, for example.) To assign one member of a union to another, go through a temporary variable.

A common (and necessary) technique when reading characters from stdin (or a file) is to store them in an int rather than a char since the special EOF value needs to be represented. If the characters were stored into a char, the EOF value truncated to a char may not test equal to EOF since char may be an unsigned type, while EOF may be negative.

Recommendation: When assigning characters returned from functions with int return type, use an int, not a char, so that EOF can be properly detected.

Compound Assignment

Assignment operators of the form =*op* are not supported by ANSI C. (K&R hinted that they were already archaic back in 1978.) However, numerous compilers continue to support them, and several obscure problems can result. For example,

```
f()
{
        int i=-10;
        static int j=-10;
        int k;

        for (k=-5; k<=5; ++k)
                ...
}
```

If the old-style assignment operators are supported (typically unknown to the programmer) the following problems occur: The int i is not initialized to -10. Instead, its current value (undefined since it has class auto) is reduced by 10 giving an undefined value. If the class static is added to the declaration, as for j, the situation is more interesting since subtracting 10 from the initial value of 0 (guaranteed for static objects) gives -10, which is the same as if we had assigned -10 to j. That is, we achieve the intended result, but by accident.

The most surprising and difficult bug to find is with the first expression in the for statement. Here, k is reduced by 5 rather than being set to -5, and depending on the initial (undefined) value of k, the loop will be executed too many or too few times, or even the correct number of times or not at all.

> **Recommendation:** If your compiler supports the old-style assignment operators of the general form =*op*, do not use them as such—use *op*= instead. Use white space to separate tokens in expressions such as i = -10 and c = *p so the operators are not misinterpreted.

ANSI C requires that assignment operators of the form *op*= be treated as a single token. Therefore, they cannot contain embedded white space.

> **Recommendation:** Do not write assignment operators as a series of tokens—they must be written without embedded white space.

The following expression is unsafe since the order of evaluation of operands is undefined.

```
x[i] = x[i++] + 10;
```

This can be resolved by using an assignment operator as follows:

```
x[i++] += 10;
```

since you are guaranteed that the left-hand operand is evaluated only once.

♦ Comma Operator ♦

This operator is well defined and has no implementation-defined or undefined characteristics. Note though that it cannot appear in constant expressions, except as an operand to sizeof.

♦ Constant Expressions ♦

ANSI C constrains the expression following the #if directive. It must expand to integer constants, the new defined operator, and other operators with no side effects. It cannot include any environmental enquiries (sizeof might be available, but this is not guaranteed) and all arithmetic is done using long int type at translation-time. Casts are not permissible. Enumeration constants occurring in this context will be treated as undefined macros with a value of 1.

Static initializer expressions are permitted to be evaluated during program startup rather than at compile-time.

The translation environment must use at least as much precision as the execution environment. If it uses more, a static value initialized at compile-time may have a different value than if it were initialized during startup on the target machine.

ANSI C has introduced `float`, `long double`, and `unsigned` integral constants.

6

Declarations

Perhaps the biggest impact ANSI C has had on the C language is in the area of declarations. New type-related keywords have been added along with terminology to classify them. The most significant aspect, from the programmer's viewpoint, is the adaptation of function prototypes from C++. The notion of tenative definitions of externals is also new.

◆ Empty Declarations ◆

K&R allowed declarations that were empty. An empty declaration is one that does not contain an identifier. ANSI C does not permit empty declarations except for a special case with structure and union tags and enumerations. The tag example follows:

```
struct a {
        /* ... */
};

{
        struct b {
                struct a *x;
        };

        struct a {
                struct b *y;
        };
}
```

Presumably, the intent here is to have the local structures b and a contain pointers to types of each other. However, the definition of b will use the

definition of the outermost block, not the current block. To hide the outer definition of `struct` a you can use an empty declaration as follows:

```
struct a {
        /* ... */
};

{
        struct a;            /* hide outer a */

        struct b {
                struct a *x;
        };

        struct a {
                struct b *y;
        };
}
```

In such cases, what was previously an empty declaration now has meaning.

Recommendation: Do not use empty declarations (except as noted
previously) since ANSI C does not support them. The exceptions
shown previously might not be supported in non-ANSI C implementations.

The enumerated data type case follows:

```
enum {red, blue, green, brown};
```

This declaration contains no variable name; however, it is still very useful in that
it defines the values of the four enumeration constants `red`, `blue`, `green`, and
`brown` to be 0, 1, 2, and 3, respectively. Of course, the constants could have
explicit initializers.

♦ Storage-Class Specifiers ♦

Position of Class Keyword

C's grammar has always allowed the storage-class specifier to go before or after
the type specifier as follows:

```
int extern ei1;
extern int ei2;

test()
{
        double static sd1 = 1.234;
        static double sd2 = 1.234;

        int auto ai1 = 10;
        auto int ai2 = 10;

        register int ri1 = 123;
        int register ri2 = 123;
}
```

The members of each pair of declarations above have identical meaning. While this capability in itself seems harmless, the situation is made a little more complex with typedef. Grammatically, typedef is a storage-class specifier, even though it does not cause storage space to be allocated. This gives rise to the following possibilities:

```
/* first pair of declarations */

typedef int INT1;
int typedef INT2;

INT1 a, b, c;
INT2 e, f, g;

/* second pair of declarations */

typedef struct tag1 {
        int i;
        long l;
        double d;
} STR1;

struct tag2 {
        int i;
        long l;
        double d;
} typedef STR2;

STR1 i, j, k;
STR2 x, y, z;
```

In the second pair involving the structures, it is not immediately obvious that they are `typedefs` since the keyword is not at the beginning of the declaration, where most programmers expect it.

Recommendation: Place any storage-class specifier at the beginning of a declaration. Not only is this where almost all programmers expect it to be, but deficient implementations might not permit it elsewhere. Also, ANSI C indicates that the practice of specifying it elsewhere is an obsolescent feature. That is, this capability might be removed from the language in some future version of the Standard.

The `register` Class

The `register` storage-class is a hint to the implementation to place the object where it can be accessed as "fast as possible." Such a location is typically a machine register. The number of `register` objects that can actually be placed in registers and the set of supported types are implementation-defined. An object with class `register` that cannot be stored in a register, for whatever reason, is treated as though it had class `auto`. ANSI C very carefully states "The type ... of such declarations ... that are effective are implementation-defined." It does not disallow any types from being used with `register`. K&R states "... only variables of certain types will be stored in registers; on the PDP-11, they are `int`, `char` and pointer."

Recommendation: Although both K&R and ANSI C permit `register` to be used with any type, numerous implementations are deficient in this area. (For example, they generate an error when encountering something like `register int i[10];` or `register struct tag s;`. Therefore, use `register` only with the `signed` and `unsigned` versions of `long`, `int`, and `char` and pointers. However, if all your implementations accept `register` with another type, feel free to use it. For example, some implementations recognize, and generate code for, `register float` and `register double` declarations.

An interesting situation arises with Intel 8088-class machines where pointers can be either 16 or 32 bits depending on the memory model selected at compile-time. Consider the following code:

```
#include <stdio.h>

char *findchar(c, string)
int c;
register char *string;
{
        while (*string != '\0') {
                if (*string == c)
                        return (string);
                ++string;
        }
        return (NULL);
}
```

The formal parameter string is a pointer. The register class suggests that, if possible, string should be copied from the call stack frame (or from wherever arguments are stored) to a register each time the function begins execution. When compiling with the small Intel memory model, string requires 16 bits, whereas 32 are needed for the large memory model. The problem is that the processor's registers are only 16 bits wide so it is impossible to store a 32-bit pointer in a register. (An implementation could store the pointer in a pair of adjacent registers, however.)

Consider the case where you have a program with a register class pointer compiled with the small memory model and the pointer is actually placed into a register. At some later time you recompile, the program using the large model (perhaps because the program won't fit in 64 KB any more). You may notice a drop in performance if the pointer is now not placed into a register (or register pair).

Recommendation: Given the advances in compiler optimization technology in recent years, the value of the register storage-class on hosted implementations has largely evaporated. (In fact, this was predicted in K&R, which stated, "... future improvements in code generation may render [register declarations] unnecessary.") It is, therefore, suggested you not use them at all, unless you can prove they are providing some value for one or more of your target implementations.

ANSI C does not permit an implementation to widen the allocation space for a variable with the register class. That is, a register char cannot be treated as if it were register int. It must behave in all ways as a char, even if it is stored in a register whose size is wider than a char. (Some implementations can actually store more than one register char object in the same register.)

The auto Class

The method used to allocate, and the amount of storage available for, automatic variables is implementation-defined. Implementations that use a stack (or other) approach may place severe limits on the amount of space available for auto-class objects. For example, 16-bit machines may limit the stack to 64 KB or, if the entire address space is 16-bits, the sum of code, static data, and stack might be 64 KB. In that case, as the size of the code or static data grows, the stack size decreases, perhaps to the point where sufficient auto space cannot be allocated.

Stack space can be overlaid with careful design as follows. Consider the case of a program that has three phases, each of which uses a large amount of stack space for auto variable storage. If each phase is executed serially, then at most only one set of auto variables need exist at any one time.

```
main()
{
        char c[1000];

        phase1();
        phase2();
        phase3();

        /* ... */
}


phase1()
{
        char sc1[1000];

        /* ... */
}


phase2()
{
        char sc2[500];

        /* ... */
}


phase3()
{
        char sc3[1200];

        /* ... */
}
```

The 1000 bytes of stack used by c in main remain allocated throughout the life of the program. However, since functions phase1, phase2, and phase3 are mutually exclusive, they can share the same stack space for their auto variables sc1, sc2, and sc3. Therefore, the maximum amount of stack they need is 1200 bytes (ignoring stack management overhead and usage for other purposes). This gives a total stack requirement of 2200 bytes (1000 for c and a maximum of 1200 for sc3). If all three service functions were part of main, the total requirement would be 3700 bytes since all auto variables would exist simultaneously.

Recommendation: Determine the maximum amount of space available for auto-class objects. (On many implementations, this is the maximum size of the run-time stack.) Use the lowest common denominator of your targets. Note that if auto space is limited, you may be forced to use a storage-class other than auto just to get the program implemented. Limited auto space may also impact your ability to use recursive functions.

Numerous implementations check for the possibility of stack overflow when each function is entered. That is, they check the amount of stack space available before allocating that required for the function. And if insufficient space is available, they terminate the program. Some implementations actually call a function to perform the check, in which case, each time you call one of your functions having automatic class variables, you are implicitly calling another function as well.

Recommendation: On implementations that "probe the stack" each time a function is called, there is often a compile-time switch allowing such checking to be disabled. While the disabling of such checking can increase the amount of stack available, possibly to the extent of allowing a program to run when it wouldn't otherwise, it is strongly suggested you not do so during testing.

Declarations are permitted at the start of any block. However, while this means an auto object's scope is limited to block scope, it does not mean that the space for that auto object is allocated dynamically at the start of the block and released at the end of that block. Many implementations allocate auto space once, at the start of the function, regardless of which subordinate blocks the automatic declarations occur in. (Of course, they still restrict the scope correctly, as if the variables really existed only during their parent block's execution.) For example,

```
test ()
{
        int i[100];

        /* ... */
        {
                int j[100];

                /* ... */
        }


        {
                int k[100];

                /* ... */
        }
}
```

This function may have space allocated for 300 ints each time it is entered. More conscientious compilers will allocate space for only 200 ints since they can share space between arrays j and k.

Consider the following example where i is defined immediately after the array d. In this particular case, i actually occupied the next memory location beyond the end of d.

```
#include <stdio.h>

main()
{
        int d[5];
        int i;

        for (i = 1; i <= 5; i = i + 1) {
                d[i] = i * i;
                printf("loop # %d\n", i);
        }
}
```

```
loop # 1
loop # 2
loop # 3
loop # 4
loop # 25
```

As we can see, i gets overwritten when (the nonexistent object) d[5] is stored into. If another declaration such as int k separated these two declarations, the error would not have been apparent if the value of k were not of interest at that time. Depending on the way in which the optimizer works, the above example may result in the last line of output being loop # 5. This would happen if i were not reloaded from memory after the assignment and before the call to printf. It is possible that a program will appear to work quite well and yet be overwriting unknown areas of memory. In such cases, the bugs might be detected only when the code is moved to another implementation.

Recommendation: Do not rely on an implementation to have a particular auto space allocation scheme. In particularly, don't rely on auto variables being allocated space in exactly the same order in which they are declared. You might wish to look at some generated code to "get a feel" for the methods used for allocation, however.

Recommendation: As mentioned previously, the space allocated for pointers on Intel 8088-class systems can vary. Be careful when changing to a larger memory model since, if pointers go from 16 bits to 32 bits, you will be doubling the space needed for each auto pointer. Don't forget about pointers in auto structures and unions as well. Also, the size of an auto structure may change across implementation due to member alignment requirements. Again, this may impact the ability to implement recursive routines. Many compilers for this machine-class support the extended keywords near and far allowing you to override the size of pointers (both code and data), on a per declaration basis.

The static Class

A problem can occur when trying to forward-reference static functions as follows:

```
test()
{
        extern void f();
        static void g();
        int (*pfi)() = g;

        f();
        (*pfi)();
}
```

```
void f()
{
        /* ... */
}

static void g()
{
        /* ... */
}
```

Function `test` has a block scope declaration in which `g` is declared to be a `static` function. This allows `test` to call the `static` function `g` rather than any `extern` function by the same name. ANSI C does not permit such declarations. It does, however, allow function declarations with file scope to have class `static` as follows:

```
static void g();

test()
{
        extern void f();
        int (*pfi)() = g;

        f();
        (*pfi)();
}


        ...
```

Recommendation: Do not use the `static` class on a block scope function declaration since it is not supported by ANSI C.

♦ Type Specifiers ♦

Three keywords have been added to ANSI C and may be used in type specifiers. They were not part of K&R. They are `signed`, `enum`, and `void`.

Recommendation: Check to see if the code you are porting uses the names `signed`, `enum`, or `void` as identifiers since doing so will cause an error with ANSI C compilers.

These new type specifiers give rise to the following base-type declarations:

```
void /* function returning, only */
signed char
signed short
signed short int
signed
signed int
signed long
signed long int
enum [tag] /* ... */
```

ANSI C also permits existing keywords to be used in different combinations giving rise to the following new type declarations. Note that many implementations have supported unsigned char and unsigned long for a number of years already.

```
unsigned char
unsigned short
unsigned short int
unsigned long
unsigned long int
long double
```

Recommendation: Non-ANSI implementations might not support the signed keyword. Also, these implementations might not support unsigned char, unsigned short, or unsigned long. Check each of your targets for such support if you need it.

When a declaration contains more than one type specifier, ANSI C allows them to occur in any order. For example, the following declarations are valid, and all of them declare an object of type unsigned long int.

```
unsigned long int uli;
unsigned int long uil;
long unsigned int lui;
long int unsigned liu;
int long unsigned ilu;
int unsigned long iul;
unsigned long ul;
long unsigned lu;
```

It is debatable whether K&R permits arbitrary ordering of type specifiers. The grammar on page 192 of K&R indicates that they are supported, but on page 193, it states, "the following [type specifier] combinations are acceptable: `short int`, `long int`, `unsigned int` and `long float`." It is unclear whether this should be taken as explicitly disallowing `int short`, `int long`, etc.

Recommendation: Write multiple type specifiers in the most logical order. For example, `unsigned long int` is the way to write this combination of specifiers. While ANSI C implementations support arbitrary ordering, deficient implementations may not.

While K&R permitted `long float` to be a synonym for `double`, this practice is not supported by ANSI C.

Recommendation: Do not use `long float` as a synonym for `double` since this is not supported by ANSI C.

ANSI C has added the new type `long double`.

Recommendation: Non-ANSI C implementations might not support the `long double` type. Check your targets if you need this type. If an implementation does not support `long double`, you cannot use either `typedef` or `#define` to change `long double` to `double` (or `float`) since `typedef` can redefine only in terms of supported types, and `#define` can redefine only single names such as `long` or `double`, not something like `long double`. However, you could use something like the following example:

```
#if LONG_DOUBLE
typedef long double LDBL;
#else
typedef double LDBL;
#endif

LDBL d1, d2;
```

◆ Structure and Union Specifiers ◆

ANSI states that the padding and alignment of members of structures is implementation-defined. This can present a problem if binary data written by one implementation are read by another (either via a file or transmitted via a communication link.) A hole may not exist at the beginning of a structure, however. Members occupy increasing storage addresses, and if necessary, a hole may be placed at the end so that proper alignment is maintained in arrays of structures. Holes placed in the middle of a structure, or at its end, may be larger than absolutely necessary (perhaps, in the interest of enhanced access time.)

If you are concerned about the possible existence and nature of such holes, you can determine this by using something like the following program:

```
#include <stdio.h>

struct {
        char c1;
        double d;
        char c2;
        float f;
        char c3;
        long l;
        char c4;
        int *pi;
        char c5;
        int (*pf)();
        char c6;
        int i;
        char c7;
        short s;
        char c8;
} s;


main()
{
        printf("      Address, Size\n");
        printf("&s    = %p, %2lu\n",
               &s, (unsigned long) sizeof(s));
        printf("&s.c1 = %p, %2lu\n",
               &s.c1, (unsigned long) sizeof(s.c1));
        printf("&s.d  = %p, %2lu\n",
               &s.d, (unsigned long) sizeof(s.d));

        printf("&s.c2 = %p, %2lu\n",
               &s.c2, (unsigned long) sizeof(s.c2));
        printf("&s.f  = %p, %2lu\n",
               &s.f, (unsigned long) sizeof(s.f));
        printf("&s.c3 = %p, %2lu\n",
               &s.c3, (unsigned long) sizeof(s.c3));
        printf("&s.l  = %p, %2lu\n",
               &s.l, (unsigned long) sizeof(s.l));
```

```
                printf("&s.c4 = %p, %2lu\n",
                        &s.c4, (unsigned long) sizeof(s.c4));
                printf("&s.pi = %p, %2lu\n",
                        &s.pi, (unsigned long) sizeof(s.pi));
                printf("&s.c5 = %p, %2lu\n",
                        &s.c5, (unsigned long) sizeof(s.c5));
                printf("&s.pf = %p, %2lu\n",
                        &s.pf, (unsigned long) sizeof(s.pf));

                printf("&s.c6 = %p, %2lu\n",
                        &s.c6, (unsigned long) sizeof(s.c6));
                printf("&s.i  = %p, %2lu\n",
                        &s.i, (unsigned long) sizeof(s.i));
                printf("&s.c7 = %p, %2lu\n",
                        &s.c7, (unsigned long) sizeof(s.c7));
                printf("&s.s  = %p, %2lu\n",
                        &s.s, (unsigned long) sizeof(s.s));
                printf("&s.c8 = %p, %2lu\n",
                        &s.c8, (unsigned long) sizeof(s.c8));
        }
```

This program produced the following output using Microsoft's DOS V5.0 compiler which aligned everything on an even boundary as shown. A compiler running on the same system, which packs structures more densely, required only 32 bytes instead of 40.

```
         Address, Size
&s     = 0736,   40
&s.c1  = 0736,    1
&s.d   = 0738,    8
&s.c2  = 0740,    1
&s.f   = 0742,    4
&s.c3  = 0746,    1
&s.l   = 0748,    4
&s.c4  = 074C,    1
&s.pi  = 074E,    2
&s.c5  = 0750,    1
&s.pf  = 0752,    2
&s.c6  = 0754,    1
&s.i   = 0756,    2
&s.c7  = 0758,    1
&s.s   = 075A,    2
&s.c8  = 075C,    1
```

Recommendation: Make no assumptions about the existence, or location or size, of holes in structures. The layout of a structure can vary considerably, even for different compilers running on the same hardware and operating system. Some compilers even provide compile-time switches or keywords to specify alignment requirements explicitly. Non-ANSI C implementations may even permit holes at the beginning of structures.

Consider two structures that, because of alignment constraints, have holes in them. If they are automatic structures, these holes will contain unpredictable data. All members in `static` and external structures and without initializers have the value 0 cast to their type. Does this include holes too? This is unspecified according to ANSI C. Structures stored in dynamic memory allocated by `calloc` have each member (and hole) initialized to "all-bits zero," which might not be the same as a member with a value of 0, particularly in the case of floating-point variables. Even if two structures have identical member values, their hole values may differ, in which case a byte-by-byte or word-by-word comparison of these structures might not work. The only predictable way to compare structures is by comparing each and every one of their members separately. The same applies to comparison of unions containing structures.

Recommendation: Do not compare two structures of the same type using a "block compare" unless you are sure that they contain no holes or that the current contents of the corresponding holes in each structure are identical. The ANSI C library function `memset` can be used to initialize an area with a user-specified bit pattern.

ANSI C requires that the type of a bit-field be `int`, `unsigned int` or `signed int` only. K&R did not restrict the types that could be used with bit-fields; however, it is very unlikely that any non-integral type would be implemented. ANSI C's tighter specification should cause no problem for existing code.

Most implementations support only unsigned bit-fields, although they do not always require the keyword `unsigned`. That is, the type `int` may actually be interpreted as `unsigned int`. So whether a plain `int` bit-field is treated as a `signed int` bit-field or as an `unsigned int` bit-field, it is implementation-defined. The following program can be used to determine the signedness of an `int` bit-field:

```
#include <stdio.h>

struct {
        int i : 4;
        int    :12;
} s;

main()
{
        s.i = 0x08;

        if (s.i > 0)
                printf("s.i is unsigned\n");
        else
                printf("s.i is signed\n");
}
```

Recommendation: If you mean a bit-field to be unsigned, declare it as
`unsigned`. Do not just use `int` and let it default to `unsigned int`
since some implementations (on a VAX, for example) do support
signed bit fields.

K&R required that consecutive bit-fields be packed into machine integers and
that they not span word boundaries. ANSI C declares that the container object in
which bit-fields are packed is implementation-defined. The same is true for
whether bit-fields span container boundaries. Both K&R and ANSI C permit the
order of allocation of bit-fields within a container to be implementation-
defined—it may be left-to-right or right-to-left (or perhaps even some other
order). The following program should help to determine this ordering. However, the use of the union is implementation-defined.

```
#include <stdio.h>

struct tag {
        unsigned int i1 : 4;
        unsigned int i2 : 4;
        unsigned int i3 : 4;
        unsigned int i4 : 4;
};

#define NUM (sizeof(struct tag) /sizeof(char))

union {
        struct tag s;
        char c[NUM];
} u;
```

```
main()
{
        int i;

        u.s.i1 = 0x0;
        u.s.i2 = 0x1;
        u.s.i3 = 0x2;
        u.s.i4 = 0x3;

        for (i = NUM - 1; i >= 0; --i)
                printf("u.c[%d] = %02x\n",
                             i, u.c[i]);
}
```

Two of the possible outputs from this test are

```
u.c[1] = 01
u.c[0] = 23

u.c[1] = 32
u.c[0] = 10
```

Recommendation: Do not assume the ordering of bit-fields is left-to-right or right-to-left. Either look at the generated code of a test program or use something like the above program to see how your implementations pack bit-fields.

Use the following program to investigate whether bit-fields span container byte or word boundaries.

```
#include <stdio.h>

struct tag {
        unsigned int i1 : 5;
        unsigned int i2 : 6;
        unsigned int i3 : 9;
        unsigned int i4 : 7;
        unsigned int i5 : 3;
        unsigned int i6 : 10;
};

main()
{
        printf("size = %lu\n",
            (unsigned long) sizeof(struct tag));
}
```

Recommendation: Do not assume that consecutive bit-fields are packed densely—they may not be able to span container boundaries.

K&R required that a bit-field's width be no larger than a machine word. Since ANSI C allows bit-fields to be packed into an implementation-defined size container, the size of this container limits the size of a bit-field.

Recommendation: Be careful when porting from a larger word-size machine to a smaller since it may be impossible to represent large bit-fields on the smaller machine. For example, it is unlikely that a bit-field of width 24 bits can be handled by a compiler running on a 16-bit machine.

K&R and ANSI C do not permit the address of a bit-field to be taken. However, some implementations permit *&bit-field*, in which case the address of the bit-field's container is returned.

Recommendation: Do not try to take the address of a bit-field by using the & address-of operator since support for this capability is not widespread, and the practice violates K&R and ANSI C.

ANSI C permits bit-fields to exist in unions without their first being declared as part of a structure, as follows:

```
union tag {
        int i;
        unsigned int bf1 : 6;
        unsigned int bf2 : 4;
};
```

Recommendation: Allowing bit-fields as members of a union is an ANSI C invention. It might not be supported in non-ANSI implementations.

Neither K&R nor ANSI C allow two structures or union types to exist with the same name in the same scope. For example, the following example should generate an error even though the structure template definitions are identical. That is, it is not possible to have "benign" redefinition of structure or union types.

```
struct tag {
        int i;
        long l;
};


struct tag {
        int i;
        long l;
};
```

Recommendation: Some implementations allow two structures or union types to exist with the same name in the same scope provided they have exactly the same definition. This practice is not supported by either K&R or ANSI C.

ANSI C disallows empty declarations except for two cases stated earlier in this chapter.

One common extension of implementations is to allow empty arrays at the end of structure definitions as follows:

```
#include <stdio.h>

struct tag {
        char c1;
        char c2;
        char c3[0];
};


main()
{
        printf("size = %lu\n",
            (unsigned long) sizeof(struct tag));
}



size = 2
```

Recommendation: Do not declare empty arrays at the end of a structure since that practice is not supported by either K&R or ANSI C.

K&R required that all the members in a union "begin at offset 0." ANSI C spells it out even more precisely by saying that a pointer to a union, suitably cast, points to each member and vice versa. (If any of the members is a bit-field, the pointer points to the container in which that bit-field resides.)

◆ Enumeration Specifiers ◆

Enumerated types were not part of K&R—they were added in the UNIX C compiler some years ago and are supported by most popular commercial C compilers. ANSI C requires that an enumeration type be implemented as an integral type, the choice of which is implementation-defined. For example,

```
#include <stdio.h>

enum tag {red, blue, green};

main()
{
        printf("size = %lu\n",
            (unsigned long) sizeof(enum tag));
}
```

Recommendation: Do not assume that an enumerated type is represented as an `int`—it may be any integral type.

Note that enumeration constants such as `red` and `blue` above are defined by ANSI C to have type `int`. Therefore, the type of an enumerated data object need not be the same as that of its "members."

◆ Tags ◆

K&R and ANSI C permit structure and union types without tags. However, a tagless type can be used only in very limited circumstances—it cannot be used where a type is needed since its type is not "known." The contexts in which a tagless structure or union type cannot be used are casts, `sizeof`, and function declarations and definitions. They can, however, be used in `typedefs`. Tagless types have been used quite liberally in the past as follows:

```
struct {
        int i;
        long l;
} a = {1, 10L};


test()
{
        struct {
                int i;
                long l;
        } b;

        struct tag {
                int i;
                long l;
        } c;

        void f();

        b = a;
        c = a;
        f(&b);
        f(&c);
}
```

By definition, a, b, and c have different types even though their members' definitions are identical. Therefore, they are not assignment-compatible under the ANSI C rules.

Recommendation: Beware of playing freely with tagless structures and unions since each tagless type is a distinct type and is not assignment-compatible with any other type. Also, a tagless type cannot be passed to a function if a prototype is in scope for that function since the prototype can never include a tagless typed argument declaration.

◆ Type Qualifiers ◆

The const type qualifier has been added to ANSI C to allow an implementation to ensure that an object is not used as a modifiable lvalue. const is particularly useful for generating code destined for read-only memory locations.

If you attempt to modify a `const` object by means of a pointer to a type without the `const` attribute, the result is undefined. For example,

```
f()
{
        const int ci;
        int *pi;

        pi = &ci;
        *pi = 10;               /* undefined */
}
```

Recommendation: Do not attempt to modify a `const` object by means of a pointer to a type without the `const` attribute.

The `volatile` type qualifier has been added to ANSI C to allow an implementation to optimize code with regard to special external storage areas. The `volatile` attribute indicates that the object can be manipulated in ways unknown to that program (perhaps from within another program or within a signal handler in the same program).

If an external hardware port is mapped into by the variable `port`, then the following program might cause that port to be pulsed 10 times.

```
extern int port;

f()
{
/* pulse 5 times */
        port = 5;

/* pulse 5 more times */
        port = 5;
}
```

The classic problem here is to make sure that a "smart" optimizing compiler doesn't treat one of the assignment statements as "unnecessary." By declaring port to be `volatile`, both assignments are retained. Because the removal of one of the statements can obviously be disastrous, a compiler must perform less optimization on such a program to ensure the right answer. In the process, it may be sacrificing efficiency.

If a `volatile` object is referenced by a pointer to a type without the `volatile` attribute, the results are undefined. For example,

```
f()
{
        volatile int vi;
        int *pi;

        pi = &vi;
        (*pi)++;                /* undefined */
}
```

Recommendation: Do not access a volatile object by means of a pointer to a type without the volatile attribute.

If you are porting code containing the const and volatile keywords to an implementation that does not recognize them, you may have to make many changes depending on how your declarations were written. For example, the following compiles without error, although the results of doing this may be undefined.

```
#define const
#define volatile

f()
{
        const int ci = 45;
        volatile long int vli;
}
```

ci may be used as an lvalue and no constraint error would be generated. Since a type qualifier can be used without a type specifier, using the macro approach above will not work if the declaration for ci were written as follows:

```
#define const

f()
{
        const ci = 45;
}
```

Here, the type of ci is implied to be int since the type specifier is omitted, yet if const is removed, an incomplete declaration remains.

Recommendation: Do not use const or volatile to imply a type of int since this eliminates your ability to remove the const and volatile keywords globally via a macro.

Recommendation: Since the `const` and `volatile` keywords are ANSI C inventions (actually, `const` was adopted from C++), they might not be supported in non-ANSI implementations.

ANSI C permits `const` and `volatile` to apply to a function's return type; however, no semantics are given for such declarations.

◆ Declarators ◆

General Information

Both K&R and ANSI C treat a declarator in parentheses as equivalent to one without. For example, the following is syntactically correct.

```
f()
{
        int (i);
        int (g)();
}
```

The second declaration may be used to hide the function declaration from a macro with arguments that has the same name as that function.

ANSI C requires that a declaration support at least 12 pointer, array, and function declarators modifying a base type. For example, `***p[4]` has four modifiers. K&R gave no limit except to say that multiple type modifiers may be present. The original Ritchie compiler supported only six type modifiers in a declarator, and this limit may well exist in current compilers.

Recommendation: If you intend to use quite complex declarations check your targets to see the level of complexity permitted in compound type modifiers. One way to do this follows:

```
int **************pi;
char c[2][2][2][2][2][2][2][2][2][2][2][2][2];
```

ANSI C requires that an array dimension have a positive, nonzero value. That is, an array may not have size zero, as permitted by some implementations.

Recommendation: Do not define arrays to have zero elements since this is not supported by ANSI C.

ANSI C permits array declarations to be incomplete by omitting the size information as follows:

```
extern int i[];
int (*pi)[];
```

However, the use of such objects may be restricted until size information is made available. For example, `sizeof(i)` and `sizeof(*pi)` are unknown and should generate an error. Implementations commonly return a value of zero when they really mean "I don't know."

Function Declarators

Some implementations allow the `fortran` type specifier to be used in a function declaration to indicate that function linkage suitable for FORTRAN (call by reference) is to be generated or that different representations for external names are to be generated. Others, most noticeably DOS compilers, also use the `pascal` and `cdecl` keywords for calling Pascal and C routines, respectively.

ANSI C's addition of function prototypes for the standard library will, no doubt, cause some problems with existing code particularly for those library functions that now have different argument and/or return value types. Problems specific to particular headers and/or library functions are discussed in the corresponding library chapter.

Recommendation: Whenever possible, use function prototypes since they can assist in locating assumptions about type compatibilities that may not be true when code is ported.

It is possible that not all of your target implementations support function prototypes in which case you can either not use them at all or use them selectively. The latter option can be implemented in a number of ways as can be demonstrated by headers for compilers that support hybrid environments as follows:

```
/* extract from math.h */

#if _PROTO
double acos(double);
double asin(double);
double atan(double);
#else
double acos();
double asin();
double atan();
#endif
```

While this approach is overt, it requires that each function be declared twice. The two declarations can be combined as follows, as is done with Whitesmiths compilers:

```
/* extract from Whitesmiths math.h */

#ifndef __
#ifdef _PROTO
#define __(a)          a
#else
#define __(a)          ()
#endif
#endif

double acos __((double x));
double asin __((double x));
double atan __((double x));
```

Recommendation: Both of these approaches require conditional compilation based on some compiler-specific predefined macro. Since implementers are permitted to use any names beginning with an underscore, and each will use different names for the same purpose (or the same names for different purposes) it is suggested that application programmers invent their own name (without a leading underscore), to indicate the support or lack thereof, for facilities such as function prototypes. This way, their headers will port to other environments, provided the macro names chosen don't conflict with anything in the new environment.

The ellipsis ... can be used at the end of a prototype to disable argument list type checking in function calls. The required syntax for this is

```
int f(int, double, ...);
```

Some implementations permit the trailing ellipsis to be omitted; however, this is not supported by ANSI C.

ANSI C requires that all calls to functions having a variable argument list be made only in the presence of a prototype. Specifically, the following well-known program from K&R is not ANSI-conforming:

```
main()
{
        printf("hello, world\n");
}
```

The reason for this is that, in the absence of a prototype, the compiler is permitted to assume that the number of arguments is fixed. Therefore, it may use registers or some other (presumably) more efficient method of passing arguments than it would otherwise use. Clearly, the `printf` function is expecting a variable argument list. Typically, it would not be able to communicate properly with code calling `printf`, if the calling code were compiled with the fixed list assumption. To correct the above example, you must either `#include <stdio.h>` (the preferred approach) or explicitly write a prototype for `printf` (including the trailing ellipsis) in the example prior to the function's use.

Recommendation: Always have a prototype in scope when calling a function having a variable argument list. Make sure the prototype contains the ellipsis notation.

It is permitted to have a dummy identifier name in prototype declarators; however, using them can cause problems as the following program demonstrates:

```
#define test 10

int f(int test);
```

Although the scope of the identifier `test` in the prototype begins at its declaration and ends at the end of the prototype, that name is seen by the preprocessor. Consequently, it is replaced by the constant 10, thus generating a syntax error. Even worse, if the macro `test` were defined as `*`, the prototype would be quietly changed from taking an argument of `int` to one of a pointer to an `int`. A similar problem can occur if your implementation's headers use dummy names that are part of the programmer's name space (i.e., without leading underscores.)

Recommendation: If you must put identifiers in prototypes, name them so that they won't conflict with macro names. This can be avoided if you always spell macros in upper-case and all other identifiers in lower-case.

◆ Type Definitions and Type Equivalence ◆

ANSI C states that a `typedef` may be redeclared only in an inner block with a declaration that explicitly contains a type specifier.

ANSI C does not allow a type specifier (such as `short`, `unsigned`, or `long`) to be added to a `typedef` type. For example,

```
typedef int INT;
unsigned INT;
```

is not permitted.

Recommendation: Do not combine type specifiers and derived types
in the same declaration.

Many C programmers believe they can use #define instead of typedef to
achieve the same purpose, and in some cases, that is true. Yet, even in those cases
that appear to work with non-ANSI compilers they might fail with an ANSI C
implementation.

Let's look at some cases where #define and typedef can both be used
to achieve the same results.

```
/* source file 1 - substituting strings */

#define COUNT int
#define STRING char *

test1()
{
        COUNT value1, value2;
        STRING s1;
}

/* source file 2 - defining types */

typedef int COUNT;
typedef char *STRING;

test2()
{
        COUNT value1, value2;
        STRING s1;
}
```

These are very simple cases to the point of being trivial. Yet, even the
STRING definition does not suffice in a typical situation as follows:

```
#define STRING char *

test3()
{
        STRING s1, s2;

        s1 = s2;     /* incompatible assignment */
}
```

The problem here is that `s1` and `s2` do not have the same type; `s1` is a pointer to `char`, while `s2` is a `char`. That is, the macro name `STRING` was literally substituted by `char *`. `s1` and `s2` did not inherit the "type" `STRING`. For this to happen, `typedef` must be used instead. Consider another case.

```
#define COMPLEX struct {          \
                double real;      \
                double imag;      \
                }

COMPLEX c1, c2;


test4()
{
        c1.real = c2.real;
        c1.imag = c2.imag;
}
```

Again, this works fine; the macro `COMPLEX` is replaced leaving a declaration in which `c1` and `c2` have the same structure type. The same result can be achieved using `typedef` as follows:

```
typedef struct {
        double real;
        double imag;
} COMPLEX;
```

Let's change the `#define` example to the following:

```
#define COMPLEX struct {          \
                double real;      \
                double imag;      \
                }

COMPLEX c1, c2;
COMPLEX c3;

test5()
{
        c1 = c2;
        c1 = c3; /* incompatible assignment */
}
```

Since `c1` and `c2` are part of the same declarator list, they have the same type, and the assignment `c1 = c2` is OK. However, `c3` does not have the same type as c1 or c2. Even though the types of c1 and c3 are "struct of some unknown type," they are different "unknown struct" types, and are not assignment-compatible. In ANSI-conforming implementations, this would generate an error. In non-ANSI mode, it will probably work even though it may be illogical. If typedef were used, c1, c2, and c3 would all have the same type by definition.

♦ Initialization ♦

If the value of an uninitialized object that has automatic storage duration is used before a value is assigned, the behavior is undefined.

External and static variables not explicitly initialized are assigned the value of 0, cast to their type. This may differ from the area allocated by calloc, which is initialized to all-bits-zero. This is particularly true for floating-point variables with value 0, which might not be represented as all-bits-zero. Note also that the null pointer constant (represented by NULL) need not be represented by all-bits-zero.

K&R did not allow automatic arrays, structures, and unions to be initialized. ANSI C does, however, provided the initializing expressions in any initializer list are constant expressions. An automatic structure or union can also be initialized with a (nonconstant) expression of the same type. For example,

```
f()
{
        int f1(), f2(), f3();

        struct tag {
                int i, j;
        } fs1(), fs2();

        union u {
                int i;
                double d;
        } f4();


/* the following are permitted */

        int i[] = {1, 2, 3};
        char c[] = "abcdef";
        struct tag s = {1, 2};
        struct tag t = fs1();
        union u u1 = {10};
        union u u3 = f4();
```

```
/* the following are not permitted since the
initializer expressions are not constants */

        int j[] = {f1(), f2(), f3()};
        struct tag st[2] = {fs1(), fs2()};
        union u u2 = {f1()};
}
```

Recommendation: Since K&R did not allow automatic arrays, structures, and unions to be initialized and ANSI C does, check your target compilers before using this feature.

ANSI C permits a union to be initialized explicitly. The value is stored in the union by casting it to the type of the first member specified. Using this rule, we see that if a `static` or external union is not explicitly initialized, it contains 0 cast into the first member (which may not result in all-bits-zero, as stated above). Prior to ANSI C, the explicit initialization of unions was not widely supported.

Recommendation: Do not rely on the initial value of a union unless your implementation allows you to initialize it explicitly.

Since ANSI C (and many other compilers) permits structures and unions to be assigned and returned from functions by value, the following automatic initializations are now possible.

```
struct s {
        int i;
        /* ... */
};

f()
{
        struct s fs();
        struct s s1 = fs();
        struct s s2 = s1;
}
```

Here, `s1` is initialized by the structure returned from function `fs` as if the code were written

```
        struct s fs();
        struct s s1;

        s1 = fs();
```

ANSI C permits bit-fields to be initialized. Other implementations might not. For example,

```
struct {
        unsigned int bf1 : 5;
        unsigned int bf2 : 5;
        unsigned int bf3 : 5;
        unsigned int bf4 : 1;
} bf = {1, 2, 3, 0};
```

Note though that unnamed bit-fields in a structure or union are ignored during initialization.

K&R and ANSI C require that the number of expressions in an initializer be less than or equal to the number expected, but never more. There is one case, however, where it is possible to specify implicitly one too many, yet not get a compilation error. For example,

```
char text[5] = "hello";
```

Here, the array text is initialized with the characters 'h', 'e', 'l', 'l', and 'o' and does not contain a trailing '\0'.

Some implementations allow a trailing comma in an initialization list. This practice is endorsed by ANSI C but might not be widely supported, even though it was permitted by K&R.

The following example shows a partially bracketed initializer list:

```
static int a[2][2] = {{1}, {2}};
```

The question here is, "Is the array initialized as 1, 2, 0, 0 or as 1, 0, 2, 0?" Existing implementations disagree, and so you should specify all initial values to make it unambiguous.

Recommendation: With nested initializers, such as are used with multi-dimensional arrays, and arrays of structures and unions, use all pairs of braces, or make sure that all initializers are present along with only the outermost set of braces, to avoid ambiguity in initializer interpretation.

♦ External Definitions ♦

An external definition is an external declaration that also defines an object or function. The term *external* refers to a declaration occurring outside the body (and formal argument list) of a function and outside all struct, union, and enum template definitions.

Function Definitions

ANSI C has introduced an alternate style of defining a function. For example,

```
/* this example */

double test(a, b, c)
int a;
double b;
char *c;
{
}



/* can be replaced with */

double test(int a, double b, char *c)
{
}
```

The one place where the new style definition differs from the old is with "narrow" types. For example,

```
f(c, s, f)
char c;
short s;
float f;
{
}
```

f expects to find its arguments widened to `int`, `int`, and `double`, respectively, whereas in the following example, it does not. That is, using the new-style definition, the narrow types can be preserved.

```
f(char c, short s, float f)
{
}
```

If a function that accepts a variable number of arguments is defined without the ellipsis notation, the behavior is undefined. For example, if `test` takes a variable number of arguments, then the definition

```
int test(char *pc, ...)
{
        /* ... */
}
```

is OK but

```
int test(char *pc)
{
        /* ... */
}
```

is not.

Recommendation: If a function takes a variable number of arguments, and function prototypes are supported, use the trailing ellipsis
notation in the function definition.

Recommendation: If your implementation supports prototypes,
always have a prototype in scope when a function is defined so the
definition also matches all calls to it.

The formal parameters in a function definition have automatic storage duration.
However, in some environments you might not be able to modify them. For
example,

```
char *scopy(char *d, char *s,
        unsigned int count)
{
        while (count-- > 0)
                *d++ = *s++;

        *d = '\0';
}
```

this program works OK when called from other C functions, but it may not when
called by other languages. DEC's VAX Fortran, for example, does not pass a
copy of its subroutine arguments on the stack as VAX C expects it to—it generates a CALLG instruction instead of a CALLS—and, consequently, the program behaves unexpectedly at run-time. In fact, the VAX Calling Standard
specifies that all formal parameters should be considered to be read-only. Note
that VAX C has been given special dispensation to violate this standard in a
number of ways.

The layout of storage for formal parameters is unspecified, and you should
use the mechanism provided in stdarg.h to traverse formal argument lists
rather than using your own "magic" pointer arithmetic.

Using a prototype, type widening can be avoided so any function that relies
on such widening may behave differently in the scope of such a prototype.

Prior to ANSI C, the following program would have compiled without error, and the automatic a would have hidden the formal argument rending that argument inaccessible:

```
f(a)
int a;
{
        double a;
}
```

ANSI C prohibits such hiding since it provides no capability whatsoever. ANSI C treats all formal parameters as though they were declared at the top-most block level of the function. Therefore, the two identifiers named a are declared at the same level, and an error results.

Note that ANSI C has declared *obsolescent* the use of function declarations and definitions that do not have the prototype format. In theory, this means that support for these "old-style" formats could be dropped in a future version of the Standard.

If you chose to use the new style of function definition, note that this includes using the keyword void to indicate the absence of formal arguments. You must also use the elipsis notation when the function takes a variable number of arguments.

External Object Definitions

ANSI C introduced the notion of tentative definitions. That is, a declaration may be a definition depending on what follows it. For example,

```
/* tentative definition, external */
int ei1;

/* definition, external */
int ei1 = 10;

/* tentative definition, internal */
static int si1;

/* definition, internal */
static int si1 = 20;
```

Here, the first references of ei1 and si1 are tentative definitions. If they were not followed by a declaration for the same identifier containing an initializer list, these tentative definitions would be treated as definitions. However, as shown, they are followed by such declarations so they are treated as declarations. The purpose of this is to allow two mutually referential variables to be initialized to point to each other. For example,

```
/* tentative definition */
static int *pi1;

static int *pi2 = &pi1;

/* actual definition */
static int *pi1 = &pi2;
```

Recommendation: Take care when using tentative definitions since this capability is not widely supported outside ANSI C.

7

Statements

No new statements have been added to C since its original design. However, various aspects of existing statements have been "tightened up" over the years. ANSI C has contributed to this, particularly with the `switch` construct.

◆ Labeled Statements ◆

K&R C had labels and "ordinary" identifiers sharing the same namespace. That is, a label name was hidden if an identifier with the same name was declared in a subordinate block. For example,

```
f()
{
label: ;
        {
                int label;

                ...
                goto label;
        }
}
```

would generate a compilation error since the object of the `goto` statement is an identifier declared to be an `int` variable, not a label.

In ANSI C labels have their own namespace allowing the above example to be compiled without error.

Recommendation: Whether or not your implementation gives labels their own namespace, treat them as if they shared the same namespace as "ordinary" identifiers. Not only will this make the usage portable, it will also probably avoid some confusion on the part of the programmer.

K&R C specified that the length of significance in an internal identifier (such as a label) was eight characters. ANSI C requires at least 31 characters of significance. Since a label name is an internal identifier, ANSI C can recognize the first 31 characters of a label name, at least. However, K&R implementations may not since they are only required to recognize the first eight.

Recommendation: Either restrict labels to eight characters or guarantee that different labels in the same function have at least the first eight characters distinct.

♦ Compound Statement, or Block ♦

A `goto` can be used to jump into a block. While this technique can be considered portable, whether any automatic variables in the block are initialized predictably is not. For example,

```c
/* a bizarre but correct program */

#include <stdio.h>

main()
{
        goto label;

        {
        int i = 100;
        int j = f();
        register k = -34;

label:  printf("i = %d, j = %d, k = %d\n",
                i, j, k);
        }
}
```

```
f()
{
        return (123);
}
```

```
i = 1040, j = 15, k = 129
```

As demonstrated, neither i, j, nor k is initialized as expected since the initialization assignments are never executed. However, storage space is allocated for the variables as required by both K&R and ANSI C.

Another possible way to jump into blocks is via the switch statement as follows:

```
/* another bizarre but correct program */

#include <stdio.h>

main()
{
        int i = 2;

        switch (i) {

case 1: break;

        {
        int j = 100;
        register int k = -34;
case 2:

        printf("j = %d, k = %d\n", j, k);
        }
        }

}
```

```
j = 1032, k = 129
```

Yet another possibility exists concerning a switch statement whose body is a compound statement. For example,

```
/* yet another bizarre but correct program */

#include <stdio.h>

main()
{
        int i = 1;

        switch (i) {
        int j = 100;
        register k = -34;
        extern void f();

        f();    /* not executed */

case 1: printf("j = %d, k = %d\n", j, k);
        }
}


void f()
{
        printf("executing function f\n");
}


j = 1054, k = 129
```

Here, it is never possible for the automatic and register initializers to be evaluated since it is not possible to "drop into the block." Control can be passed into the block only to a case label. The other interesting aspect is that, for the same reason, the call to function f is never executed. The initialization lists at the start of the block are treated the same as if they had been written as follows:

```
int j;
register k;

j = 100;
k = -34;
```

Recommendation: It is generally considered bad programming practice to jump into a compound statement. However, if you must (and you can justify it), adequately annotate any automatic and register variable declarations indicating that they will only be initialized according to their given initializer lists if the block is entered normally.

K&R permitted blocks to nest, but it gave no indication as to how deeply. ANSI C requires compound statements to nest to at least 15 levels.

Recommendation: If you are using a pre-ANSI C compiler and you rely heavily on deep nesting of compound statements, check the permissible depth for each target implementation.

Recommendation: Always place declarations before statements in a block even if your implementation permits otherwise. Both K&R and ANSI C require declarations to precede statements.

◆ Expression and Null Statements ◆

An expression statement has the form *expression;*, and it contains no keywords. It is evaluated for its side-effects. Examples are

```
f();
i++;
i = 10;
```

Consider the following example, containing several expression statements:

```
test1()
{
        extern int i[5];
        int *pi = &i[2];

        i[0];
        pi;
        *pi;
        *pi++;
}
```

Neither K&R nor ANSI C require that the first three expression statements be evaluated, although it is conceivable that on some implementations some or all of them will be. In the last statement, the autoincrement is required to be done, however, the dereferencing of the location (indicated by the `*` operator) is not.

The situation can be different with compilers supporting the `volatile` type modifier. For example,

```
test2()
{
        extern volatile int vi[5];
        volatile int *pvi = &vi[2];

        vi[0];
        pvi;
        *pvi;
        *pvi++;
}
```

Optimizers must tread very carefully when dealing with objects having the `volatile` attribute since they can make no assumptions about the current state of such an object. In the simplest case, an implementation may evaluate every expression containing a `volatile` expression simply because doing so may generate a side-effect. For example, the statement `*pvi;` could generate code to access `vi[2]`. That is, it might place the address of `vi[2]` on the bus such that it can be seen by hardware waiting to synchronize on such an access. Note that even if an implementation does this, it should not generate code for the statement `pvi;` since `pvi` is not itself `volatile` and evaluating the expression `pvi` does not involve the accessing of a `volatile` object. `pvi` can be made a `volatile` pointer as follows:

```
volatile int *volatile pvi = &vi[2];
```

Recommendation: Do not rely on expressions statements such as `i[0];`, `pi;`, and `*pi;` to generate code. Even if `i` is a `volatile` object, it is not guaranteed that the `volatile` object would be accessed as a result.

◆ Selection Statements ◆

ANSI C guarantees at least 15 levels of nesting of selection control structures, iteration control structures and compound statements. K&R provided no minimum limit.

Recommendation: If you are using a pre-ANSI C compiler and you rely heavily on deep nesting of selection control structures, iteration control structures and compound statements, check the permissible depth for each target implementation.

The `switch` Statement

K&R required that the controlling expression in a `switch` statement have type `int`. ANSI C requires that it have an integral type thus allowing both `signed` and `unsigned long int` types and the `unsigned int` type. K&R also required that each `case` constant expression have type `int`. ANSI C requires each `case` expression to be of integral type, and each is converted to the type of the controlling expression, if necessary.

An interesting question arises with K&R implementations. Can `sizeof` be used in a `case` expression? This would depend on whether an implementation declared the type of `sizeof` as `int` or `unsigned int`. If it were `unsigned int`, it would not be allowed. And even if it were permitted, would the unsigned size value of a very large object be treated as a negative number since the controlling expression has type `signed int`? In ANSI C environments, `sizeof` has type `size_t` (which, in actuality, must be either `unsigned int` or `unsigned long`) which would be converted if the controlling expression were a signed integral type.

Recommendation: Be careful when using `sizeof` in a `case` constant expression. Depending on the type of `sizeof`, K&R may not allow it. With ANSI C, such a case label will be treated as a signed integral type.

Since ANSI C supports enumerated data types (which are represented by an integral type), it permits their use in `switch` expressions and in `case` constant expressions. Enumerated types are not defined in K&R.

Some implementations have a notation for specifying a range of values for a `case` constant expression. Note that since several different and incompatible syntaxes are in use, this feature was not incorporated into ANSI C.

Recommendation: Avoid the use of ranges of values in `case` constant expressions unless all your implementations support the same syntax for this extension.

Some implementations permit multi-character character constants such as `'ab'` and `'abcd'`. Character constants are permitted in `case` constant expressions.

Recommendation: Since the internal representation of multi-character character constants is implementation-defined, they should not be used in `case` constant expressions.

K&R did not specify the maximum number of `case` values permitted in a `switch` statement. ANSI C guarantees support for at least 257 `cases` for each `switch` statement.

Neither K&R nor ANSI C guarantee the order of `case` tests in a `switch` statement. For example, in the following program, the `cases` may be tested in the order 1, 2, and 3 or 3, 2, and 1 or any other order—the ordering is undefined. The only thing guaranteed is that if there is no unconditional jump statement (such as `break`, `goto`, `continue`, `return`, `exit(n)`, etc.) at the end of a `case` "statement set," control will pass to the next `case` "statement set," as written in the source code.

```
test(i)
int i;
{
        switch (i) {

case 1:         /* ... */
        break;

case 2:         /* ... */
        break;

case 3:         /* ... */
        break;
        }
}
```

This issue does not affect the code's portability *per se*; however, it may well affect program efficiency when the code is moved to a different implementation. For example, if you have 20 transaction types to process using a `switch` with 20 cases, you may be inclined to order the `case` labels in decreasing order of transaction frequency. If the highest percentage of transactions are of type 5, you might put that `case` first assuming that it will be tested for first. However, the compiler may test `cases` in the order specified, in the reverse of that order, or some other order. A common way of implementing a contiguous range of `case` values is to set up a jump table in which `cases` are processed efficiently without regard to their label value. To guarantee the order of evaluation of tests, use nested `if/else` statements rather than `switch`.

Recommendation: Do not rely on a `switch`'s cases being evaluated in the order they are specified. The order of `case` testing is undefined and depending on the set of `case` values, and their contiguity, the implementation may test in one of several different methods. They may even use a combination of methods within the same `switch`.

Refer to the previous section entitled "Compound Statement, or Block" above for a discussion of transferring into compound statements within `switch` statements.

◆ Iteration Statements ◆

The controlling expressions in `while`, `do`, and `for` statements may contain expressions of the form *expr1* `==` *expr2*. If *expr1* and *expr2* are floating-point expressions, equality may be difficult or impossible to achieve due to the implementation-defined nature of floating-point representation, rounding, etc.

Recommendation: If the controlling expressions in `while`, `do` and `for` statements contain floating-point expressions, note that the results of floating-point equality tests are implementation-defined. Having something like `fabs`(*expr1* − *expr2*) `< 0.1e-5` may be more desirable than *expr1* `==` *expr2*, for example.

ANSI C guarantees at least 15 levels of nesting of selection control structures, iteration control structures, and compound statements. K&R provided no minimum limit.

Recommendation: If you are using a pre-ANSI C compiler and you rely heavily on deep nesting of selection control structures, iteration control structures, and compound statements, check the permissible depth for each target implementation.

The do Statement

The syntax of the `do` statement is

```
do statement while (expression);
```

so the body is itself another statement. If multiple statements are required in the body, they must be written as a block of statements as follows:

```
#include <stdio.h>

main()
{
        int c;

        c = getchar();
        do {
                putchar(c);
                c = getchar();
        } while (c != EOF);
}
```

Several implementations have been found to be deficient in that they allow the braces to be omitted. Both K&R and ANSI C require them if the `do while` body contains multiple statements.

The `for` Statement

Often, programmers write assignment (and other) expressions without embedded white space, as in `i=10`. One common place for this is in the first expression of a `for` statement. This form of expression is perfectly valid. However, it can cause some surprises on implementations that still support the old-style compound assignment operators. Refer to the section "Compound Assignment" for details.

♦ Jump Statements ♦

The `goto` Statement

Refer to the previous section entitled "Labeled statements" for a discussion of the implications of a separate label namespace. Refer to the section entitled "Compound Statement, or Block" to learn about the ramifications of jumping into compound statements.

The `return` Statement

If the value of a function is used, but no value is `returned`, the result is undefined. One place where this may cause some grief is in function `main`. Consider the following examples:

```
main()
{
        return;
}
```

`main` has a return type of `int` yet no value is `returned`, so the return value is undefined.

```
main()
{
}
```

Dropping into the closing brace of a function is equivalent to `return` without a value; so, again, the return value is undefined.

```
main()
{
        return 0;
}
```

Here, the value of 0 is explicitly returned.

```
main()
{
        exit(0);
}
```

This example does not return a value—it terminates by a call to exit. According to ANSI C, this should result in the same behavior as return 0; above.

Since few programs ever explicitly return (with or without a value) from main, many implementations' startup code ignores the value "returned" from main. They then terminate the program with an exit code of 0 (or some other "success" value), as if exit(0) or return 0 had been specified by the programmer.

Recommendation: In non-ANSI implementations, do not rely on the exit code of a program being set to the value you explicitly specify in a return statement in main since that return value may be replaced by some other "success" value such as 0. Use the exit library function instead.

Note that ANSI C guarantees that an explicitly returned value from main shall be used as the program's exit code.

Recommendation: Do not rely on the "returned" value of a function if none is explicitly returned.

ANSI C supports the void function type, which allows the compiler to ensure that a void function has no return value. K&R did not include the void type.

Recommendation: If you use the void function type, make sure that it is declared in both the function definition and in all places where the function is called. Not all implementations may support the void function type.

ANSI C supports the ability to return structures and unions by value. It places no constraint on the size of the object being returned, although the size of such objects that can be passed to a function by value may be limited. K&R did not include the returning of structures and unions by value.

Recommendation: Since ANSI C and many modern compilers permit the returning of structures and unions by value, the statements `return str;` and `return &str;` may be different. In the first case, the structure `str` will be returned by value while in the second, its address will be returned. On compilers not supporting aggregate return by value, both expressions are interpreted as "pointer to a structure."

It is unsafe to return certain values from a function. For example, the address of an automatic variable should never be returned.

```
#include <stdio.h>

main()
{
        int *pi, *f();

        pi = f();
        printf("%d\n", *pi);
}


int *f()
{
        int i = 100;

        return &i;
}
```

```
100
```

In this trivial example, even though the automatic variable `i` no longer exists after function `f` returns, the place it occupied on the run-time stack is still intact and so the program produces the "correct" answer. However, this is not guaranteed to occur.

Recommendation: Never `return` the address of an automatic variable from a function since once that function returns, the location pointed to is no longer allocated to that variable.

K&R (pages 68 and 70) show the general form of the `return` statement to be `return` (*expression*); yet, `return` *expression*; is shown as the formal definition on page 203. This may appear to be a contradiction. Page 203 is correct—the parentheses are not part of the syntax; they are merely redundant grouping parentheses and are part of the expression. The confusion comes from the fact that most (if not all) of the examples using `return` in K&R have the returned value within parentheses. From a style point of view, the parentheses are useful since they help to separate the `return` keyword from the expression, and they clearly delimit the expression if it is rather complex. However, they are never needed. (Note that in the second edition of K&R, the parentheses have been removed from the examples, and, often, `main` is terminated using `return 0;`.)

◆ Extensions ◆

The `asm` "statement" may be used by some implementations to insert assembly-language code directly into the translator output. The most common implementation is via a statement like

```
asm text
```

The `asm` keyword is not part of K&R or ANSI C.

Recommendation: Avoid embedding assembly code within C source. Not only will this not be portable, but the technique relies heavily on an intimate understanding of the code generated by the compiler. Trying to anticipate what an optimizer will do can be fraught with danger. If you need the speed or capability of assembly code, write the whole function in assembler and call it from C. Then when you move the application, the assembler function only need be rewritten—the programmer need have no knowledge of the code generator and optimizer.

Some implementations also have a `fortran` keyword; however, this is used in declarations, not as a statement.

◆ ◆ ◆ ◆ ◆ ◆

8

The Preprocessor

According to the ANSI C Standard Rationale document, "Perhaps the most undesirable diversity among existing C implementations can be found in preprocessing. Admittedly a distinct and primitive language superimposed upon C, the preprocessing commands accreted over time, with little central direction, and with even less precision in their documentation."

◆ General Information ◆

Preprocessor Versus Compiler

Many C compilers involve multiple passes, the first of which often contains the preprocessor. Using this knowledge, a compiler can often take short cuts by arranging information to be shared between the preprocessor and the various phases of the compiler proper. While this may be a useful feature for a particular implementation you should keep in mind that other implementations may use completely separate, and noncooperating, programs for the preprocessor and the compiler.

Recommendation: Keep the ideas of preprocessing and compilation separate. One possible problem when you fail to do this will be demonstrated when the `sizeof` operator is used as discussed below.

Although C is a free-format language, the preprocessor need not be since, strictly speaking, it is not part of the C language. The language and the preprocessor each have their own grammars, constraints, and semantics.

The Directive Name Format

A preprocessing directive always begins with a # character. However, not all preprocessors require the # and the directive name to be one token. That is, the # prefix may be separated from the directive name by spaces and/or horizontal tabs. For example, the following macro definitions:

```
#define MAX 26
# define MAX 26
#    define MAX 26
#<tab><tab>define MAX 26
```

may all be treated equally (and correctly) by some preprocessors; yet, all but the first will be rejected by other preprocessors.

K&R shows the # as part of the directive name, with no intervening white space. No statement is made as to whether such white space is permitted.

ANSI C permits an arbitrary number of horizontal tabs and spaces between the # and the directive name. The # and the directive name (such as define and include) are considered to be separate tokens.

Recommendation: The directive name should immediately follow the # character with no intervening white space unless all of your preprocessors support otherwise.

Start Position of Directives

Many preprocessors permit directives to be preceded by white space allowing indenting of nested directives as follows.

```
#if condition-1a
        #if condition-2a
                #if condition-3a
                ...
                #endif
        #else
                ...
        #endif
#else
        #if condition-2b
                #if condition-3b
                ...
                #endif
        #else
                ...
        #endif
#endif
```

Less flexible preprocessors require the # character to be the first character of a source line, thus requiring the above construct to be written instead as

```
#if condition-1a
#if condition-2a
#if condition-3a
...
#endif
#else
...
#endif
#else
#if condition-2b
#if condition-3b
...
#endif
#else
...
#endif
#endif
```

This latter format completely lacks any implied meaning regarding the scope of the conditional inclusion directives.

Some implementations require directives to begin in the first column; yet, they permit white space between the # and the directive name. In such cases, indenting can still be achieved as follows:

```
#if condition-1a
#       if condition-2a
#               if condition-3a
                ...
#               endif
#       else
                ...
#       endif
#else
#       if condition-2b
#               if condition-3b
                ...
#               endif
#       else
                ...
#       endif
#endif
```

K&R states that "Lines beginning with # communicate with this preprocessor." No definition for "beginning with" is given.

ANSI C permits an arbitrary amount of white space before the # character. This white space is not restricted to horizontal tabs and spaces—any white space is allowed.

Recommendation: Always begin directives at the first character on a line.

White Space Within Directives

ANSI C requires that all white space appearing between the directive name and the directive's terminating new-line be horizontal tabs and/or spaces. Therefore, the following directives contain syntax errors since the white space includes non-space, nontab characters. (The sequences <VT>, <CR>, <FF>, and <BS> represent a vertical tab, carriage return, form feed, and backspace, respectively.)

```
#define<VT>YES<CR>1
#define<FF>NO<BS>0
```

K&R makes no statement about the validity or nature of such embedded white space.

If you use at least one white space character to separate tokens in a directive, the actual number of such characters (and the mix of tabs and spaces) is almost always immaterial to the preprocessor. The one exception has to do with benign redefinition of macros using the #define directive. This is discussed later in this chapter.

Recommendation: Do not use white space other than spaces and horizontal tabs to separate tokens within a directive.

Directive Continuation Lines

K&R declared that macro definitions (with and without arguments) could be continued across multiple source lines if all lines to be continued contained a backslash immediately preceding the terminating new-line.

ANSI C has generalized this notion and permits any token (not just those seen by the preprocessor, but by the language as well) to be continued using the backslash/new-line sequence.

In the following case, the second source line starting with #define does not begin a macro definition directive since it is a continuation line and the #, therefore, is preceded by other than spaces and/or horizontal tabs.

```
#define NAME ... \
#define ...
```

> **Recommendation:** Restrict the backslash new-line continuation convention to macro definitions only, unless all your target implementations support its use elsewhere.

Trailing Tokens

Strictly speaking, the preprocessor should diagnose any tokens in excess of those expected. However, some implementations process only the tokens they expect, then ignore any tokens remaining on the directive line. If this is the case, the source line

```
#include <header.h> #define MAX 23
```

(which seems to indicate that a new-line was somehow omitted, perhaps lost during conversion for porting) would cause the header to be included. However, the macro definition will be ignored. Another example is

```
#ifdef DEBUG fp = fopen(name, "r");
```

In this case, the file is never opened regardless of whether DEBUG is defined.
K&R gives no indication as to what should happen in these cases.
ANSI C requires a diagnostic if excess tokens are present.

> **Recommendation:** Since the examples shown can never be interpreted correctly, their use is clearly an error. The real problem is, whether the error is detected. If any of your target preprocessors accept the above examples without error, write a program to locate any directive that follows non-white space characters on a line. This will find errors of the first type but not the second since any valid C statement could potentially follow the #ifdef directive.

Comments in Directives

Comments of the form /*...*/ are treated as a single space so they can occur anywhere that white space can. Since all, or various kinds of, white space can occur in preprocessing directives, so too can C-style comments. For example, in the directives

```
#define NUM_ELEMS 50   /* ... */
#include "global.h"   /* ... */
/* ... */ #define FALSE 0
/* ... */ #ifdef SMALL
/* ... */ #define TRUE 1 /* ... */
```

each comment is replaced by a single space during preprocessing. While the first two directives should port without error, the last three have leading horizontal white space, something not universally accepted, as noted above.

Of course, comments can occur between directive tokens, but this makes the directive more difficult to read. Therefore, it is to be avoided.

Note that comments can be continued indefinitely across source lines without requiring backslash/new-line terminators.

Recommendation: Restrict comments to the end of a directive source line. Beware though, of placing a comment after a backslash continuation character since when the comment gets replaced with a space during tokenization, the backslash will be followed by a space, not a new-line. Consequently, the sequence will not be recognized as that for continuation.

Phases of Translation

ANSI C contains a detailed discussion of the manner and order in which source text is translated into tokens for processing by the compiler. Prior to ANSI C there were no hard and fast rules governing this area allowing code such as the following to be interpreted in different ways by different preprocessors:

```
#ifdef DEBUG
#define T
#else
#define T /\
*
#endif
...
T          printf(...); /* ... */
```

The intent here, perhaps, is to disable the `printf` function call by having `T` become the start of a comment whenever `DEBUG` is not defined. As one programmer put it, "To define `T` as `/*` we need to fool the preprocessor, since it detects comments before doing anything else. To do this, we place the asterisk on a continuation line. Since the preprocessor doesn't see the token `/*`, everything works as expected. It works fine with C compilers in UNIX environments."

But does the preprocessor detect comments before doing anything else? Since the answer to this question varies by implementation, let's look at what ANSI C says. The phases of translation in ANSI C, as they affect the preprocessor, follow:

- Backslash/new-line pairs are removed so that continuation lines are spliced together.

- The source is broken into preprocessing tokens and sequences of white space characters (including comments).

- Each comment is replaced with a space character. However, whether consecutive white space characters are compressed to one such character is implementation-defined.

- Preprocessing directives are executed, and macro invocations are expanded. For each header included here, the steps outlined, are followed over again.

An ANSI C compiler, therefore, is obliged to diagnose an error when given the previous code since the #endif directive will be included in the comment started on the macro definition line.

Recommendation: Do not write tricky code that uses idiosyncrasies of a preprocessor unless you realize the implications and you document it appropriately. Deal with the preprocessor in an overt manner and do not try to circumvent it. Regarding the example above, at the expense of adding a few keystrokes and making the code more readable, the recommended solution is to use

```
#ifdef DEBUG
        printf(...);
#endif
```

Some UNIX implementations expand macros before looking for preprocessor commands thus accepting the following code:

```
#define d define
#d MAX 43
```

Recommendation: Do not use the preprocessor to construct preprocessor directive names. In any case, this is disallowed by ANSI C.

Inspecting Preprocessor Output

Some implementations have a preprocessor separate from the compiler, in which case an intermediate text file is produced. Other implementations, which combine the preprocessor and compiler, have a listing option that allows the final effect of all directives to appear in the compilation listing file. They may also allow intermediate expansions of macros whose definitions contain other macros to be listed. Note that some implementations are not able to preserve comments or white space when saving the intermediate code since comments may already have been reduced to spaces prior to the preprocessor directives being processed.

This is the case with ANSI C's phases of translation.

Recommendation: See which of your implementations allows the output of the preprocessor to be saved. One particularly useful quality assurance step is to compare the output text files produced by each of your preprocessors. This allows you to check if they expand macros and conditionally include code in the correct manner. So when you transport a source file to a new environment, you may also wish to transport the preprocessed version of that file.

♦ Source File Inclusion ♦

The `#include` directive is used to treat the contents of the named header as if it were in-line as part of the source file being processed. A header need not correspond exactly to a text file (or be of the same name), although it often does. Therefore, the term header will be used rather than header file or include file.

ANSI C requires that a header contain complete tokens. Specifically, you may not put only the start or finish of a comment, string literal, or character constant in a header. A header must also end with a new-line. This means that you cannot paste tokens together across `#includes`.

Recommendation: Do not put the leading or trailing (only) part of a comment, string literal, or character constant in a header. Always terminate a header with a new-line.

A very real port problem with C is the lack of control of identifier namespace between implementer and programmer, or, even between programmers. For example, you may define a macro called TOTAL. If no other macro by that name is defined in any header in your implementation, the program behaves as expected. However, when you port that program to another implementation, a macro by that name already exists in one of the headers you include, `stdio.h`, for example. Except for implementers beginning their identifier names with underscores, you cannot ensure your choice of names won't conflict when you move the code elsewhere.

The index in K&R contains only three macros—EOF, FILE, and NULL. It also lists some 20-30 library functions. No others are mentioned or required. ANSI C, on the other hand, contains several hundred reserved identifiers, most of which are macros or library function names. Add to that the system-related identifiers used by your compiler (VAX C has several thousand) and those identifiers used by any third-party layered products, and you have a very real potential for naming conflicts.

> **Recommendation:** For each of your target environments, generate a reserved identifier list in sorted alphabetical order by header, and across headers. Use this list of identifiers for two purposes: to identify names to stay away from when inventing your own identifier names and to find the union of all sets so you know what names are common and can be used meaningfully in common code. Note that just because a macro of the same name appears in different environments does not mean it is used for the same purpose. For names you invent, use some unique prefix (not leading underscores), suffix, or naming style so the likelihood of conflict is reduced.

`#include` Directive Format

K&R defines two forms of the `#include` directive. For directives of the form

```
#include "header-name"
```

"the header is searched for first in the directory of the original source file, then in a sequence of standard places." ANSI C states that the header is searched for in an implementation-defined manner.

K&R (and ANSI C) requires that only the implementation-defined standard places are searched for directives of the form

```
#include <header-name>
```

> **Recommendation:** Use the `<...>` format when referencing the standard headers (e.g., `stdio.h`) provided with your compiler and any layered products. For all project-specific headers, use the `"..."` form.

ANSI C adds a third form,

```
#include identifier
```

provided `identifier` ultimately translates to the form `"..."` or `<...>`. Since a macro name is an identifier, this format allows a header name to be constructed or otherwise defined either using the (new) token-pasting preprocessing operator `##` or by defining the macro on the compiler command line. Many compilers support a command-line argument of the form `-Didentifier` or `/define=identifier`, which is equivalent to having `#define identifier 1` in the source being compiled.

DEC's VAX C uses this format to specify an entry point within a text library. When VAX C is installed you can chose between having the standard headers as separate ASCII files of the same name or combined in a text library or both.

If your target compilers support the –D (or /d) option discussed above and the #include identifier format, you can specify a header's full device/directory path name at compilation-time rather than hard-code that information into the #include directive.

One technique to help isolate hard-coded header locations follows. A master header contains

```
/* hnames.h - header names, fully qualified */

#define MASTER "DBA0:[data]master.h"
#define STRUCTURES "DUA2:[templates]struct.h"
```

Now, if this header is included in another header, these macro names can be used as follows:

```
#include "hnames.h"

#include MASTER
#include STRUCTURES
```

If you move the code to another system or you move the headers to a different location on the same system, you simply modify the hnames.h header and recompile all modules that include it.

Recommendation: If your implementation supports the #include identifier format use, it only if your compilers support the –D (or /d) command-line option or you have some other way of constructing header names in a portable fashion.

Header Names

The format and spelling of the header name in the "..." and <...> formats is implementation-dependent.

A peculiar problem occurs with file systems (such as MS-DOS) that use the backslash to separate subdirectory and file names in file pathnames. The completely qualified name of a DOS disk file has the following format:

```
\dir1\dir2\ ... \filename.ext
```

The problem arises with directory and filenames such as

```
\totals\accum.h
\summary\files.h
```

```
\times\filecopy.h
\volume\backup.h
```

Here, either the directory or the filename (or both) begin with the sequence '\x', where x is a recognizable special character sequence within a C literal string. The problem then becomes, "How do I name this header file when including it?"

When using compilers that recognize and translate escape sequences prior to including headers, you will need to use

```
#include "\\totals\accum.h"
#include "\summary\\files.h"
#include "\\times\\filecopy.h"
#include "\volume\\backup.h"
```

Newer compilers may also support either or both of the escape sequences '\a' and '\v' (alarm and vertical tab, respectively). In this case,

```
#include "\\totals\accum.h"
#include "\volume\\backup.h"
```

must be changed to

```
#include "\\totals\\accum.h"
#include "\\volume\\backup.h"
```

The situation is further complicated if the escape sequence is of the form '\nnn', where nnn is an octal constant. The same is true if the compiler supports the new escape sequence '\xhhh', where hhh is a hexadecimal constant. In these cases, header names of the format

```
#include "\0401.h"
#include "\xable.h"
```

will need to be changed to

```
#include "\\0401.h"
#include "\\xable.h"
```

An implementation that processes headers before interpreting escape sequences will generate an error if any of the above strings is encountered since \\ denotes a directory with no name, something DOS does not support.

In ANSI C, the phases of translation are specified such that headers are included before escape sequences in string literals are converted to single characters. Therefore, the \\ are not necessary in the above examples as the text within "..." is merely a sequence of characters whose meaning is implementation-defined.

Recommendation: If possible, do not embed file system device, directory, or subdirectory information into header names. (This also applies to code being ported from one DOS C compiler to another since each may have a different idea about phases of translation.)

Recommendation: On DOS, if you must embed directory information in header names, make sure the path name does not contain characters that correspond to C's escape sequences.

Recommendation: Use only lower-case letters in header names and limit the number to six (as is the case for all ANSI C standard headers). If the header actually is a file, limit the file type (if one is possible) to one character (traditionally h). Some file systems are case-sensitive in which case STDIO.H, stdio.h, and Stdio.h could be three separate files. Most file systems support files with names of six letters and many support names containing digits and a one-to-three character file type of the form .xxx.

Nested Headers

A header may include other #include directives. The level of header file nesting permitted is implementation-defined. K&R states that headers may be nested but gives no minimum requirement. ANSI C requires at least eight levels of header-nesting capability.

Recommendation: If headers are designed properly, they should be able to be included multiple times and in any order. That is, each header should be made self-sufficient by having it include any headers it relies on. Put only related things in a header and restrict nesting to three, or at most four, levels. Use #ifdef wrappers around the contents of a header so they are not included more than once in the same scope.

Some hierarchical file systems (as used in DOS, UNIX, and VAX/VMS, for example) allow a file path to be relative to some default directory rather than as an absolute specification. For example, on DOS, assuming that the user's current directory is \main, then

```
#include "data\master.h"
```

causes the preprocessor to search for the header `master.h` located in directory `data`, which, itself, is a subdirectory of the user's current directory `\main`. The fully qualified filename is `\main\data\master.h`. But what if `master.h` contains another relative path reference?

```
/* master.h */

#include "struct\files.h"
```

Is this directory reference relative to the user's default or to that of the header including this header? That is, is the fully qualified filename

```
\main\struct\files.h
```

or

```
\main\data\struct\files.h
```

K&R requires a header to be searched for relative to the original source file, in which case the fully qualified filename would be

```
\main\struct\files.h
```

ANSI C declares that the search method is implementation-defined.

Recommendation: If you must nest headers and embed directory path names in header names, make sure you understand the way in which your implementation constructs a fully qualified name. Use the `hnames.h` header idea proposed above.

#include Path Specifiers

K&R and ANSI C provide only two mechanisms to specify header location search paths, namely, `<...>` and `"..."`. Sometimes it is necessary or desirable to have more than this, or perhaps for testing purposes, you temporarily want to use some other location instead. Many implementations allow one or more include search paths to be specified as command-line arguments at compile-time. For example,

```
cc -Ipath1 -Ipath2 -Ipath3 source-file
```

tells the preprocessor to first search for `"..."` format headers using `path1` then `path2` and `path3` and, finally, in some system default location. The lack of this feature or the support of less than the required number of paths may cause problems when porting code. Even though your compiler may support a sufficient number of these arguments, the maximum size of the command-line buffer may be such that it will be too small to accommodate a number of verbose path specifiers.

Recommendation: If this capability is present in all your implementations, check the number of paths supported by each.

Modification of Standard Headers

On many implementations, the headers supplied with the compiler are text files that can be read and even modified. Except for a "small" number of macro definitions, library function declarations, and `typedefs`, the contents of standard headers such as `stdio.h` may vary widely from one implementation to the next. Perhaps one of your implementation's `stdio.h` contains a definition of the macros `TRUE`, `FALSE`, `YES`, and `NO`, while the others do not. In this case, it is very tempting to add these definitions to these other versions of `stdio.h`. However, doing so will likely lead to both maintenance and porting problems. When a new release of the compiler is installed, you must remember to modify the new header versions. The same is true when you port the code to some other environment in which the standard headers are "deficient."

Recommendation: Do not modify standard headers by adding definitions, declarations, or other `#includes`. Instead, create your own miscellaneous or local header and include that in all the relevant places. When upgrading to new compiler versions or when moving to different compilers, no extra work need be done beyond making that local header available as before. About the only change to standard headers that is permissible is to add a conditional inclusion mechanism such that the header is not preprocessed multiple times if it is included more than once in the same scope. The purpose of this is to reduce compilation time, and as such its omission has no real effect when upgrading or moving to new compilers. One technique for achieving this follows:

```
/* stdio.h */
#ifndef STDIO_H
#define STDIO_H
...
...   /* body of header */
...
#endif
```

Another common approach used by implementers is to use a macro name such as `__STDIO__`. In any case, it is wise to use a name that is a function of the header name. By doing this, you have effectively reserved the corresponding identifier from other use. Obviously, this technique can be applied to your own user-written headers, provided, of course, you don't use the leading underscores since this is reserved for implementers use.

◆ Macro Replacement ◆

The `#define` directive is used to associate a string definition with a macro name. Since a macro name is an identifier, it is subject to the same naming constraints as other identifiers. K&R required eight characters of significance, and ANSI C requires 31.

Recommendation: Use the lowest common denominator length of significance for macro names.

Recommendation: Since the vast majority of C programmers have been directly or indirectly influenced by K&R, it is suggested you spell macro names using upper-case letters, digits, and underscores. This will be the most common convention you are likely to encounter.

ANSI C requires that tokens specified as a part of a macro definition must be well formed (i.e., complete). Therefore, a macro definition cannot contain just the start or end part of a comment, literal string, or character constant. While this may seem reasonable, and it is, it can surprise you with `#error` and `#pragma` directives such as

```
#error that's all folks
```

since the single quote is seen as the beginning of a (nonterminated) character constant.

Some compilers allow partial tokens in macros such that when the macro is expanded, it is pasted to the token preceding and/or following it.

Recommendation: Avoid having partial tokens in macro definitions.

The definition of a macro may contain an arithmetic expression such as

```
#define MIN 5
#define MAX MIN + 30
```

The preprocessor does not recognize this as an expression, but rather as a sequence of tokens that it substitutes wherever the macro is called. It is not permitted to treat the definition of MAX as if it were

```
#define MAX 35
```

Preprocessor arithmetic comes into play only with the conditional inclusion directive #if. However, the original definition of MAX above will be treated as an expression if the following code is used:

```
#if MAX
        ...
#endif
```

This will be expanded to

```
#if MIN + 30
        ...
#endif
```

then

```
#if 35
        ...
#endif
```

An implementation may place a limit on the size of a macro's definition.

Recommendation: If you plan on having macros whose definitions are longer than 80 characters, test your environments to see what their limits are.

Macros with Arguments

A macro with arguments has the general form

```
#define name(arg1, arg2, ...,argn) definition
```

K&R does not state the maximum number of arguments allowed. However, ANSI C guarantees at least 31.

Recommendation: If you plan on using macros with more than four or five arguments, check the limits of your target implementations.

While there can be no white space between the macro name and the (that begins the argument list in a macro definition, this constraint is not often present in macro calls and not at all in ANSI C.

Recommendation: In a macro call, do not put a space between the macro name and the (that begins the argument list. For example, use

```
PROCESS(a, b, c);
```

instead of

```
PROCESS (a, b, c);
```

Some implementations allow a macro call to have less than the number of arguments declared in the macro's definition. K&R and ANSI C require that the number of arguments be the same in each.

In the following example, whether or not an error is generated is undefined. ANSI C declares this to be a constraint violation, so it must be diagnosed. The construct is certainly nonportable.

```
#define M(a)  f(a)    /* one argument */

    M();         /* no argument */
```

Recommendation: Make sure all calls to a macro have the same number of arguments as the macro definition.

There is no requirement that all of the arguments specified in a macro definition argument list must appear within that macro's definition.

Rescanning Macro Names

A macro definition can refer to another macro, in which case that definition is rescanned as necessary.

ANSI C requires the definition of a macro to be "turned off" for the duration of the expansion of that macro so that "recursive death" is not suffered. That is, a macro name that appears within its own definition is not re-expanded. This allows the name of a macro to be passed as an argument to another macro.

Replacement Within Strings and Character Constants

Some implementations allow macro arguments within string literals and character constants to be replaced as follows:

```
#define PR(a) printf("a = %d\n",a)
```

Then the macro call

```
PR(total);
```

is expanded to

```
printf("total = %d\n",total);
```

On implementations that do not allow this, the macro would be expanded to

```
printf("a = %d\n",total);
```

K&R states that "text inside a string or character constant is not subject to replacement."

ANSI C does not support the replacement of macro arguments within strings and character constants. However, it does supply the (new) # stringize operator so that the same effect can be achieved. For example,

```
#define PR(a) printf(#a " = %d\n",a)
...
PR(total);
```

expands to

```
printf("total" " = %d\n",total);
```

and since ANSI C permits adjacent strings to be concatenated, this becomes

```
printf("total = %d\n",total);
```

Recommendation: Unless all your compilers handle this situation in the same manner, avoid this construct. If some of your compilers allow string substitution and the others support the # operator, you could use conditional inclusion to switch between the two based on the definition of a specific macro.

Command-Line Macro Definition

Many compilers allow macros to be defined using a command-line argument of the form -Didentifier or /define=identifier, which is equivalent to having #define identifier 1 in the source being compiled. Only a very few compilers allow macros with arguments to be defined in this manner. VAX C is one such implementation.

The size of the command-line buffer, or the number of command-line arguments, may be such that there is insufficient room to specify all the required macro definitions, particularly if you use this mechanism to specify identifiers used in numerous `#include` directives.

Recommendation: Qualify if this capability is present in all your implementations. At least five or six identifiers should be supported provided you keep the lengths of each to a minimum. (Note that if you use 31 character identifier names on DOS, you will very quickly exceed its command-line buffer size of 128-odd bytes.)

Benign Redefinition

Many implementations permit an existing macro to be redefined without its first being `#undefed`. The purpose of this (generally) is to allow the same macro definition to occur in multiple headers, all of which are included in the same scope. However, if one or more of the definitions is not the same as the others, a serious problem can occur. For example,

```
#define NULL 0
...
#define NULL 0L
...
```

causes the first part of the code to be compiled using zero as the value for `NULL` and the last part using zero `long`. This can cause serious problems when using `f(NULL);` since the size of the object passed to `f` may not the same as that expected by `f`.

Very few compilers warn about such redefinitions.

ANSI C allows a macro to be redefined provided the definitions are the same. This is known as *benign redefinition*. Just what does "the same" mean? Basically, it requires that the macro definitions be spelled EXACTLY the same, and depending on how white space between tokens is processed, multiple consecutive white space characters may be significant. For example,

```
1.        #define MACRO a macro
2.        #define MACRO a macro
3.        #define MACRO a<TAB>macro
4.        #define MACRO a    macro
5.        #define MACRO example
```

Macros 1 and 2 are the same. Macros 3 and 4 may also be the same as 1 and 2 depending on the handling of the white space. Macro 5 would definitely be flagged as an error. Note that this does not solve the problem of having different definitions for the same macro that are not in the same scope.

Recommendation: It is legitimate to have a macro defined exactly the same in multiple places (typically in headers). In fact, this idea is encouraged for reasons stated elsewhere. However, avoid having different definitions for the same macro. Since the use of multiple, consecutive white space characters may result in different spellings (as in macros 3 and 4 above), you should separate tokens by only one white space character, and the character you use should be consistent. As horizontal tabs may be converted to spaces, space separators are suggested.

By macro redefinition, we mean either the redefinition of a macro without arguments to a macro of the same name, also without arguments, or the redefinition of a macro with arguments with the same macro name with the same number and spelling of arguments.

Recommendation: Even if your implementation allows it, do not redefine a macro without arguments to one with arguments or vice versa. This is not supported by ANSI C.

Predefined Macros

ANSI C requires the following five predefined macros:

- `__DATE__` -- Date of compilation in the form `"Mmm dd yyyy`.
- `__TIME__` -- Time of compilation in the form `hh:mm:ss`.
- `__FILE__` -- Name of file being compiled.
- `__LINE__` -- Line number of file being compiled.
- `__STDC__` -- Has the value 1 if the compiler is ANSI-conforming.

At least `__LINE__` and `__FILE__` are available in UNIX as of Version 7. The date format of the string produced by `__DATE__` can vary. ANSI C produces `"Mmm dd yyyy"`, VAX C uses the format `"dd-mmm-yyyy"`, while others use the ISO format `"yyyy-mm-dd"`. The format of the date string is important if you attempt to parse a string initialized with `__DATE__`. For example, you can initialize a character array using

```
char compile_date[] = __DATE__;
```

and then extract day, month, and year information at run-time. For this to be reliable, the format of the date string must be predictable.

Recommendation: If you only display the __DATE__ string or write it to a file, you need not be concerned if its format changes across implementations. Different formats will cause problems if your code expects them to be a certain way.

These macros (and the identifier defined) cannot be #defined or #undefed. ANSI C also requires that any other predefined names begin with an underscore. Since few pre-ANSI implementations have predefined names of this format, these names would not be available in ANSI-mode.

K&R contains no predefined macros. Even NULL and EOF are defined in the standard headers.

Macro names describing the translation and execution environments may be defined by the implementation before translation begins. Generally, these can be removed via the #undef directive. Multiple predefined macros may have the same value, and different implementations may use different identifiers to mean the same thing. For example, in VAX C, the macros vms, VMS, vax, VAX, vaxc, VAXC, vax11c, VAX11C, vms_version and VMS_VERSION are known by the compiler—they are not the subject of a #define directive.

Note that identifiers defined on the compiler command line are not considered to be predefined macros, even though they conceptually are defined prior to the source being processed.

Except for the five predefined macros specified by ANSI C, all other predefined names are implementation-defined. There is no established set of names for the most common CPUs and operating systems or for the various memory models possible on the Intel 8088-class machines, for example.

Recommendation: You may use those names defined by a particular implementation if you are likely to be bound to that implementation. If not, invent a set of meaningful names using upper-case letters only so they can be distinguished from other identifiers and use them throughout. Names of the format CPU_xxx and OS_xxx would help readability and should reduce the possibility of conflict with macro names elsewhere.

Macro Definition Symbol Table

The maximum number of entries that can fit in an implementation's preprocessor symbol table may vary considerably as can the amount of total string space available for macro definitions.

ANSI C requires that at least 1024 macro identifiers be able to be simultaneously defined in a source file (including all included headers, of course). While this guarantee may allow 1024 macros, a conforming implementation might require that each macro definition be restricted in length. It certainly does not guarantee 1024 macro definitions of unlimited length and complexity.

K&R makes no statement about the limit on the number or size of concurrent macro definitions.

Recommendation: If you expect to have a large number (greater than a few hundred) of concurrent macro definitions, write a program that can generate test headers containing macros of arbitrary number and complexity, to see what each of your implementations can handle. There is also some incentive to include only those headers that need be included and to modularize headers such that they contain only related material. It is perfectly acceptable to have the same macro definition in multiple headers. For example, some implementers define NULL in several headers just so the whole of stdio.h need not be preprocessed for one macro name.

Stacking Macro Definitions

Some implementations allow the stacking of macros. That is, if a macro name is in scope and a macro of the same name is defined, the second definition hides the first. If the second definition is removed, the first definition is back in scope again. For example,

```
#define MAX 30
...
... /* MAX is 30 */
...
#define MAX 35
...
... /* MAX is 35 */
...
#undef MAX
...
... /* MAX is 30 */
...
```

ANSI C does not permit the stacking of macro definitions. K&R states that the use of #undef "causes the identifier's preprocessor definition to be forgotten," presumably forgotten completely.

Recommendation: Since macro stacking is a covert operation and it is not universally implemented, avoid it. If used, it can lead to some very nasty debugging problems since the macro name is no longer a mnemonic for a constant.

The # Stringize Operator

This is an ANSI C invention. Its use is discussed previously with the `#define` directive.

The ## Token-Pasting Operator

This is an ANSI C invention. It allows a macro expansion to construct a token that can then be rescanned. For example, with a macro definition of

```
#define PRN(x) printf("%d", value ## x)
```

the macro call

```
PRN(3);
```

generates the code

```
printf("%d", value3);
```

A common solution to this problem prior to ANSI C follows:

```
#define M(a, b)   a/* */b
```

Here, instead of the definition being a b (since the comment is replaced with a space), the implementation made it ab, thus forming a new token that was then rescanned. This practice is not supported by either K&R or ANSI C. The ANSI C approach to this is

```
#define M(a, b)   a ## b
```

where the spaces around the `##` operator are optional.

Recommendation: Do not rely on comments in macro definitions being replaced by nothing.

ANSI C specifies that in `A ## B ## C`, the order of evaluation is implementation-defined.

An interesting situation exists in the following example:

```
#define INT_MIN -32768

int i = 1000-INT_MIN;
```

Here, the macro expands producing `1000--32768`, which looks perhaps as if it should generate a syntax error since 1000 is not an lvalue. However, ANSI C resolves this with its "phases of translation" by requiring that the preprocessing tokens – and `32768` retain their meaning when handed off to the compiler. That is, the two minus signs are not recognized as the autodecrement token `--`, even though they are adjacent in the expanded text stream. A non-ANSI implementation, however, might rescan the text producing a different token sequence.

Some implementations allow the output from their preprocessor to be saved as a file that, presumably, can be compiled at some later stage. In such cases, the expressions above, `1000--32768` will now be interpreted to be three tokens, not four as before. To be absolutely correct, the preprocessor would have to separate the tokens with white space when writing them to output such that when read by the compiler, they are interpreted correctly.

Recommendation: To avoid such macros definitions being misinterpreted, surround them with parentheses.

Redefining Keywords

Some implementations (including ANSI C) permit C language keywords to be redefined. For example,

```
#if __STDC__ != 1
        #define void int
#endif
```

Recommendation: Do not gratuitously redefine language keywords.

◆ The #undef Directive ◆

#undef can be used to remove a library macro to get access to a real function. If a macro version does not exist, the `#undef` is ignored since a nonexistent macro can be the subject of an `#undef` without error.

You may need to remove macro definitions when you have finished with them (before you reach the end of the source file) if you are reaching the limits of the preprocessor's symbol table.

Recommendation: Don't #undef a macro so you can define it differently unless you have fully thought out the maintenance repercussions.

Refer to "Stacking Macro Definitions" above for a discussion of the use of #undef in stacked macro implementations.

ANSI C does not permit the predefined macros __DATE__, __TIME__, __FILE__, __LINE__, and __STDC__ to be #undefed.

♦ Conditional Inclusion ♦

This capability is one of the most powerful parts of a C environment available for writing code that is to run on different target systems.

Recommendation: Make as much use as possible of conditional inclusion directives. This is made easier if you have, or you establish, a meaningful set of macros that distinguish one target environment from another. See limits.h and float.h for details of host characteristics.

#if Arithmetic

The object of an #if directive is a constant expression that is tested against the value 0.

Some implementations allow the sizeof operator to be used in the constant expression as follows:

```
#if sizeof(int) == 4
        int total;
#else
        long total;
#endif
```

Strictly speaking, the preprocessor is a macro processor and string substitution program and need not have any knowledge about data types or the C language. Remember that sizeof is a C language compile-time operator, and at this stage we are preprocessing, not compiling.

ANSI C requires that the constant expression not contain a cast or an enumeration constant. K&R uses the same definition of constant expression for the preprocessor as it does for the language, thus implying that sizeof is permitted here. No mention is made of the use of casts in constant expressions (even in the language). Whether the sizeof operator is supported in this context is implementation-defined. That is, while it is permitted, it is not guaranteed. Note that if an enumeration constant were present, it would be treated as an unknown macro and, as such, would default to a value of 0.

Recommendation: Do not use `sizeof`, casts, or enumeration constants in conditional constant expressions. To get around the inability of using `sizeof`, you may be able to determine certain attributes about your environment by using the header `limits.h`. For example, given that `INT_MAX` and `LONG_MAX` are defined in `limits.h` to represent the maximum and minimum values, respectively, of a `signed int`, the following code checks to see of the size of an `int` is the same as a `long`:

```
#include <limits.h>

#if INT_MAX < LONG_MAX
        int total;
#else
        long total;
#endif
...
#endif
```

ANSI C evaluates the constant expression using `long int` arithmetic according to the host environment. (In cross-compilation environments, the results of such arithmetic may vary between host and target.) All operands in the constant expression are treated as signed or unsigned `long int` quantities. Floating-point constants are not permitted. Consider the following (admittedly contrived) case on a 16-bit, twos-complement machine:

```
#if 32767 + 2 + 32767
        ...
#endif
```

If the expression were evaluated using signed `int` arithmetic, overflow would occur and the (expected) result would be `0`, which tests false, and the subordinate code is not compiled. (`32767 + 2` gives `-32767` and `-32767 + 32767` gives `0`.) Using long arithmetic, as required by ANSI C, the expression is treated as if it were written

```
#if 32767L + 2L + 32767L
        ...
#endif
```

Now, the result is `65536L`, which tests true, and the subordinate code is compiled.

> **Recommendation:** Your preprocessor might not perform arithmetic in `#if` directives using `long int` precision. To force this, always use the `L` (or `l`) suffix on constants (or macro definitions that expand to integral constants). Do not rely on underflow or overflow since arithmetic properties vary widely on ones- and twos-complement and packed-decimal machines. Do not use floating-point constants. Do not use the right-shift operator if signed operands are present since the result is implementation-defined when the sign bit is set.

A character constant can legitimately be part of a constant expression (where it is treated as an integer). Character constants can contain any arbitrary bit pattern (by using `'\nnn'` or `'\xhhh'`). Some implementations, such as DEC's PDP-11 and VAX, would therefore support character constants whose value was negative (e.g., `'\377'` and `'\xFA'` have their high bits set).

ANSI C states that whether or not a single-character character constant may have a negative value is implementation-defined. K&R makes no statement.

Some implementations (e.g., VAX C and various Whitesmiths compilers) support multi-character constants, as does ANSI C.

> **Recommendation:** Do not use character constants whose value may be negative. Also, since the order and meaning of characters in multi-character constants is implementation-defined, do not use them in `#if` constant expressions.

In ANSI C, if the constant expression contains a macro name that is not currently defined, the macro is treated as if it were defined with the value 0. The macro name is only interpreted that way; it does not actually become defined with that value. K&R makes no provision for this case.

> **Recommendation:** Do not use the fact that undefined macros evaluate to 0 in constant expressions. If a macro definition is omitted, either from a header or from the command line at compile-time, then using this default rule results in its being erroneously interpreted as being defined with the value 0. It is not always practical to test if a macro is defined first before using it—we all assume that `EOF` and `NULL` are defined in `stdio.h`, for example. However, for macros expected to be defined on the command line, it is worth the check since it is very easy to omit the macro definition if you are typing the compile command line manually. To further help avoid such problems use command procedures or scripts to compile code, particularly when numerous and lengthy include paths and macros are present on the command line.

It is possible for the constant expression to produce an error, for example, if division by 0 is encountered. (This is possible if a macro name used as a denominator has not been defined and defaults to 0.) Some implementations may flag this as an error, while others won't. Some may continue processing, assuming the value of the whole expression is 0.

Recommendation: Do not assume your implementation will generate an error if it determines the #if constant expression contains a mathematical error.

K&R does not include the ! unary operator in the operators permitted within constant expressions. This is generally considered to be either an oversight or a typographical error.

The defined Operator

Sometimes it is necessary to have nested conditional inclusion constructs such as

```
#ifdef VAX
        #ifdef VMS
                #ifdef DEBUG
                ...
                #endif
        #endif
#endif
```

This is supported by both K&R and ANSI C. ANSI C (and other implementations) provides the defined preprocessor unary operator to make this construct more elegant. For example,

```
#if defined(VAX) && defined(VMS) \
        && defined(DEBUG)
        ...
#endif
```

ANSI C essentially reserves the identifier defined—it may not be used elsewhere as a macro name.

Recommendation: Do not use the defined operator unless all your environments support it.

The #elif Directive

The following cumbersome construct is also commonly used in writing portable code. It is supported by K&R and ANSI C.

```
#if MAX >= TOTAL1
        . . .
#else
        #if MAX >= TOTAL2
                . . .
        #endif
#else
        #if MAX >= TOTAL3
                . . .
        #endif
#else
        . . .
#endif
```

The directive #elif simplifies nested #ifs greatly as follows.

```
#if MAX >= TOTAL1
        . . .
#elif MAX >= TOTAL2
        . . .
#elif MAX >= TOTAL3
        . . .
#else
        . . .
#endif
```

Recommendation: Do not use the #elif directive unless all your environments support it.

Nested Conditional Directives

ANSI C guarantees at least eight levels of nesting. K&R states that these directives may be nested but gives no guaranteed minimum.

Recommendation: Use no more than two or three levels of nesting with conditional directives unless all of your implementations permit more.

◆ Line Control ◆

K&R defined the syntax of the `#line` directive to be

```
#line line-number filename
```

The line number and filename are used to update the `__LINE__` and `__FILE__` predefined macros (if they are supported), respectively.

ANSI C allows either a macro name or string literal in place of the filename. It also permits a macro in place of the line number, provided its value is a decimal digit sequence.

VAX C (among other compilers) allows an obsolete version of this directive where the token line is omitted. The resulting directive looks something like

```
# line-number filename
```

which is not to be confused with the null directive.

The purpose of this directive is to have the compiler produce messages based on the line numbers and filenames provided by `#line` rather than on its own accounting of these items. Therefore, the compiler (rather than the preprocessor) is expected to recognize `#line` directives. Whether the preprocessor recognizes, passes on, eliminates, or modifies `#line` directives is implementation-defined. Some compilers may complain about `#line` directives; others will ignore them.

◆ The Null Directive ◆

ANSI C permits a null directive of the form

```
#
```

This directive has no effect and is typically found only in machine-generated code. While it has existed in implementations for many years, it was not defined in K&R.

◆ The #pragma Directive ◆

`#pragma` is an ANSI C invention. The intent of this directive is to provide a mechanism for implementations to extend the preprocessor's syntax. This is possible since the preprocessor ignores any pragma it does not recognize. The syntax and semantics of a `#pragma` directive are implementation-defined, although the general format is

```
#pragma token-sequence
```

Possible uses of pragmas are to control compilation listing pagination and line format, to enable and disable optimization, and to activate and deactivate lint-like checking. Implementers can invent pragmas for whatever purpose they desire.

One possible problem with pragmas is that the same pragma may be interpreted differently by different implementations.

Recommendation: If you use pragmas, make sure you find out all the pragmas understood by your implementations so there is no conflict of interpretation. Use the conditional inclusion directives if only some of your implementations support pragmas or they support the same pragma names, each with different semantics.

◆ The #error Directive ◆

This is an ANSI C invention. Its format is

```
#error token-sequence
```

and it causes the implementation to generate a diagnostic message that includes the token sequence specified.

One possible use is to report on macros you expected to be defined, but which were found not to be.

◆ Non-Standard Directives ◆

Numerous implementations accept other preprocessor directives. For example, VAX C supports #dictionary and #module. UNIX System V.3 supports others. Since these extensions directly relate to the implementation's specific environment, they have little or no utility in other environments. Therefore, they must be identified in code that is to be ported and implemented in some other way, if at all.

The C Run-Time Library

Library Introduction

♦ Definition of Terms ♦

Many standard library routines deal with strings. A *string* is an array of `char` terminated by a `'\0'` character.

A *letter* is one of the 52 upper- and lower-case alphabetic characters required to be in the execution character set. It is not to be confused with a multibyte character that may represent a non-English "letter" (e.g., a Kanji character) or with "extended" characters (e.g., such as those Western European alphabetic characters containing diacritical marks.)

ANSI C has introduced the notion of locales such that the traditional C environment is defined by the `"C"` locale. A *locale* contains information about currency, date, and time (and other attributes') formatting requirements for the given locale. This is discussed further under `locale.h`. The behavior of numerous library functions (including some declared in `ctype.h` and `time.h`) is affected by the current locale.

Numerous library routines are documented as dealing with a *decimal point* when, in fact, they use a radix point. In the `"C"` locale, the period character is used for this purpose; however, another character may be used in a different locale. The standard routines using a radix point that is affected by the locale are: `atof`, `fprintf`, `fscanf`, `localconv`, `printf`, `scanf`, `sprintf`, `sscanf`, `strtod`, `vfprintf`, `vprintf`, and `vsprintf`.

◆ The Standard Headers ◆

Each library routine defined by ANSI C is declared in a corresponding header, the names and purposes of which follow:

Header	Purpose
assert.h	Program diagnostic purposes
ctype.h	Character testing & conversion
errno.h	Various error checking facilities
float.h	Floating type characteristics
limits.h	Integral type sizes
locale.h	Internationalization support
math.h	Math functions
setjmp.h	Nonlocal jump facility
signal.h	Signal handling
stdarg.h	Variable argument support
stddef.h	Miscellaneous
stdio.h	Input/output functions
stdlib.h	General utilities
string.h	String functions
time.h	Date and time functions

The headers are defined as having lower-case names and must be correctly located by a conforming implementation using the above spellings. Since some file systems support mixed-case file names, you should not spell the standard header names in any other way.

Each header is self-contained. That is, it contains all the declarations and definitions needed to invoke the routines declared within it. Note though that a header does not necessarily contain all the macro definitions whose value can be returned by these routines. For example, strtod in stdlib.h could return a value of HUGE_VAL, and ERANGE may be stored in errno; yet, these three macros are not defined in stdlib.h. To use them, both errno.h and math.h must be included as well.

In order to be self-contained, several headers either define the same names (identically) or include other standard headers so the required names become defined. Examples of this are NULL and size_t, which are required to be defined in a number of different headers.

All external identifiers declared in any of the standard headers are reserved, whether or not their associated header is referenced. That is, don't presume that just because you never include time.h that you can define your own external routine called clock. Note that macros and typedef names are not included in this reservation since they are not external names. Appendix A contains a list of all of the identifiers defined and declared by the standard headers.

External identifiers that begin with an underscore are reserved. All other library identifiers should begin with two underscores or an underscore followed by an upper-case letter. For example, on many UNIX implementations, `fopen` calls `_open`, yet that name is not reserved—`_open` can be used by a programmer as a macro name or a local variable name or a static function name. Of course, doing so on such implementations may have disastrous effects, and as a consequence, implementers using this approach will have to pick a name other than `_open` (`_Open` or `__open`, for example).

Standard headers may be included in any order and multiple times in the same scope without producing ill effects. The one exception is `assert.h`, which if included multiple times, can behave differently depending on the existence of the macro `NDEBUG`.

To be strictly conforming, ANSI C prohibits a program from including a standard header from inside an external declaration or definition. This means you should not include a standard header from within a function since a function is an external definition.

Many of the prototypes for the standard library routines contain keywords and derived types invented or adopted by ANSI C. These include `const`, `fpos_t`, `size_t`, and `void *`. Where these are applied to functions that have existed for a number of years, they remain compatible with existing calls to those functions.

The standard library is defined for a hosted C implementation only; it is not required in a free-standing environment.

◆ Use of Library Functions ◆

Not all the Standard library routines validate their input arguments. In such cases, if you pass in an invalid argument, the behavior is undefined.

An implementation is permitted to implement any required routine as a macro, defined in the appropriate header, provided that macro expands "safely." That is, no ill effects should be observed if arguments with side-effects are used. If you include a standard header, you should not explicitly declare any routine you plan to use from that header since any macro version of that routine defined in the header will cause your declaration to be expanded (probably incorrectly or producing syntax errors.)

You should take care when using the address of a library routine since it may currently be defined as a macro. Therefore, you should `#undef` that name first or reference it using `(name)` instead of just `name`. Note that it is possible to call both a macro and a function version of the same routine in the same scope without first having to use `#undef`. For example,

```
int isupper(int);

#include <stdio.h>
#include <ctype.h>

main()
{
        int i = 'Z';

        if (isupper(i))
                printf("macro\n", i);

        if ((isupper)(i++))
                printf("function\n");
}
```

Here, the second usage of isupper is surrounded by parentheses; it is not recognized as a macro invocation. However, without an explicit declaration of that function, the compiler complains that the identifier isupper is not defined. Only if the token immediately following an identifier is a (does C assume that identifier designates a function returning int. And since the next token is a), the implicit recognition is not made.

To make this program compile, we need to declare isupper. However, if such a declaration is placed after the inclusion of ctype.h, the macro version of isupper will cause the declaration to be seen as a macro call. And since we cannot assume the header contains this declaration as well as a macro definition, we must place the declaration before the inclusion of ctype.h. Of course, this requires the implementation to have a function version of the routine, and many don't, even though ANSI C requires them to.

When using a library routine, it is strongly suggested you include the appropriate header. If you choose not to, you should explicitly declare the functions yourself using prototype notation, especially for routines such as printf, that take variable argument lengths. The reason for doing this is that the compiler may pass arguments using a different mechanism when prototypes are used than when they are not. For example, with the correct prototype in scope, the compiler knows exactly how many arguments are expected and their types. And for fixed length argument lists, it may choose to pass the first two or three (or so) arguments in registers instead of on the stack. Therefore, if you compile your code without prototypes and the library is compiled with them, the linkage may fail. For this reason, the following well-known program (from K&R, first edition, page 6) is not strictly conforming since printf is called without being in the scope of an appropriate prototype:

```
main()
{
        printf("hello, world\n");
}
```

◆ Non-Standard Headers ◆

The *de facto* Standard C library provided by AT&T with UNIX contains both general-purpose and operating system-specific routines. Almost all the general-purpose ones were adopted by the ANSI C Committee, while most of the operating system-specific ones were picked up by the IEEE POSIX Committee. A few were wanted by both or neither groups and have since been divided up amicably between the two groups. It should be noted that a (very) few macros and functions are defined and declared differently by both groups. In particular, their versions of `limits.h` are not identical. However, it is the intent of both standards groups that a C program be able to be both ANSI- and POSIX-conforming at the same time. Other *de facto* and industry standards include AT&T's SVID and the X/OPEN vendor consortium Portability Guide. All four standards are discussed in Appendix B.

There are numerous headers commonly provided in UNIX and/or MS-DOS environments that are not included in the ANSI C library. These include `bios`, `conio`, `curses`, `direct`, `dos`, `fcntl`, `io`, `process`, `search`, `share`, `stat`, `sys/locking`, `sys/stat`, `sys/timeb`, `sys/timeb`, `sys/types`, and `values`.

Other headers whose names were not adopted by ANSI C have all or some of their capabilities made available through various ANSI C headers. These include `malloc`, `memory`, and `varargs`, which have been reborn or combined with `stdlib.h`, `string.h`, and `stdarg.h`, respectively.

10

`assert.h` — Diagnostics

◆ Program Diagnostics ◆

The `assert` Macro

Calling sequence:

```
#include <assert.h>

void assert(int expression);
```

Description: `assert` is a macro that writes a diagnostic message to `stderr` provided its argument evaluates to false and the macro `NDEBUG` is not currently defined. If `NDEBUG` is defined when `assert.h` is included, the `assert` macro is equated to `((void)0)` such than a statement of the form `assert(arg);` becomes a void expression statement.

Comments:

- `assert` must be implemented as a macro, not a function. Since `assert` is a macro, the prototype shown above should not exist in `assert.h`—it is shown simply to indicate the correct usage of `assert`, as if it really were a function.

- If `assert` is the object of an `#undef` directive, the behavior is undefined.

- To disable the effects of assert, the macro `NDEBUG` must be defined prior to `assert.h` being included.

- The format of the message output is implementation-defined. However, ANSI C intends that the expression used as the argument to `assert` be output in its text form (as it exists in the source code) along with the source filename and line number (represented by `__FILE__` and `__LINE__`, respectively) of the invocation of the failing `assert`. Specifically, the expression `MAX - MIN` should be output as `100 - 20`, not `80` (assuming `MAX` is defined to be `100`, and `MIN`, `20`).

- ANSI C requires that `assert` call the library function `abort`. Some implementations call `exit` instead.

- ANSI C requires the `assert` argument to be an integral expression; however, some implementations permit any arbitrary scalar type. In the example at the end of this section, the expression is `pi != NULL`, which has type `int`. Note that this is treated the same as the expression `pi` even though `pi` is not an `int` expression since `assert` is typically expanded to either an `if` construct or a conditional operator expression. In such contexts, when a pointer is logically tested, it is implicitly compared with 0, the null pointer constant.

- Since `assert` is a macro, take care not to give it expressions that have side-effects—you cannot rely on the `assert` macro evaluating your expression only once.

- ANSI C requires `assert` to write to `stderr`. Some implementations write to `stdout` instead. `assert` need not expand into a call to `fprintf` to `stderr` directly; it could expand to a call to another function, such as `_Assert`, which then writes out the diagnostic. If the `assert` macro does refer to `stderr`, and `stderr` is not declared within `assert.h` (either explicitly, or implicitly via an `#include <stdio.h>` directive), you will need to declare `stderr` prior to invoking the `assert` macro. This declaration is best achieved by including `stdio.h`.

- If `assert` directly calls `fprintf`, it should explicitly declare that function or include `stdio.h` since `fprintf` has a variable argument list and requires a prototype with ellipses notation. Since some implementations do not do this, you should include `stdio.h` yourself, prior to invoking `assert`.

- While most library headers are designed to be included only once (with multiple inclusions having no extra effect), `assert.h` can be included multiple times such that, with the appropriate `#define`s and `#undef`s of `NDEBUG`, you can enable and disable assertions over various sections of code in the same source file.

Example:

```
#include <assert.h>
#include <stdlib.h>
#include <stdio.h>

main()
{
        int *pi;

        pi = malloc(100 * sizeof(int));
        assert(pi != NULL);

        /* ... */
}

Assertion failed: pi != 0L, file ..., line ...
Abnormal program termination
```

11

ctype.h — Character Handling

In ANSI C all the routines made available via `ctype.h` take one `int` argument. However, the `int` argument passed must either be representable in an `unsigned char` or be the macro `EOF`. If an argument has any other value, the behavior is undefined.

Recommendation: Do not rely on an implementation truncating the `int` argument since it is not obliged to. Some implementations supporting the ASCII character set implement these capabilities as macros, as follows:

```
#define isupper(c)  (_ctype_[(c) & 0x7F] & _U)
#define islower(c)  (_ctype_[(c) & 0x7F] & _L)
#define isalpha(c)  (_ctype_[(c) & 0x7F] & (_U | _L))
#define isdigit(c)  (_ctype_[(c) & 0x7F] & _D)
```

As a result, expressions such as `isupper (12345)` and `isdigit (9876)` are well behaved. However, this is not universally so.

ANSI C has introduced the notion of a locale. By default, a C program runs in the `"C"` locale unless the `setlocale` function has been called (or the implementation's normal operating default locale is other than `"C"`.) In the `"C"` locale, the `ctype.h` routines have the meaning they have always had. When a locale other than `"C"` is selected, the set of characters qualifying for a particular character type test may be extended to include other implementation-defined characters. For example, implementations running in western Europe will likely include characters with diacritical marks, such as the umlaut, caret, and tilde. Therefore, whether Ä, for example, tests true with `isalpha` is implementation-defined, based on the current locale.

Many implementations use a character representation that has more bits than are needed to represent the host character set—on 8-bit character machines, ASCII is the most common example. However, such implementations often support an extended character set using the otherwise unused bits. For example, MS-DOS uses the eighth bit to represent extended ASCII characters (many of which are non-English punctuation and currency symbols). Also, a C programmer is at liberty to treat a char as a small integer, storing into it any bit pattern that will fit.

When a char contains a bit-pattern that represents something other than the machine's native character set, it should not be passed to a ctype.h routine, unless permitted by your current locale. Even then, the results are implementation-defined. Also, you should determine whether a char is signed or not since an 8-bit char containing 0x80 may be treated quite differently when it is signed than, unsigned. For example, in the following case, a value of 0x80 for c will result in either _ctype[129] or _ctype[-127] being accessed (on a twos-complement system):

```
#define isupper(c) (_ctype[(c) + 1] & _IS_UPP)
```

Recommendation: Do not rely on the ctype.h routines handling an argument of EOF correctly, even though ANSI-conforming implementations are obliged to. This can be avoided by testing for EOF before calling these routines and is generally necessary when getting characters from getchar, fgetc, etc.

ANSI C requires that all ctype.h routines be implemented as functions. They may also be implemented as macros provided it is guaranteed they are safe macros. That is, their arguments are only evaluated once. This permits an argument of something like i++ or --j. This is not guaranteed in non-ANSI implementations.

Recommendation: In non-ANSI implementations, do not assume any ctype.h routine implemented as a macro only evaluates its argument once; it may evaluate it more times. Generally, do not use arguments with side-effects. Also, do not assume function versions of the macros are available.

Implementations that provide the ctype.h routines as macros often use a table of chars, each entry of which contains a bit mask defining the attributes of a particular character in the implementation's character set. To access these masks, a number of macros are defined. ANSI C requires an implementer to use names beginning with an underscore and an upper-case letter (or two underscores) for such macros. However, this may not be the case with non-ANSI implementations.

Recommendation: If you include `ctype`, do not subsequently declare a prototype for any of its routines yourself without first using `#undef` since the header may implement the routines as macros. In such a case, your prototype may be misinterpreted, or it may generate a syntax error when expanded by the macro definition.

The sets of printing and control characters is implementation-defined due to character set differences and locale requirements.

It is permissible to `#undef` any `ctype.h` routine to get at a corresponding function version.

◆ Character Testing Functions ◆

Recommendation: The actual value returned when the argument tests true is implementation-defined. Therefore, you should use a logical, rather than an arithmetic, test on such values.

ANSI C has reserved all function names beginning with `is` followed by a lower-case letter (followed by any other valid identifier characters) for future additions to the run-time library. Therefore, don't invent your own functions with names of this format.

The `isalnum` Function

Calling sequence:

```
#include <ctype.h>

int isalnum(int c);
```

Description: `isalnum` tests if its argument is `isalpha` or `isdigit`.

Comments:

• Since the result of `isalpha` is locale-specific, so too is `isalnum`.

The **isalpha** Function

Calling sequence:

```
#include <ctype.h>

int isalpha(int c);
```

Description: isalpha tests if its argument is an alphabetic character.

Comments:

- In the "C" locale, this means it's isupper or islower. In other locales, other implementation-defined characters may be included in the isalpha set provided they are not in the iscntrl, isdigit, ispunct, or isspace sets as well.

- Use isalpha rather than something like

```
if ((c >= 'A' && c <= 'Z') || (c >= 'a' && c <= 'z'))
```

since in some character sets (EBCDIC, for example) the upper- and lower-case letter groups do not occupy a contiguous range of internal values.

The **isascii** Function

Calling sequence:

```
#include <ctype.h>

int isascii(int c);
```

Description: isascii accepts any int value and tests if its value is within the range for a valid ASCII code (0–127). If it is, nonzero is returned, else zero is returned.

Comments:

- This routine is not part of the ANSI C library since ANSI C is not character set-specific. Also, there is no guarantee that this routine will be available in all ASCII environments.

The **iscntrl** Function

Calling sequence:

```
#include <ctype.h>

int iscntrl(int c);
```

Description: iscntrl tests to see if its argument is one of an implementation-defined set of control characters.

Comments:

- In ASCII, the control characters have values 0 through 0x1f, and 0x7f.
- In EBCDIC, the control characters have values less than 0x40 (except that 0x29, 0x30, 0x31, and 0x3e are not control characters.)

The **iscsym** Function

Calling sequence:

```
#include <ctype.h>

int iscsym(int c);
```

Description: iscsym tests if its argument is a character that can be used in a C identifier name (in other than the first position).

Comments:

- This routine is not part of the ANSI C run-time library.
- Normally, the set of valid characters is A–z, a–z, 0–9, and _ . However, some implementations may permit other characters such as $.
- iscsymf can be used to check the first character of an identifier name.

The **iscsymf** Function

Calling sequence:

```
#include <ctype.h>

int iscsymf(int c);
```

Description: iscsymf tests if its argument is a character that can be used in the first position of a C identifier name.

Comments:

- This routine is not part of the ANSI C run-time library.
- Normally, the set of valid characters is A–Z, a–z, and _ . However, some implementations may permit other characters such as $.
- iscsym can be used to check the trailing characters of an identifier name.

The isdigit Function

Calling sequence:

```
#include <ctype.h>

int isdigit(int c);
```

Description: isdigit tests to see if its argument is one of the decimal digits 0–9.

Comments:

- This routine is not locale-specific.

The isgraph Function

Calling sequence:

```
#include <ctype.h>

int isgraph(int c);
```

Description: isgraph tests to see if its argument is any printable character except a space.

Comments:

- This routine is locale-specific.

The islower Function

Calling sequence:

```
#include <ctype.h>

int islower(int c);
```

Description: `islower` tests if its argument is a lower-case alphabetic character.

Comments:

- In the `"C"` locale, lower-case letters are the Roman letters `a-z` inclusive. In other locales, other implementation-defined characters may be included in the `isalpha` set, provided they are not in the `iscntrl`, `isdigit`, `ispunct`, or `isspace` sets as well.

- Use `islower` rather than something like

      if (c >= 'a' && c <= 'z')

since in some character sets (EBCDIC, for example) the lower-case letters do not occupy a contiguous range of internal values.

The `isodigit` Function

Calling sequence:

```
#include <ctype.h>

int isodigit(int c);
```

Description: `isodigit` tests if its argument is a valid octal digit. The set of valid characters are the digits `0-7`.

Comments:

- This routine is not part of the ANSI C run-time library.

The `isprint` Function

Calling sequence:

```
#include <ctype.h>

int isprint(int c);
```

Description: `isprint` tests to see if its argument is any printable character including a space. (It subsumes `isgraph`'s functionality.)

Comments:

- This routine is locale-specific.

The ispunct Function

Calling sequence:

```
#include <ctype.h>

int ispunct(int c);
```

Description: ispunct tests to see if its argument is any printable character except a space or any character for which isalnum tests true.

Comments:

- This routine is locale-specific.

The isspace Function

Calling sequence:

```
#include <ctype.h>

int isspace(int c);
```

Description: isspace tests to see if its argument is any of the white space characters.

Comments:

- In the "C" locale, the set of characters is space, form feed, new-line, carriage return, horizontal tab, and vertical tab. (The vertical tab character, '\v', has not always been recognized by the C language or this library function.)

- In other locales, other implementation-defined characters may be added to the above set, provided they do not test true for isalnum.

- Some implementations have a function called iswhite, which has the same capability as isspace.

The isupper Function

Calling sequence:

```
#include <ctype.h>

int isupper(int c);
```

Description: `isupper` tests if its argument is an upper-case alphabetic character.

Comments:

- In the `"C"` locale, upper-case letters are the Roman letters `A–Z` inclusive. In other locales, other implementation-defined characters may be included in the `isalpha` set, provided they are not in the `iscntrl`, `isdigit`, `ispunct`, or `isspace` sets as well.

- Use `isupper` rather than something like

      if (c >= 'A' && c <= 'Z')

  since in some character sets (EBCDIC, for example) the upper-case letters do not occupy a contiguous range of internal values.

The `isxdigit` Function

Calling sequence:

```
#include <ctype.h>
int isxdigit(int c);
```

Description: `isxdigit` tests if its argument is a valid hexadecimal digit. The set of valid characters are the digits `0–9` and the letters `A–F` and `a–f`.

Comments:

- This routine is not locale-specific.

♦ Character Case Mapping Functions ♦

ANSI C has reserved all function names beginning with `to` followed by a lower-case letter (followed by any other valid identifier characters) for future additions to the run-time library. Therefore, do not invent your own functions with names of this format.

The `toascii` Function

Calling sequence:

```
#include <ctype.h>

int toascii(int c);
```

Description: toascii accepts any int value and retains only the low-order seven bits producing a valid ASCII code (0–127). If the argument is already a valid ASCII code, it is returned unchanged.

Comments:

- This routine is not part of the ANSI C library since ANSI C is not character set-specific. Also, there is no guarantee that this routine will be available in all ASCII environments.

The tolower Function

Calling sequence:

```
#include <ctype.h>

int tolower(int c);
```

Description: If the argument is an upper-case character, its lower-case equivalent is returned, else the argument is returned intact.

Comments:

- In non-"C" locales, the mapping from upper- to lower-case may not be one-for-one. For example, an upper-case letter might be represented as two lower-case letters taken together, or, perhaps, it may not even have a lower-case equivalent.

- In the "C" locale, only those characters testing true for isupper are converted to their corresponding lower-case equivalent.

- In non-ANSI implementations, tolower may be an unsafe macro. That is, its argument is evaluated more than once and that will cause problems if the argument has side-effects.

The _tolower Function

Calling sequence:

```
#include <ctype.h>

int _tolower(int c);
```

Description: Some implementations provide this routine in macro form as a (possibly faster) alternative to a safe function version of tolower.

Comments:

- For `_tolower` to be a safe macro, its argument is required to already be an upper-case letter. `_tolower` can be implemented in ASCII environments using

  ```
  #define _tolower(c) ((c) + 'a' - 'A')
  ```

- ANSI C permits an implementation to make a `ctype.h` routine a (safe) macro as well as a function. `_tolower` is not part of the ANSI C library.

The **toupper** Function

Calling sequence:

```
#include <ctype.h>

int toupper(int c);
```

Description: If the argument is a lower-case character, its upper-case equivalent is returned, else the argument is returned intact.

Comments:

- In non-"C" locales, the mapping from lower- to upper-case may not be one-for-one. For example, a lower-case letter might be represented as two upper-case letters taken together, or, perhaps, it may not even have an upper-case equivalent.

- In the "C" locale, only those characters testing true for `islower` are converted to their upper-case equivalent.

- In non-ANSI implementations, `toupper` may be an unsafe macro. That is, its argument is evaluated more than once and that will cause problems if the argument has side-effects.

The **_toupper** Function

Calling sequence:

```
#include <ctype.h>

int _toupper(int c);
```

Description: Some implementations provide this routine in macro form as a (possibly faster) alternative to a safe function version of `toupper`.

Comments:

- For `_toupper` to be a safe macro, its argument must be a lower-case letter. `_toupper` can be implemented in ASCII environments using

  ```
  #define _toupper(c) ((c) + 'A' - 'a')
  ```

- ANSI C permits an implementation to make a `ctype.h` routine a (safe) macro as well as a function. `_tolower` is not part of the ANSI C library.

C H A P T E R

◆ ◆ ◆ **12** ◆ ◆ ◆

`errno.h` — Errors

This header contains the declaration of a macro `errno` and a number of macros against which the value of `errno` can be compared. Numerous Standard library functions assign values to `errno` when they detect errors.

◆ The `errno` Macro ◆

Historically, `errno` has been declared as an `extern int`; however, ANSI C requires that `errno` be a macro. (The macro could, however, expand to a call to a function of the same name.) Specifically, `errno` is a macro that expands to a modifiable lvalue that has type `int`. As such, `errno` could be defined as something like `*_Errno()`, where the implementation-supplied function `_Errno` returns a pointer to `int`. Even though `errno` is a macro, it is still possible to find its address since the macro must expand to an lvalue.

ANSI C requires that `errno` be defined in `errno.h` so that it immediately becomes available when `errno.h` is included. Some implementations' versions of `errno.h` contain only the `errno` value macros, requiring the programmer to declare `errno` explicitly in his own code. Still other implementations declare `errno` in the header `math.h` (not endorsed by ANSI C) and don't even have a header called `errno.h`. It is likely that implementations will declare `errno` to have the `volatile` attribute, although this is not required by ANSI C.

Various standard library functions are documented as setting `errno` to a nonzero value when certain errors are detected. ANSI C requires that this value be positive. It also states that no library routine is required to clear `errno` (giving it the value 0), and, certainly, you should never rely on a library routine doing so. Unfortunately, during the evolution of the UNIX C Standard library `errno` was used as a scratch work area by various library (and other) functions. This has lead to the rule that you shouldn't assume a function leaves `errno` alone just because it isn't documented as changing it.

It is the programmer's responsibility to clear errno each time immediately before calling a library routine that is documented as having the ability to set it. They must also test the value of errno immediately after the library function returns, or they must save the value of errno in another variable. This is to ensure that the value of errno doesn't get overwritten by the next documented (or undocumented) library routine call. For example,

```c
#include <errno.h>
#include <math.h>
#include <stdio.h>

test(d)
double d;
{
        double val;

        errno = 0;          /* clear errno */
        val = sqrt(d);
        if (errno == EDOM)
                printf("domain error\n");
}
```

Here, we clear errno, call sqrt, and then immediately test errno as suggested above.

```c
errno = 0;          /* clear errno */
strcpy(dest, source);
val = sqrt(d);
if (errno == EDOM) /* unsafe */
```

In this case we are not guaranteed that the value of errno will correctly reflect the action taken by sqrt. Although we cleared errno, we called strcpy before calling sqrt. And even though strcpy isn't documented as setting errno we cannot assume that it doesn't. If it does and sqrt works without error, errno will no longer be 0 and the if test will fail. Alternatively, strcpy could set errno to the value EDOM for some strange reason, and if sqrt completes without error, we would get a bogus EDOM indication. Similar problems are possible with the next example where we call strcpy after sqrt and before testing errno.

```c
errno = 0;          /* clear errno */
val = sqrt(d);
strcpy(dest, source);
if (errno == EDOM) /* unsafe */
```

Consider the following example:

```
a = sqrt(b) + sqrt(c);
```

Since the order of evaluation of the addition is undefined, we don't know which call to `sqrt` is executed first. And even if we did, both, either, or neither of the calls could result in `errno` being set. If `errno` were set, we could not tell which call caused it; perhaps both set it. The best solution to this type of problem is to validate the arguments before calling the library functions. However, if you can't or won't, you will have to split such expressions into multiple assignment statements.

ANSI C guarantees that `errno` is cleared during program startup.

In an early draft of ANSI C, `errno` was declared in the header `stddef.h`. However, it was subsequently moved to `errno.h`. Do not expect `errno` to be declared in `stddef.h`.

The ANSI C library functions `perror` and `strerror` can be used to process messages corresponding to the documented values for `errno`. Note that to implement these functions some libraries declare an external array `sys_errlist` as an array of pointers to `char`. This is a table of pointers to the message strings. Also, a macro `sys_nerr` defines the maximum `errno` message number stored in the table `sys_errlist`. While support for this table and macro are common (particularly with UNIX systems), they are not part of ANSI C.

Often, implementations have a secondary error storage location whose value is inspected when `errno` contains a specific value. The name of this location varies widely—VAX C uses `vaxc$errno`, Microtec C uses `local_errno`, and various DOS compilers use `_doserrno`. The notion of an implementation-defined secondary error status code is not addressed by ANSI C.

The following ANSI C library functions are documented as setting or using `errno`: `acos`, `asin`, `cosh`, `exp`, `fgetpos`, `fsetpos`, `ftell`, `ldexp`, `log`, `log10`, `perror`, `pow`, `signal`, `sinh`, `strtod`, `strtol`, and `strtoul`.

◆ The **errno** Value Macros ◆

Historically, macros that define valid values for `errno` have been named starting with `E`. And although a standard set of names has evolved for UNIX systems, and one is emerging for DOS systems, there is otherwise wide divergence on the spelling and meaning of such names. As a result, ANSI C defines only two macros: EDOM and ERANGE. EDOM is used to indicate a domain error, while ERANGE indicates a range error.

The list of standard macros in UNIX SVID follows (the POSIX Standard may be slightly different):

```
E2BIG              /* arg list too long */
EACCES             /* permission denied */
EAGAIN             /* no more processes */
EBADF              /* bad file number */
EBUSY              /* mount device busy */
ECHILD             /* no children */
EDEADLK            /* deadlock avoided */
EDOM               /* math argument */
EEXIST             /* file exists */
EFAULT             /* bad address */
EFBIG              /* file too large */
EINTR              /* interrupted system call */
EINVAL             /* invalid argument */
EIO                /* i/o error */
EISDIR             /* is a directory */
EMFILE             /* too many open files */
EMLINK             /* too many links */
ENFILE             /* file table overflow */
ENODEV             /* no such device */
ENOENT             /* no such file or directory */
ENOEXEC            /* exec format error */
ENOLCK             /* no locks available */
ENOMEM             /* not enough core */
ENOSPC             /* no space left on device */
ENOTBLK            /* block device required */
ENOTDIR            /* not a directory */
ENOTTY             /* not a typewriter */
ENXIO              /* no such device or address */
EPERM              /* not owner */
EPIPE              /* broken pipe */
ERANGE             /* result too large */
EROFS              /* read-only file system */
ESPIPE             /* illegal seek */
ESRCH              /* no such process */
ETXTBSY            /* text file busy */
EXDEV              /* cross-device link */
```

Note that other macros are possible for network and operating system-specific purposes, and it is expected more will be added in future product releases. This is permitted by ANSI C, which has reserved the space of identifier names beginning with E followed by an upper-case letter or digit for just this purpose.

A number of implementations define a macro EZERO with a value of 0. We presume that this can be used instead of the constant 0. However, this is not required by ANSI C, and it is suggested you use 0 instead.

ANSI C requires that EDOM and ERANGE (and presumably any implementation-defined macros) be distinct nonzero integral constant expressions. In fact, they should also be positive.

As mentioned above, a secondary error status location may also exist. If it does, it is inspected based on some implementation-defined value of errno indicating some implementation-specific error. For example, on VAX C, if errno is set to EVMSERR, vaxc$errno is inspected. Other implementations use a macro called ELOCAL. There is no standard name for, or guarantee that, the secondary storage actually exists.

Since errno is available to the programmer, you may wish to use it for your own error-reporting purposes. While this is not encouraged, you will probably be safe if you stick to macros with negative values.

C H A P T E R
◆ ◆ ◆ 13 ◆ ◆ ◆

`float.h` — **Numerical Limits**

A conforming implementation must document all the following items, which are specified in the header `<float.h>`. The values given below are replaced by implementation-defined values that must be equal or greater in magnitude (absolute value).

Strictly speaking, this header is not part of the C run-time library since it doesn't refer to any run-time library functions. (However, some of the values in `float.h` might actually be produced at run-time as a result of a function call.) This header is discussed in more detail in Chapter 2 "The Environment." It is mentioned here along with all the other standard headers for completeness.

This header has much the same purpose as `limits.h` except that it defines the floating-point characteristics of the target system. The meaning and formulas applied to each of these can be complex, and you are referred to your compiler manual or a copy of the ANSI Standard for specific details. (The `FLT`, `DBL`, and `LDBL` prefixes designate the types `float`, `double`, and `long double`, respectively. Note that several generic floating-point attributes have the prefix `FLT`, even though they are not `float`-specific.)

```
FLT_RADIX            2
FLT_ROUNDS
FLT_MANT_DIG
DBL_MANT_DIG
LDBL_MANT_DIG
FLT_EPSILON          1E-5
DBL_EPSILON          1E-9
LDBL_EPSILON         1E-9
FLT_DIG              6
DBL_DIG              10
LDBL_DIG             10
FLT_MIN_EXP
DBL_MIN_EXP
LDBL_MIN_EXP
```

```
FLT_MIN              1E-37
DBL_MIN              1E-37
LDBL_MIN             1E-37
FLT_MIN_10_EXP         -37
DBL_MIN_10_EXP         -37
LDBL_MIN_10_EXP        -37
FLT_MAX_EXP
DBL_MAX_EXP
LDBL_MAX_EXP
FLT_MAX              1E+37
DBL_MAX              1E+37
LDBL_MAX             1E+37
FLT_MAX_10_EXP         +37
DBL_MAX_10_EXP         +37
LDBL_MAX_10_EXP        +37
```

ANSI C requires that the macro `FLT_RADIX` be defined as a compile-time constant expression. Therefore, it can be used with the preprocessing directive `#if`. No other macros in `float.h` have this requirement.

Recommendation: If the name of a macro not yet defined appears in an `#if` directive, its value defaults to 0. Therefore, if you suspect one or more of your implementations' `float.h` headers is less than complete, use `#ifdef` to test for a particular macro's existence before attempting to use its value in a `#if` expression.

ANSI C defines the values `-1` through `3` for the macro `FLT_ROUNDS`. All other values specify implementation-defined rounding behavior. The meaning of the defined rounding mode values is as follows:

-1	indeterminable
0	toward zero
1	to nearest
2	toward positive infinity
3	toward negative infinity

The type `long double` was invented by ANSI C. Although it is expected to be used by implementations that have more than two floating-point representations to support three separate floating-point representations, this need not be the case. For example, `long double` can legitimately be mapped into the same representation as `double` (or even `float`). The only requirement is that the precision and range of `long double` be greater than or equal to that of `double`, which is, in turn, greater than or equal to that of `float`. It is likely that `double` and `long double` will both map to the same floating-point representation in many implementations, either permanently or, at least, initially. In the latter case, an implementation can claim ANSI-conformance by properly supporting `long double` mapped into `double`. Then later, `long double` can be changed to support a "bigger" type.

The macros in `float.h` can be used to tell if the types `float`, `double`, and `long double` are mapped to the same or different representations. (Note that `sizeof` is not an accurate measure for this. For example, `sizeof(float)` might equal `sizeof(double)`, but in the case of `float`, not all the bits allocated are actually used to represent the value.)

Some implementations define more macros in `float.h` than are required by ANSI C. For examples, some DOS compilers define a series of macros that describe the floating-point characteristics of the Intel 8087, 80287, and 80387 floating-point chips. The names of these macros often have one of the general forms `SW_*`, `MCW_*`, `EM_*`, `IC_*`, `RC_*`, `PC_*`, and `CW_*`, where `*` represents one or more upper-case letters and/or digits and underscores. At least one major DOS implementation also provides a series of macros named `FPE_*`, which are used to detect and process floating-point interrupts using `signal`.

Some implementations also declare various floating-point hardware-specific functions in `float.h` rather than in `math.h`. Examples are functions to set and/or test the status of various floating-point processor registers or states.

ANSI C does not require `HUGE_VAL` to be defined in `float.h`. This macro must be defined in the header `math.h`. (Of course, an implementation could define it in `float.h` as well, but don't expect it to be there on other implementations.)

C H A P T E R

14

`limits.h` — Numerical Limits

A conforming implementation must document all the following items, which are specified in the header `<limits.h>`. The values given below are replaced by implementation-defined values that must be equal or greater in magnitude (absolute value).

Strictly speaking, this header is not part of the C run-time library since it doesn't refer to any run-time library functions. This header is discussed in more detail in Chapter 2 "The Environment." It is mentioned here along with all the other standard headers for completeness.

```
CHAR_BIT                 8
CHAR_MAX
CHAR_MIN
SCHAR_MAX             +127
SCHAR_MIN             -127
UCHAR_MAX             255
SHRT_MAX           +32767
SHRT_MIN           -32767
USHRT_MAX          65535
INT_MAX            +32767
INT_MIN            -32767
UINT_MAX           65535
LONG_MAX      +2147483647
LONG_MIN      -2147483647
ULONG_MAX      4294967295
MB_LEN_MAX               1
```

ANSI C requires that all the macros be defined as compile-time constant expressions. Therefore, they can be used with the preprocessing directive `#if`. Note that the minima specified by ANSI C accommodate a ones-complement machine. For example, `SHRT_MIN` is -32767, but on a twos-complement implementation, it might well be -32768. However, this is not guaranteed. An implementation is not obliged to state exactly what the minimum value of a short int it supports is, although that is intended by ANSI C. Therefore, an implementation that can represent -32768 in a signed short might define SHRT_MIN to be -32767 and still be conforming.

ANSI C requires a conforming implementation to support types short and int with at least 16 bits of precision and type long int with at least 32 bits. However, long and int (and short) can still be mapped to the same representation.

It may seem intuitive that knowing the number of bits in a char and the number of chars in a particular integral object type, you can immediately deduce the range of values for that type as follows:

```
#include <stdio.h>
#include <limits.h>

main()
{
        printf("# bits in an int = %d\n",
                CHAR_BIT * sizeof(int));
}
```

However, this is not a reliable technique since not all of the "bytes" allocated to an object need be used to represent that object. This is the case on at least one known C implementation where sizeof(short) equals 8 while only three bytes (24 bits) are used to represent a short's value.

Every effort has been made by the ANSI C and IEEE POSIX standards to be compatible. To that end, operating system-specific functions are provided by POSIX while non-operating system-specific ones are provided by ANSI C. However, some overlap exists, primarily in limits.h. The POSIX version provides the following macros there: ARG_MAX, CHILD_MAX, CHILD_MAX_CEIL, CLK_TCK, CUR_MAX_LET, FCHR_MAX, LINK_MAX, MAX_CANON, MAX_CHAR, MAX_LET, NAME_MAX, NGROUPS_MAX, OPEN_MAX, OPEN_MAX_CEIL, PASS_MAX, PATH_MAX, PID_MAX, PIPE_BUF, PIPE_MAX, and UID_MAX. If you are attempting to write C code that is both ANSI- and POSIX-conforming you will need to study carefully the versions of this header provided by each of your implementations. (Note that CLK_TCK is defined by ANSI C in time.h.)

An implementation may well define other macros in limits.h beside the ones required by ANSI C. Also, historically, users (and some implementations) have supplied a header called portable.h that provided some of the capabilities supplied by limits.h.

The values of the macros CHAR_MIN and CHAR_MAX are affected by the signedness of a plain char. Numerous implementations allow a plain char to be either signed or unsigned. One common way of specifying this is via a compile-time switch. In such an implementation, the values must be correct for the chosen signedness yet still be ANSI-conforming compile-time expressions.

Turbo C (V1.5) uses the following technique:

```
#if (((int)((char)0x80)) < 0)
#define CHAR_MAX 0x7F
#define CHAR_MIN 0x80
#else
#define CHAR_MAX 0xFFU
#define CHAR_MIN 0x00
#endif
```

While this approach is quite ingenious, it is not ANSI-conforming since the cast operator is not permitted in constant expressions used with the `#if` directive. (Likewise, the `sizeof` operator and enumeration constants are not allowed here.)

The types of the values of the `limits.h` macros are not specified by ANSI C. For example, a macro can be given the same value on two implementations running on the same machine and operating system, yet the values have different types. On a 16-bit twos-complement implementation, `INT_MIN` could be defined as follows:

```
#define INT_MIN        0x8000
```

or

```
#define INT_MIN        0100000
```

or

```
#define INT_MIN -32768
```

The type of `INT_MIN` in the first two cases is `unsigned int`, whereas it is `long int` in the third. (32768 has type `long` and -32768 is that value negated.)

Recommendation: Whenever you pass a `limits.h` macro to a function, explicitly cast it (or pass it in the presence of a prototype) so you are guaranteed that the argument has the type expected by the function being called. For example,

```
#include <limits.h>

void f(int);

...

    f((int) INT_MIN));
```

Since the type of a macro can be unsigned, don't compare the value of a macro with a negative value since the results of such comparisons are implementation-defined.

MB_LEN_MAX is the maximum number of bytes in a multibyte character, for any supported locale. If an implementation supports only the "C" locale, then this value is 1, and no extra price is paid for "supporting" multibyte characters since there aren't any. MB_LEN_MAX is an ANSI C invention.

C H A P T E R

15

`locale.h` — **Localization**

This header was created by ANSI C as a place to declare routines and types useful in establishing library run-time environments that support cultural and language representations in other than the "USA English" mode provided by traditional C. (This traditional locale is known as the `"C"` locale.)

The key to defining a locale is in the type struct `lconv`, defined in `locale.h`. This structure must contain at least the following members in any order. In the `"C"` locale, the members shall have the values specified in the comments.

```
char *decimal_point;        /* "." */
char *thousands_sep;        /* "" */
char *grouping;             /* "" */
char *int_curr_symbol;      /* "" */
char *currency_symbol;      /* "" */
char *mon_decimal_point;    /* "" */
char *mon_thousands_sep;    /* "" */
char *mon_grouping;         /* "" */
char *positive_sign;        /* "" */
char *negative_sign;        /* "" */
char int_frac_digits;       /* CHAR_MAX */
char frac_digits;           /* CHAR_MAX */
char p_cs_precedes;         /* CHAR_MAX */
char p_sep_by_space;        /* CHAR_MAX */
char n_cs_precedes;         /* CHAR_MAX */
char n_sep_by_space;        /* CHAR_MAX */
char p_sign_posn;           /* CHAR_MAX */
char n_sign_posn;           /* CHAR_MAX */
```

Implementations may add other members as they wish.

The macros defined in this header are NULL, LC_ALL, LC_COLLATE, LC_CTYPE, LC_MONETARY, LC_NUMERIC, and LC_TIME. (NULL is discussed in the chapter on `stddef.h`.) The macros with names of the form `LC_ *` must expand to distinct integral constant expressions, and they are used as the first argument to the function `setlocale`. ANSI C has reserved the space of names beginning with `LC_` followed by an upper-case letter for use by implementations so they may add more locale subcategories.

The only locale defined by ANSI C is `"C"`; the strings used to identify all other locales are implementation-defined. These strings (and `"C"`) can be used as the second argument to `setlocale`. If you plan to use several locales and you wish to move affected code to a different implementation (and one that presumably supports equivalent locales), the spellings of the locale strings may differ. Therefore, do not hard-code the strings in the program. Rather, use the following approach:

```
/* myloc.h contains the following: */

#define LOC_SPANISH "Spanish"
#define LOC_FRCANADA "FrenchCanadian"
#define LOC_SWGERMAN "SwissGerman"
...


/* In your code write */

#include <locale.h>
#include "myloc.h"

setlocale(LC_ALL, LOC_SPANISH);
...
setlocale(LC_ALL, LOC_FRCANADA);
...
setlocale(LC_ALL, LOC_SWGERMAN);
```

Now, you can provide a different version of the header `myloc.h` for each implementation, with the strings changed as necessary. Perhaps an even better method is to use conditional compilation as follows:

```
/* myloc.h contains the following: */

#if COMPILER == 1
#define LOC_SPANISH "Spanish"
#elif COMPILER == 2
#define LOC_SPANISH "SPANISH"
#elif COMPILER == 3
#define LOC_SPANISH "ESPANOL"
#else
#error Compiler macro is not defined correctly
#endif
```

Using either of these approaches, the strings can contain any multibyte character that the host system can handle, permitting locales to be mapped to files on disk, across a network, etc.

◆ Locale Control ◆

The `setlocale` Function

Calling sequence:

```
#include <locale.h>

char *setlocale(int category, char *locale);
```

Description: `setlocale` allows the program to either change a complete locale, a subcategory of the current locale, or to interrogate the "name" of the current locale.

Comments:

- Using `LC_ALL` as the category implies "the whole locale," whereas the other `LC_*` macros imply a specific part of the given locale. `LC_COLLATE` affects the behavior of `strcoll` and `strxfrm`. `LC_TYPE` affects various character functions in `ctype.h` and the multibyte functions declared in `stdlib.h`. `LC_MONETARY` affects `localeconv`, `LC_NUMERIC` affects various I/O formatting functions such as the `printf` family, and `LC_TIME` affects `strftime`.

- In a strict ANSI environment, a program starts up in the `"C"` locale. Therefore, an explicit call to `setlocale` is needed to change the default. However, it is likely that implementations running in non-USA English environments will provide a compile-time switch to change the default startup locale to something else. If this is the case, the code may have to be changed to include a call to `setlocale`, when moved to another implementation.

- If a pointer to a locale string is given to `setlocale` and that locale is available, a locale string corresponding to the given category is returned. This string can be given back to `setlocale` in future calls. If the requested locale is not available or known, `NULL` is returned, and the locale is not changed. A `NULL` locale pointer causes the string defining the current locale to be returned.

- If you modify the contents of the string returned by `setlocale`, the behavior is undefined.

◆ Numeric Formatting Convention Inquiry ◆

The **localeconv** Function

Calling sequence:

```
#include <locale.h>

struct lconv *localeconv(void);
```

Description: A call to `localeconv` causes a structure of type `lconv` to be initialized with values corresponding to the current locale such that they can be interrogated by the programmer and used to format currency, floating-point data, etc., as needed.

Comments:

- `localeconv` returns a pointer to the initialized structure having type `lconv`. The programmer should not modify this structure.

16

`math.h` — Mathematics

The ANSI C headers are supposed to be self-sufficient; however, it may be necessary to include `errno.h` to guarantee that the macros EDOM and ERANGE are defined and that `errno` is declared properly.

The math function names created by adding a suffix of `f` or `l` are reserved for implementations of `float` and `long double` versions, respectively. However, an ANSI-conforming implementation is required to support only the `double` set. In the case of the `float` set, these functions must be called in the presence of an appropriate prototype; otherwise, `float` arguments will be widened to `double`. (Note though that specifying `float` in a prototype does not necessarily force such widening to be disabled; this aspect of prototypes is implementation-defined. However, it is necessary when supporting the `float` set.)

The functions `ecvt`, `fcvt`, and `gcvt` are not defined by ANSI C since their capability is available via `sprintf`.

`math.h` contains one macro definition, that for HUGE_VAL. This expands to a positive `double` expression that is not necessarily representable as a `float`. ANSI C does not require it to be a constant expression. Some implementations, including SVID, call this macro HUGE instead.

ANSI C does not declare `abs` in `math.h`, but it does declare it in `stdlib.h`. If `abs` is implemented as a function, and `math.h` is included rather than `stdlib.h`, the correct result should be obtained as `abs` takes and returns `int` values. However, if `abs` is a macro, `abs` will become an unsatisfied external reference at link-time. Likewise, `labs` is declared in `stdlib.h`. However, if this is called without the correct declaration, `int` instead of `long int`, will be assumed for the return value.

ANSI C has invented the `div` and `ldiv` math functions for computing quotients and remainders. These are declared in `stdlib.h`, as are the random number functions `rand` and `srand`.

The following functions are commonly declared in `math.h`; however, they are not defined by ANSI C: `cabs`, `erf`, `erfc`, `gamma`, `hypot`, `j0`, `j1`, `jn`, poly, pow10, y0, y1, and yn. The same is true for structure tags and types associated with complex arithmetic.

◆ Treatment of Error Conditions ◆

A domain error occurs if an input argument is outside the domain over which the mathematical function is defined. In this case, an implementation-defined value is returned, and errno is set to the macro EDOM. (Refer to sqrt(-0) for an example.)

A range error occurs if the result of the function cannot be represented as a double. If the result overflows, the function returns the value of HUGE_VAL, with the same sign as the correct value would have. errno is set to the macro ERANGE. If the result underflows, the function returns 0 and errno may or may not be set to ERANGE, as the implementation defines.

The matherr machinery used by SVID (and others) is not included in ANSI C partly because it requires a user-defined library function. matherr requires a structure type exception and the macros DOMAIN, OVERFLOW, PLOSS, SING, TLOSS, and UNDERFLOW to be defined.

◆ Trigonometric Functions ◆

The acos Function

Calling sequence:

```
#include <math.h>

double acos(double x);
```

Description: acos computes the arc cosine of its argument.

Comments:

- If the argument is not in the range [-1, +1], a domain error occurs.
- The value returned is the arc cosine in the range [0, π] radians.

The asin Function

Calling sequence:

```
#include <math.h>

double asin(double x);
```

Description: `asin` computes the arc sine of its argument.

Comments:

- If the argument is not in the range [-1, +1], a domain error occurs.
- The value returned is the arc sine in the range [-π/2, +π/2] radians.

The `atan` Function

Calling sequence:

```
#include <math.h>

double atan(double x);
```

Description: `atan` computes the arc tangent of its argument.

Comments:

- The value returned is the arc tangent in the range [-π/2, +π/2] radians.

The `atan2` Function

Calling sequence:

```
#include <math.h>

double atan2(double y, double x);
```

Description: `atan2` computes the arc tangent of `y/x`.

Comments:

- If both arguments are 0 a domain error occurs. On IEEE implementations, this is not an error.
- The sign of both arguments is used to determine the quadrant of the returned value.
- The value returned is the arc tangent of `y/x` in the range [-π, +π] radians.

The `cos` Function

Calling sequence:

```
#include <math.h>

double cos(double x);
```

Description: `cos` computes the cosine of its argument (measured in radians).

Comments:

- If the magnitude of the argument is large, `cos` may produce a result with little or no significance.

The `sin` Function

Calling sequence:

```
#include <math.h>

double sin(double x);
```

Description: `sin` computes the sine of its argument (measured in radians).

Comments:

- If the magnitude of the argument is large, `sin` may produce a result with little or no significance.

The `tan` Function

Calling sequence:

```
#include <math.h>

double tan(double x);
```

Description: `tan` computes the tangent of its argument (measured in radians).

Comments:

- If the magnitude of the argument is large, `tan` may produce a result with little or no significance.

◆ Hyperbolic Functions ◆

The `cosh` Function

Calling sequence:

```
#include <math.h>

double cosh(double x);
```

Description: cosh computes the hyperbolic cosine of its argument (measured in radians).

Comments:

- If the magnitude of the argument is too large, a range error occurs.

The sinh Function

Calling sequence:

```
#include <math.h>

double sinh(double x);
```

Description: sinh computes the hyperbolic sine of its argument (measured in radians).

Comments:

- If the magnitude of the argument is too large, a range error occurs.

The tanh Function

Calling sequence:

```
#include <math.h>

double tanh(double x);
```

Description: tanh computes the hyperbolic tangent of its argument.

◆ Exponential and Logarithmic Functions ◆

The exp Function

Calling sequence:

```
#include <math.h>

double exp(double x);
```

Description: exp computes the exponential function of its argument.

Comments:

- If the magnitude of the argument is too large, a range error occurs.

The **frexp** Function

Calling sequence:

```
#include <math.h>

double frexp(double value, int *exp);
```

Description: frexp breaks a floating-point number into a normalized fraction and an integral power of 2.

Comments:

- The integral power is stored at the location pointed to by exp and the fractional part is the return value.

- The value returned has magnitude of 0 or is in the interval [1/2, 1), and value equals x times 2 raised to the power *exp.

- If value is 0, both the return value and *exp are 0.

The **ldexp** Function

Calling sequence:

```
#include <math.h>

double ldexp(double x, int exp);
```

Description: ldexp multiplies a floating-point number by an integral power of 2.

Comments:

- A range error may result.

- The value returned is x times 2 raised to the power exp.

The `log` Function

Calling sequence:

```
#include <math.h>

double log(double x);
```

Description: `log` computes the natural logarithm of its argument.

Comments:

- If the argument is negative, a domain error occurs.
- If the argument is zero and the logarithm of zero cannot be represented (it could be represented as -∞ perhaps), a range error occurs. This is compatible with IEEE P854. Some implementations might generate a domain error instead.

The `log10` Function

Calling sequence:

```
#include <math.h>

double log10(double x);
```

Description: `log10` computes the base-ten logarithm of its argument.

Comments:

- If the argument is negative, a domain error occurs.
- If the argument is zero and the logarithm of zero cannot be represented, a range error occurs.

The `modf` Function

Calling sequence:

```
#include <math.h>

double modf(double value, double *iptr);
```

Description: `modf` breaks a floating-point number into integral and fractional parts.

Comments:

- Each part has the same sign as the original number.

- The integral part is stored in the location pointed to by `iptr`, and the fractional part is used as the return value.

♦ Power Functions ♦

The pow Function

Calling sequence:

```
#include <math.h>

double pow(double x, double y);
```

Description: `pow` computes `x` raised to the power `y`.

Comments:

- If `x` is negative and `y` is not an integer, a domain error occurs.

- If `x` is 0 and `y` is less than or equal to 0, and the result cannot be represented, a domain error occurs.

- A range error may occur.

The sqrt Function

Calling sequence:

```
#include <math.h>

double sqrt(double x);
```

Description: `sqrt` computes the nonnegative square root of its argument.

Comments:

- If the argument is negative, a domain error occurs.

- Some implementations (for example, IEEE P854) support a negative floating zero, in which case `sqrt(-0)` may be required to return `-0`. ANSI C requires a domain error to be generated but permits an implementation-defined value to be returned (thus permitting a result of `-0`).

◆ Nearest Integer, Absolute and Remainder ◆

The `ceil` Function

Calling sequence:

```
#include <math.h>

double ceil(double x);
```

Description: `ceil` computes the smallest integral value not less than its argument.

Comments:

- The integral value computed is returned as a `double`.

The `fabs` Function

Calling sequence:

```
#include <math.h>

double fabs(double x);
```

Description: `fabs` computes the absolute value of its floating-point argument.

The `floor` Function

Calling sequence:

```
#include <math.h>

double floor(double x);
```

Description: `floor` computes the largest integral value not greater than its argument.

Comments:

- The integral value computed is returned as a `double`.

The fmod Function

Calling sequence:

```
#include <math.h>

double fmod(double x, double y);
```

Description: fmod computes the floating-point remainder of x/y.

Comments:

- The value returned is $x - i * y$, where i is an integer such that, if y is nonzero, the result has the same sign as x and magnitude less than that of y.

- It is implementation-defined whether or not a domain error occurs, or if fmod returns 0, if y is 0.

C H A P T E R
17

`setjmp.h` — Non-Local Jumps

The non-local jump routines `setjmp` and `longjmp` work with an object of type `jmp_buf`. This type is defined in `setjmp.h`. ANSI C requires this type to be an array of some type even if it is only an array of one element. This is because, historically, `jmp_buf` was defined as an array of `int`, and since arrays are passed by address, the `jmp_buf` argument was passed to both `setjmp` and `longjmp` without a leading `&` operator.

All ANSI C requires though is that `jmp_buf` be an array of suitable size to store the "current program context," whatever that may be. The type of each element is irrelevant and varies from `char`, `int`, `unsigned int` to pointer to `char`. Since an object of type `jmp_buf` is used only as a storage place for `setjmp` and `longjmp`, programmers should not be concerned about its actual representation. (In this respect, it is much like a `FILE` object.)

Since the type `jmp_buf` is very much implementation-defined, you should always include `setjmp.h` rather than declaring `jmp_buf` explicitly in your code.

Some implementations that make `jmp_buf` an array of `int` (or `unsigned int`) also define a macro called `_JBLEN` that specifies the number of elements in the array. This macro is not supported by ANSI C.

◆ Saving the Calling Environment ◆

A program's current context (or calling environment) can be saved into an object of type `jmp_buf` (by `setjmp`), and the program can be restored to that context by a subsequent call to `longjmp`.

The setjmp Macro

Calling sequence:

```
#include <setjmp.h>

int setjmp(jmp_buf env);
```

Description: setjmp is called initially to save the current context of the program. A corresponding call to longjmp causes control to return to the function in which setjmp was first called. It does this by returning as though setjmp had been called a second time. That is, longjmp is an unconditional "jump" instruction that reappears in the middle of setjmp, which then returns to its caller as though it had been called directly by the programmer.

Comments:

- In ANSI C, if the macro setjmp is the subject of an #undef directive and a function by the same name is called, the result is undefined. Note that implementations historically have made setjmp a function not a macro as permitted by ANSI C. This means one can no longer reliably take the address of the function setjmp.

- Since setjmp can now be a macro, its definition is restricted such that it be usable in the following ways only: 1) the entire controlling expression of a selection or iteration statement; 2) one operand of a relational or equality operator with the other operand an integral constant expression, with the resulting expression being the entire controlling expression of a selection or iteration statement; 3) the operand of a unary ! operator with the resulting expression being the entire controlling expression of a selection or iteration statement; or 4) the entire expression of an expression statement (possibly cast to void).

- When the programmer explicitly calls setjmp, it returns a zero value. When setjmp returns via an unconditional jump from longjmp, it returns a user-defined nonzero value.

- Some implementations provide a routine called _setjmp, which is a special version of setjmp. _setjmp is not defined by ANSI C.

- setjmp may be called to save as many different contexts as the programmer wishes, and the class of the jmp_buf objects can be as desired. The only criteria is that longjmp be able to get at the context it needs to restore to. Clearly, you need to provide a separate jmp_buf object for each concurrent saved context.

♦ **Restoring the Calling Environment** ♦

A program's current context (or calling environment) that was saved by `setjmp` can be restored by calling `longjmp`.

The `longjmp` Function

Calling sequence:

```
#include <setjmp.h>

void longjmp(jmp_buf env, int val);
```

Description: `longjmp` causes an unconditional jump into the routine `setjmp`, which in turn causes `setjmp` to return to its caller with a return value corresponding to the `val` argument passed to `longjmp`.

Comments:

- `longjmp` does not return to its caller. Rather, it returns to the caller of `setjmp`.

- If the value of `val` is zero, it is made `1` so that a call to `setjmp` directly (which returns `0`) cannot be confused with `longjmp`'s returning through `setjmp` with a value of `0`.

- If `longjmp` attempts to restore to a context that was never saved by `setjmp`, the result is undefined.

- If `longjmp` attempts to restore to a context and the parent function, which called `setjmp` to save that context initially, has terminated, the results are undefined. Therefore, you should perform a `longjmp` only back up the program call tree, not across its branches. Also, the `longjmp` call must always follow on the same level or be below in level to the `setjmp` call.

- The actual information that constitutes a "saved environment" is implementation-defined and might be as little as a few machine registers. Therefore, it is imperative that you understand just what is preserved across a `longjmp`. All external and `static` objects are preserved but `auto` and `register` variables are not. Also, even if all machine registers are saved, there is no way of knowing which `auto`s were placed in registers or which `register` class objects were not in registers. So the state of all `auto` and `register` class objects defined in the function that calls `setjmp` are undefined after `longjmp` has returned to that function. There is one exception. Any `volatile auto` object is guaranteed to be intact. Of course, any changes you made to `static` and external (and `volatile auto`) objects between the `setjmp` and `longjmp` calls remain in effect as do any things written to disk, etc. Consider the following example:

```
#include <stdio.h>
#include <setjmp.h>

main()
{
        jmp_buf buffer;
        int i;
        int j = 10;
        register int k = 100;
        void test();

        i = setjmp(buffer);
        printf("setjmp return = %d\n", i);
        printf("j = %d, k = %d\n", j, k);

        j += 10;
        k += 20;
        if (i == 0)
                test(buffer);
}

void test(buffer)
jmp_buf buffer;
{
        longjmp(buffer, 1);
}

setjmp return = 0
j = 10, k = 100
setjmp return = 1
j = 20, k = 100
```

- The first time through, j and k have the expected values. However, although both are incremented before test is called, when longjmp returns control to setjmp, only j's value is still intact. The value of k was restored to its initial value 100 rather than to 120. For this implementation, it appears the register variable is not preserved, while the auto is, assuming, of course, the register variable actually is stored in a register. It could well be the opposite way around. In any case, the result is undefined, and therefore unreliable, as we have demonstrated.

- The behavior is undefined if longjmp is invoked from a nested signal handler. Do not invoke longjmp from an exit handler, such as those registered by the atexit function.

- Some implementations provide a routine called _longjmp, which is a special version of longjmp. _longjmp is not defined by ANSI C.

18

signal.h — Signal Handling

This header declares a type and several functions and macros that are useful in handling signals. (Signals are often called exceptions.)

The Type `sig_atomic_t`

ANSI C invented the type `sig_atomic_t`. An object of this type is guaranteed to be accessed as an atomic entity, even in the presence of asynchronous interrupts. That is, when an asynchronous event occurs, an object of this type cannot be partially updated—it has either been completely updated or not been updated at all. ANSI C requires that this type be integral, and many implementations define it to be `int`. The ANSI C library does not contain functions that take arguments or have return values of this type.

Function Pointer Macros `SIG_*`

Three function pointer macros are defined by ANSI C. They are `SIG_DFL`, `SIG_IGN`, and `SIG_ERR` and must expand to distinct constant expressions that have a type compatible with the second argument to, and the return value from, the function `signal`. The values of these expressions must not compare equal to the address of any function so they can be distinguished from pointers to actual functions. The macros are often defined as follows:

```
#define SIG_DFL ((int (*)())0)
#define SIG_IGN ((int (*)())1)
#define SIG_ERR ((int (*)())-1)
```

or as

```
#define SIG_DFL ((void (*)())0)
#define SIG_IGN ((void (*)())1)
#define SIG_ERR ((void (*)())-1)
```

The casts in the second set of definitions are required by ANSI C since that is the type of `signal`'s second argument and return type. Traditionally, a library function called `ssignal` (used along with `gsignal`) has been used to declare signal-handling actions. `ssignal` has a second argument and return type of pointer to function returning `int` and this corresponds to the first set of macro definitions above. Currently, many implementations support both `signal` and `ssignal`, and they use `SIG_DFL` and `SIG_IGN` for both, even though two different types are required. This will not be possible in strict ANSI C because a pointer to a function of type `void` is not assignment-compatible to a pointer to a function of type `int`. However, this is an implementation issue and should not bother the programmer since each target implementation's version of `signal.h` must resolve this. The important thing is not to use the integral values `0`, `1`, or `-1` in place of these macros. Not only are the types of these values not compatible with that expected, but an implementation is also not required to use these particular values. Note that `ssignal` and `gsignal` are not part of the ANSI C library.

Strictly speaking, the casts above should be

```
#define SIG_DFL ((void (*)(int))0)
#define SIG_IGN ((void (*)(int))1)
#define SIG_ERR ((void (*)(int))-1)
```

where the pointer is to a function of type `void` and has one argument, of type `int`.

`SIG_ERR` is used as a return value from `signal` and will be discussed further with that function below. Some implementations do not define `SIG_ERR`; rather, they rely on the programmer to define a macro or to specify a hard-coded constant. (VAX C V2.3 actually defines a macro called `BADSIG` for the same purpose.)

An implementation is permitted to provide other such function pointer value macros for their own purposes. ANSI C reserves names of the form `SIG_*`, where `*` represents the trailing part of an identifier that begins with an upper-case letter.

Signal Type Macros `SIG*`

The first argument to `signal` (and `ssignal`) has type `int` and is known as the signal number. It indicates which particular class of signals we wish to process with the `signal` function. These signal numbers have traditionally been defined as macros with names of the form `SIG*`, and ANSI C has defined the following six names:

- `SIGABRT` – abnormal termination (such as a call to `abort`).

- `SIGFPE` – an erroneous arithmetic operation, such as zero-divide or an operation resulting in overflow. (Its name comes from Floating-Point Exception.)

- `SIGILL` – invalid function image; possibly an illegal instruction was detected.

- `SIGINT` – receipt of an interactive attention signal (such as CTRL/C).

- `SIGSEGV` – an invalid access to storage (segment violation).

- `SIGTERM` – a termination request was sent to the program.

An implementation is not required to be able to generate any or all of the above types of signals, and they are permitted to provide other such signal number macros for their own purposes. ANSI C reserves names of the form `SIG*` (where `*`, represents the trailing part of an identifier that begins with an upper-case letter) for use as signal number macros. ANSI C requires all signal number macros to have positive values.

The signal numbers specified by SVID follow:

```
SIGALRM          /* alarm clock */
SIGBUS           /* bus error */
SIGEMT           /* EMT instruction */
SIGFPE           /* floating point exception */
SIGHUP           /* hangup */
SIGILL           /* illegal instruction */
SIGINT           /* interrupt */
SIGIOT           /* IOT instruction */
SIGKILL          /* kill */
SIGPIPE          /* write to a pipe with no reader */
SIGQUIT          /* quit */
SIGSEGV          /* segmentation violation */
SIGSYS           /* bad argument to system call */
SIGTERM          /* s/w termination signal from kill */
SIGTRAP          /* trace trap */
SIGUSR1          /* user-defined signal 1 */
SIGUSR2          /* user-defined signal 2 */
```

The complete set of signals available in a given implementation, their semantics, and their default handling is implementation-defined.

Some implementations define a macro called `NSIG`, which is one more than the maximum signal number defined. This macro is not defined by ANSI C.

Some implementations of `signal` pass more than one argument to a signal handler, in which case they provide a set of macros corresponding to the possible values of these extra arguments. Two common such sets are named `ILL_*` and `FPE_*` and identify reserved instruction and floating-point exception subcodes, respectively. Examples are:

```
ILL_PRIVIN_FAULT
ILL_RESAD_FAULT
ILL_RESOP_FAULT
FPE_DECOVF_TRAP
FPE_FLTDIV_FAULT
FPE_FLTDIV_TRAP
FPE_FLTOVF_FAULT
FPE_FLTOVF_TRAP
FPE_FLTUND_FAULT
FPE_FLTUND_TRAP
FPE_INTDIV_TRAP
FPE_INTOVF_TRAP
FPE_SUBRNG_TRAP
```

Although some of these names are in widespread use, they are not defined in ANSI C. (Some implementations define the `FPE_*` family in `float.h`.)

♦ Specify Signal Handling ♦

The `signal` Function

Calling sequence:

```
#include <signal.h>

void (*signal(int sig, void (*func)(int)))(int);
```

Description: `signal` is called to indicate the type of action to be taken when a signal of the specified type is encountered. A signal may be ignored, handled by the system in a "default" manner, or processed by a user-supplied handler.

Comments:

- `signal` returns a value equal to `SIG_ERR` if it cannot perform the requested operation. Historically, `ssignal` returned -1, and many implementations of `signal` also return this value. However, in these cases, they return -1 cast to the appropriate pointer type. Do not test explicitly for a -1 return value—use the macro `SIG_ERR` instead. Always test the return value from `signal`—do not assume it did exactly as you requested.

- If `signal` does not return `SIG_ERR`, it returns the value given to `signal` (as its second argument) in the previous call for that signal number. That is, you can save the current signal-handling context, change it temporarily, and then restore it again using this return value.

- It may not be possible to ignore a signal (`SIGKILL`, for example), in which case `signal` returns `SIG_ERR`.

- Usually, when a signal is detected and given off to a handler, that signal will be handled in the "default" manner when next it occurs. That is, you must explicitly call `signal` to reset the signal mechanism from within the signal handler if you wish to continue to trap and handle the signal. (This is required by ANSI C except in the case of `SIGILL`, where it is implementation-defined as to whether the signal is reset automatically.)

- According to ANSI C, when a signal is trapped and a user-written handler has been supplied, that handler is called with one argument, of type `int`. Some implementations provide other arguments as well, in which case their prototypes for `signal` and `ssignal` are as follows:

```
void (*signal (int, void (*)(int, ...))) (int, ...);
int (*ssignal (int, int (*)(int, ...))) (int, ...);
```

- The handler for `signal` should have a `void` return type. (The `ssignal` mechanism requires the handler to have type `int`.) The handler may terminate using `return` or a call to `abort`, `exit`, or `longjmp`. If a `SIGFPE` handler terminates using `return`, the behavior is undefined.

- When a signal is generated by other than a call to `abort` or `raise`, the signal handler is somewhat limited as to the objects it can reliably access and the functions it can call if the behavior is to be defined. For example, all non-local storage should be declared as `volatile sig_atomic_t` so it can be reliably accessed from within the handler. Also, the handler should not call other library functions except for `signal` since these are not guaranteed to be reentrant. (Note that a `const` object can be accessed reliably only if it is declared `const` everywhere in the program since the `const` attribute doesn't guarantee the object's value won't change--it simply means that, in the current scope, you can't change its value.)

- If a call to `signal` from within a handler returns `SIG_ERR`, the value of `errno` is indeterminate. In other circumstances, `SIG_ERR` is returned, and `errno` contains a positive value whose possible values can be defined by the implementation. (A value of `EINVAL` is commonly used for this purpose, although this is not a defined value of `errno` in ANSI C.)

- During program startup, an implementation is at liberty to specify that selected signals be ignored or handled by default means as appropriate. That is, the initial state of signal handling is implementation-defined.

- ANSI C makes no statement about the behavior when a second signal for the same handler occurs before the first is processed.

◆ Send Signal ◆

The `raise` Function

Calling sequence:

```
#include <signal.h>

int raise(int sig);
```

Description: `raise` can be used to send the specified signal to the program. It is useful for testing user-written signal handlers.

Comments:

- `raise` returns a value of zero if the raise was successful. Otherwise, it returns a nonzero value.

◆ An Example ◆

The following simple example shows a user-written handler for the trapping of SIGINT signals.

```
#include <signal.h>
#include <stdio.h>
#include <stdlib.h>

volatile sig_atomic_t val = 0;
void myhandler(int);

main()
{
        if (signal(SIGINT, myhandler) == SIG_ERR) {
                fprintf(stderr, "Can't setup handler\n");
                exit(1);
        }

        while (val < 100)
                printf("val = %d\n", ++val);
}
```

```
void myhandler(signum)
int signum;
{
        val = 0;

        if (signal(SIGINT, myhandler) == SIG_ERR) {
                fprintf(stderr, "Can't reset handler\n");
                exit(1);
        }
}
```

Note the declaration of the external variable `val`—it has both the `volatile` and `sig_atomic_t` specifiers as suggested earlier. The types of conditions that generate `SIGINT` are unspecified by ANSI C. One common condition is pressing the CTRL/C key combination. However, on VAX/VMS, CTRL/Y ("abort my program") is different than CTRL/C and cannot be trapped with `SIGINT`. On DOS, CTRL/Break may not behave like CTRL/C—it's up to the implementation.

♦ Non-ANSI Issues ♦

As mentioned previously, `ssignal` and `gsignal` are provided by many implementations to handle user-specified (or software) signals. While ANSI C makes no mention of these, SVID provides the signal numbers `SIGUSR1` and `SIGUSR2` for this purpose. The popular `kill` function, which can affect a process other than its own, likewise is not supported by ANSI C.

Numerous other signal-specific functions with names of the form `sig*` are provided by implementations, particularly those running in signal-intensive environments such as on DEC hardware. They usually also define a number of structures with tag names of the form `sig*`.

19

stdarg.h — Variable Arguments

The `stdarg` facility provides a way to access variable argument lists portably, such as those passed to the `printf` and `scanf` library families. The header `stdarg.h` is an ANSI C invention modeled closely on the UNIX `varargs.h` capability. Since ANSI C uses a slightly different approach, the new header `stdarg` was designed rather than retaining `varargs` with a changed meaning.

While it is possible that some implementations will provide both of the headers `stdarg.h` and `varargs.h`, others might provide only one or the other.

Except where specifically noted, the following sections assume an ANSI C implementation (i.e., `stdarg` is used).

ANSI C requires that `va_start` and `va_arg` be macros. If they are the subject of `#undef`, and an actual function of the same name is used instead, the behavior is undefined. It is unspecified whether `va_end` is a macro or a function.

In ANSI-conforming mode, certain extensions might not be available. For example, some implementations have a macro called `va_count`, which gives access to the argument count. These extensions might be retained in `varargs.h` only, or they may be conditionally made available within `stdarg.h`.

Typically, the type `va_list` is implemented using `typedef`; however, it could be done using `#define` using something like

```
#define va_list char *
```

in which case you must not use a declaration of the form

```
va_list ap1, ap2;
```

since the types of ap1 and ap2 are different. For this reason, declare ap1 and ap2 separately.

The va_start Macro

Calling sequence:

```
#include <stdarg.h>

void va_start(va_list ap, parmN);
```

Description: This macro initializes the ap (argument pointer) argument. parmN is the last of the list of fixed arguments.

Comments:

- va_start must be called before va_arg or va_end are used for any given variable argument list.
- Normally, it is permitted to specify the register storage class in a formal argument list. However, if register is used with parmN, or parmN has type function or array, the behavior is undefined.
- The varargs version has only the ap argument.

The va_arg Macro

Calling sequence:

```
#include <stdarg.h>

type va_arg(va_list ap, type);
```

Description: This macro causes the next argument, of the type *type*, to be retrieved from the argument list and returned as the value of the whole expression.

Comments:

- The ap argument must be the same as that passed to va_start.
- If there are no more arguments, or *type* is not the type of the next argument, the result is undefined.
- The varargs version requires va_arg to get the last fixed argument as well as the variable ones.

The **va_end** Macro

Calling sequence:

```
#include <stdarg.h>

void va_end(va_list ap);
```

Description: This macro performs any necessary cleanup of variable argument list processing.

Comments:

- The `ap` argument must be the same as that passed to `va_start`.

- Many implementations `#define` this macro as nothing. That is, when expanded, no code results, meaning that in these cases, it doesn't matter whether you call `va_end`. ANSI C states that if `va_end` is not invoked before the function returns, the behavior is undefined.

- Once you have called `va_end`, you must call `va_start` before attempting to reprocess the argument list; otherwise, the behavior is undefined.

- Some implementations of `va_end` set `ap` to `NULL` requiring `NULL` either to be explicitly defined by the programmer or to include the appropriate header such that `NULL` becomes defined.

- `va_end` must be invoked from the same function in which the corresponding `va_start` was invoked.

♦ Examples ♦

The following example shows how to use `stdarg` to pass a variable number of `int` arguments to the function `maxi`, which returns the maximum of the `int`s (excluding the count) passed to it. Note that if the trailing argument count is incorrect (as is the case in the last two calls to `maxi`), the results are undefined, even though predictable behavior may result for some implementations. (Note the potential problem with the argument 65432, which may be a `long` rather than an `int`.)

```
/* stdarg example with prototypes */

#include <stdio.h>

int maxi(int, ...);


main()
{
        printf("-> %d\n", maxi(4, 10, 20, -5, 17));
        printf("-> %d\n", maxi(3, -10, -5, -17));

/* is type of second argument int or long? */

        printf("-> %d\n", maxi(3, 65432, -5, -17));

/* call maxi with count too small or too big */

        printf("-> %d\n", maxi(2, 10, -5, 17));
        printf("-> %d\n", maxi(4, 10, -5, 17));
}


#include <stdarg.h>
#include <limits.h>

int maxi(int parmn, ...)
{
        va_list ap;
        int i, j;
        int max = INT_MIN;

        va_start(ap, parmn);
        printf("%2d: ", parmn);

        for (j = 1; j <= parmn; ++j) {
                i = va_arg(ap, int);
                printf("%d, ", i);
                if (max < i)
                        max = i;
        }

        va_end(ap);
        return (max);
}
```

```
4: 10, 20, -5, 17, -> 20
3: -10, -5, -17, -> -5
3: -104, 0, -5, -> 0
2: 10, -5, -> 10
4: 10, -5, 17, 250, -> 250           /* ??? */
```

While stdarg can be used without the corresponding function prototypes as follows, it is not recommended since in the absence of a prototype, an ANSI C compiler can assume the number of arguments in the call is fixed and can pass arguments in a different-than-usual manner (e.g., by register).

```
/* stdarg example without prototypes */

#include <stdio.h>

int maxi();

main()
{
        /* ... */
}


#include <stdarg.h>
#include <limits.h>

int maxi(parmn)
int parmn;
{
        /* ... */
}
```

A version of the above examples is implemented below using the varargs facility. The main difference here is the special formal argument va_alist (or va_decl, which expands to va_alist). Also, va_arg must be called to get the first actual argument, whereas with stdarg, the first argument is named as a formal. Note that if va_decl is used, it MUST NOT have a trailing semicolon since one will be added if necessary when the va_decl macro is expanded.

```
/* varargs solution */

#include <stdio.h>

int maxi();

main()
{
        /* ... */
}



#include <varargs.h>
#include <limits.h>

int maxi(va_alist)
va_list va_alist;
/* or
va_decl
*/
{
        va_list ap;
        int i, j, k;
        int max = INT_MIN;

        va_start(ap);
        k = va_arg(ap, int);
        printf("%2d: ", k);

        for (j = 1; j <= k; ++j) {
                i = va_arg(ap, int);
                printf("%d, ", i);
                if (max < i)
                        max = i;
        }

        va_end(ap);
        return (max);
}



 4: 10, 20, -5, 17, -> 20
 3: -10, -5, -17, -> -5
 3: -104, 0, -5, -> 0
 2: 10, -5, -> 10
 4: 10, -5, 17, 449, -> 449          /* ??? */
```

The preceding problem involves a variable number of arguments all of the same type. In this case, use of the stdarg and varargs facilities may be overkill. An alternate (and also portable) approach is to always pass two arguments, an array of values and a count as follows:

```
/* handling a variable number of values via an array */

#include <stdio.h>
#include <stddef.h>

int maxil(size_t, int *);

main()
{
        static int array[5] = {4, 10, -7, 17, 20};
        size_t i;

        for (i = 1; i <= sizeof(array)/sizeof(int); ++i)
                printf("-> %d\n", maxil(i, array));
}

#include <limits.h>

int maxil(size_t count, int table[])
{
        size_t i;
        int max = INT_MIN;

        for (i = 0; i < count; ++i) {
                printf("%d, ", table[i]);
                if (max < table[i])
                        max = table[i];
        }

        return (max);
}


4, -> 4
4, 10, -> 10
4, 10, -7, -> 10
4, 10, -7, 17, -> 17
4, 10, -7, 17, 20, -> 20
```

An example that cannot be implemented using an array of arguments occurs when the arguments have different types as follows. This program is a very simple version of printf. (It uses printf in the solution. In a real version, you would write/use a series of primitive type-to-character conversion functions in place of printf.)

```c
/* handling arguments with varying types */

#include <stdio.h>

int output(char *, ...);

main()
{
        output("S D C\nS X F E\n", "abcd", 123, 'A',
               "xyz", 0x12ab, 123.4, 123.4);
}

#include <stdarg.h>
#include <string.h>

int output(char *parmn, ...)
{
        va_list ap;
        int count = strlen(parmn);
        int j;

        va_start(ap, parmn);

        for (j = 1; j <= count; ++j) {
                switch (*parmn) {

/* string */    case 'S': {
                        char *pc;

                        pc = va_arg(ap, char *);
                        printf("%s", pc);
                        break;
                }

/* decimal */   case 'D': {
                        int i;

                        i = va_arg(ap, int);
                        printf("%d", i);
                        break;
```

```
/* character */ case 'C': {
                        int i;

                        i = va_arg(ap, int);
                        printf("%c", i);
                        break;
                }

/* hex digit */ case 'X': {
                        int i;

                        i = va_arg(ap, int);
                        printf("%x", i);
                        break;
                }

/* double */    case 'F': {
                        double d;

                        d = va_arg(ap, double);
                        printf("%f", d);
                        break;
                }

/* exponent */  case 'E': {
                        double d;

                        d = va_arg(ap, double);
                        printf("%e", d);
                        break;
                }

                default: {
                        putchar(*parmn);
                        break;
                }
                }
                ++parmn;
        }

        va_end(ap);
}

abcd 123 A
xyz 12ab 123.400000 1.234000e+002
```

◆ ◆ ◆ 20 ◆ ◆ ◆

stddef.h — Common Definitions

ANSI C invented this header as a repository for several miscellaneous macro definitions and types. The macros are NULL and offsetof, and the types are size_t, ptrdiff_t, and wchar_t.

Note that in early versions of the ANSI C Draft, errno was also declared in stddef.h. However, it was subsequently moved to errno.h when that header was created. Do not rely on errno being declared in stddef.h.

The ptrdiff_t Type

ptrdiff_t is the type of the difference between two pointers of the same type. The type is signed and integral. In practice, both pointers must point to elements within the same array for the subtraction to be meaningful or, in fact, reliable. In theory, there is a problem with ptrdiff_t—it can't always represent the largest possible difference for certain types of arrays (most noticeably, arrays of char).

The maximum theoretical number of elements in an array is the largest value representable by an unsigned long int. However, for non-char type arrays (and maybe not even for char arrays), the maximum number of elements is that largest value divided by sizeof (*element-Type*). In any case, the difference between the addresses of the first and last element in the largest possible char array cannot always be represented in a signed int type. The same may also be true for other array types.

In reality, however, it is very unlikely you will have arrays that take up more than half of your address space. (Even if you do, on Intel 8088-class systems with a memory limitation of 1 MB, ptrdiff_t could be of type long int, thus allowing all possible differences to be represented. Also, on VAX/VMS, a user program may not take up more than half of the address space.) Depending on how memory is organized and addressed, this might not be a real problem.

The size_t Type

size_t is the type of the result obtained from the sizeof operator. size_t must be unsigned and integral. Typically, it is typdefed as either unsigned int or unsigned long int.

The following example shows how size_t can be used:

```
#include <stdio.h>
#include <stddef.h>

main()
{
        size_t strlen(char *);

        printf("length = %lu\n",
                        (unsigned long) strlen("qwerty"));
}


size_t strlen(string)
char *string;
{
        size_t length = 0;

        while (*string++ != '\0')
                ++length;

        return (length);
}

length = 6
```

In reality, the declaration of strlen would be contained in the ANSI C header string.h, and strlen would be defined in the run-time library.

All library functions defined by ANSI C that take an argument or return a value that represents the size of an object, now use size_t as the type of that argument or return value. Historically, these functions have used int instead (although some did use unsigned int.) The following library functions use size_t: bsearch, calloc, fread, fwrite, malloc, mblen, mbstowcs, mbtowc, memchr, memcmp, memcpy, memmove, memset, qsort, realloc, strcspn, strftime, strlen, strncat, strncmp, strncpy, strspn, strxfrm, and wcstombs.

Note that since ANSI C refers to size_t in several headers and that each header is supposed to be self-sufficient (either by containing a copy of required common definitions or by including the appropriate header), size_t is available if you #include any of the following headers: stddef.h, stdio.h, stdlib.h, string.h or time.h.

The wchar_t Type

This integral type has a range of values that can represent distinct codes for all members of the largest extended character set specified among the supported locales.

wchar_t is an ANSI C invention needed when you are dealing with wide characters and wide strings. The headers locale.h and stdlib.h contain macros and functions useful for processing in other than USA-English environments.

The NULL Macro

NULL expands to an implementation-defined null pointer constant. It can be passed to various library functions as an argument and can be returned by them to indicate some special success or failure condition. It may also be used by programmers for their own purposes.

Since C portably permits a pointer to be assigned the value 0 and to be compared with the value 0, NULL is often defined as having this value. For example,

```
#define NULL 0
#define NULL 0L
#define NULL ((char *)0)
#define NULL ((void *)0)
```

It is possible that any of these definitions (or others) might be used for a given implementation. Therefore, you should not use NULL in any other context except where a null pointer is required. Certainly, you should not assume NULL is equivalent to the integral expression 0—NULL is a pointer expression.

Depending on how NULL is defined, it may need to be explicitly cast when used as a function argument. This can be the case in Intel 8088-class systems, where the size of a pointer can be changed at compile-time by selecting the appropriate memory model and NULL has been defined to be either 0 or 0L. On such implementations, you may need to define both near and far null data and null function pointers, particularly if your wish to have mixed-model programs. In fact, if you always pass NULL to a function in the presence of an appropriate prototype, only one version of the macro is needed (provided, of course, the implementation has defined it correctly.)

Note that since ANSI C refers to NULL in several headers and that each header is supposed to be self-sufficient (either by containing a copy of required common definitions or by including the appropriate header), NULL is available if you #include any of the following headers: locale.h, stddef.h, stdio.h, stdlib.h, string.h, and time.h.

ANSI C does not require the null pointer to have an internal representation of "all-bits-zero"—it can be any address guaranteed not to be used for an object or function. Because of this, you should take care when using calloc or memset. These functions can be used to initialize space to all-bits-zero, and that need not be the same as the logical value 0.

The offsetof Macro

This macro was invented by ANSI C and allows you to find the offset (in bytes) of a member from the start of its parent structure. offsetof expands into an integral constant expression that has type size_t.

One possible definition of offsetof is

```
#define offsetof(type, member)          \
        ((size_t)(&((type *) 0)->member))
```

The trick is to imagine that the structure exists at absolute location zero since we know that address and this is achieved by casting 0 to a pointer and taking the address of the member offset from that address.

If the member is a bit-field, the behavior is undefined since you cannot take the address of a bit-field.

stdio.h — Input/Output

♦ File Systems ♦

Almost all aspects of file and directory systems are implementation-defined. So much so that ANSI C cannot even make a statement about the most basic thing, a filename. Just what filenames can and must an implementation support? And as for directory and device names, there is nothing close to a common approach.

Some implementations may permit filenames to contain wildcards. That is, the file specifier may refer to a group of files using a convention such as `*.dat` to refer to all files with a type of `.dat`. None of the standard I/O routines is required to support such a notion.

Numerous operating systems can limit the number of open files on a per user basis. VAX/VMS even can limit the number of versions of any given file in a directory. And if you create one too many, the oldest one is transparently deleted. Note, too, that not all systems permit multiple versions of the same filename in the same directory, and this has consequences when you use `fopen` with `"w"` mode, for example.

Some file systems also place disk quotas on users such that an I/O operation may fail when a file grows too big—you may not know this until an output operation fails.

Back to the filename issue. After extensive investigation, the ANSI C committee found that the format of a portable filename is up to six alphabetic characters followed by a period and none or one letter. And given that some file systems are case-sensitive, these alphabetic characters should all be the same case. However, rather than restrict yourself to filenames of the lowest common denominator, the following approach is suggested:

```
/* files.h - filename header */

#if HOST == DOS
#define MASTER "\\system\\data\\master.dat"
#elif HOST == VMS
#define MASTER "DBA3:[system.data.]master.dat"
...
#endif

/* your code */
#include "files.h"

...

fp = fopen(MASTER, "r");

i = remove(MASTER);

i = rename(OLDNAME, NEWAME);
```

So by conditionally compiling within the header `files.h`, your code becomes readable and the file system dependencies are isolated from your code.

The whole concept of filename redirection at the command-line level is also implementation-defined. If possible, it means that `printf` and `fscanf`, for example, may actually be dealing with devices other than the user's terminal. They could even be dealing with files. Note that `gets` behaves slightly differently to `fgets` from `stdin`, yet `gets` could be reading from a file if `stdin` were redirected.

The details of file buffering, disk sector (or block) sizes, etc., are also implementation-defined. However, ANSI C requires an implementation to be able to handle text files with lines containing at least 254 characters, including the trailing new-line.

On some systems, (such as UNIX, VAX/VMS, and DOS), `stdin`, `stdout`, and `stderr` are special to the operating system and are maintained by it. On other systems, these may be established during program startup. Whether these files go against your maximum open file limit is implementation-defined.

`stdio.h` defines several types and macros and declares numerous functions useful for performing file and terminal I/O.

Defined Types

`size_t` is defined in several headers and is discussed in detail under `stddef.h`.

`FILE` is an object type capable of containing the "current context" of an open file. This information includes, buffering details, error and end-of-file flags, file position indicator, and other implementation-defined fields. Typically,

FILE is a structure, although it may actually be a pointer to a structure, in which case, FILE * is really a pointer to a pointer a structure. You should always traffic in FILE objects rather, than their underlying equivalents, since they vary considerably from one implementation to another. (Some implementations define FILE using #define rather than typedef.)

The type fpos_t is used by fgetpos and fsetpos. It must map to a type large enough to hold the largest possible file position indicator for the implementation. It may be an array, a structure, a long int, etc., as appropriate. You should always traffic in fpos_t objects rather than their underlying equivalents since they vary considerably from one implementation to another.

Defined Macros

NULL is defined in several headers and is discussed in detail under stddef.h.

_IOFBF, _IOLBF, and _IONBF are distinct integral constant expressions that can be used with the third argument to setvbuf.

BUFSIZ is an integral constant expression that is the size of the buffer to be used by setbuf. ANSI C requires it to be at least 256.

EOF is a negative integral constant expression that is returned by numerous functions to indicate an end-of-file condition. (Some implementations explicitly document EOF as having the value -1. However, this is not required by ANSI C.)

FOPEN_MAX is an integral constant expression that is the minimum number of files that the implementation guarantees you can have open simultaneously. ANSI C requires FOPEN_MAX to be at least eight including stdin, stdout, and stderr. Note that some operating systems (such as DOS and VAX/VMS) can limit the number of open files on a per user basis at the operating system level. Apart from files you explicitly open, those opened by tmpfile also are counted against FOPEN_MAX. This name was an ANSI C invention and earlier versions of it were called SYS_MAX and OPEN_MAX.

FILENAME_MAX is an integral constant expression that is the maximum length of a filename string that can be used with the implementation. ANSI C specifies no minimum size.

L_tmpnam is an integral constant expression that is the size of a character array large enough to contain the temporary filename generated by tmpnam.

SEEK_CUR, SEEK_END, and SEEK_SET are distinct integral constant expressions that can be used with the third argument to fseek. These are relatively new additions to C, and their values were previously hard-coded in the call. (These values are often, 1, 2, and 0, respectively; however, these values are not required by ANSI C.)

TMP_MAX is an integral constant expression that is the maximum number of unique filenames that can be generated by tmpnam. ANSI C requires TMP_MAX to be at least 25.

stdin, stdout, and stderr are expressions of type FILE * that point to file objects corresponding to "standard input," "standard output," and "standard error," respectively. These expressions need not designate modifiable lvalues (and usually don't.)

♦ Common Extensions ♦

A number of other macros are often defined in stdio.h, particularly in UNIX implementations. These include: L_ctermid, L_cuserid, L_lcltmpnam, L_nettmpnam, P_tmpdir, max, and min. Two very common ones are TRUE and FALSE. None of these are defined by ANSI C.

The UNIX I/O functions that deal in file descriptors rather than FILE pointers have been widely emulated outside UNIX. UNIX implementations have also defined numerous other I/O functions over the years. These functions include: open, close, read, write, fileno, creat, read, write, getw, putw, getch, getche, and lseek. On some systems the macros STDIN, STDOUT, and STDERR were defined to deal with special file descriptors. None of these are defined by ANSI C.

DOS C implementations often support the extra file pointers stdprn and stdaux that point to the default printer and auxiliary device (often COM1:), respectively.

♦ Operations on Files ♦

The remove Function

Calling sequence:

```
#include <stdio.h>

int remove(const char *filename);
```

Description: remove causes the file whose name is pointed to by filename to be made inaccessible by that name.

Comments:

- On many systems, the file is actually deleted. However, it may be that you are removing a synonym for a file's name, rather than deleting the file itself. In such cases, when the last synonym is being removed, the file is typically deleted.

- If the file being removed is currently open, the behavior is implementation-defined. (In a shared file system, another program may be accessing the file you are removing.)

- If remove succeeds, it returns a zero value; otherwise it returns a nonzero value. (Don't assume a -1 value for an error, even though some implementations use this value.) ANSI C does not document errno as being used to convey failure information, although some implementations do.

- remove has the same (or very similar) functionality as the UNIX routine unlink. In fact, on some implementations, remove is a macro that expands to a call to unlink (or vice versa). unlink returns −1 on error, and errno is set appropriately. (SVID specifies that errno may be one of ENOTDIR, ENOENT, EACCES, EPERM, EBUSY, ETXTBSY, or EROFS.) unlink is not defined by ANSI C.

- Temporary, scratch files created using tmpfile need not be explicitly removed since they are removed when they are closed or during program termination.

The rename Function

Calling sequence:

```
#include <stdio.h>

int rename(const char *old, const char *new);
```

Description: rename causes a file, currently known by the name pointed to by old, to be known by the name pointed to by new.

Comments:

- ANSI C states that the old filename is removed (as if it had been the subject of a call to remove). Presumably, this permits a filename synonym to be renamed as well. Since old is removed, if old is currently open, the behavior is implementation-defined. (In a shared file system, another program may be accessing the file you are renaming.)

- If a file called new already exists, the behavior is implementation-defined. For example, DOS will not permit you to rename to an existing filename. However, VAX/VMS will create the next highest version numbered file of the name new. Some implementations may even remove the new file first.

- A file system with a hierarchical (or other) directory structure might not directly permit renaming of files across directories. In these cases, the rename might fail, or the file might actually be copied and the original removed. ANSI C hints that if a file copy is needed, rename could fail; however, it does not require it to. Generally, file systems do not permit renaming across devices, although this could also be achieved by copying and removing old.

- If rename succeeds it returns a zero value; otherwise it returns a nonzero value. (Don't assume a −1 value for an error even though some implementations use this value.) ANSI C does not document errno as being used to convey failure information, although some implementations do. On failure, the file still has the name old. On failure, POSIX specifies a set of valid errno codes. rename is not part of SVID.

The `tmpfile` Function

Calling sequence:

```
#include <stdio.h>

FILE *tmpfile(void);
```

Description: `tmpfile` creates a temporary binary file that is removed when it is closed or at program termination.

Comments:

- `tmpfile` opens the file for update as if it had been opened by `fopen` using the mode `"wb+"`. If this mode is inappropriate, use `setvbuf` or `setbuf` to change it. Alternatively, you can get a unique filename from `tmpnam` and `fopen` it yourself. Under UNIX, binary and text files are the same so the file is opened with mode `"w+"`.

- If the program terminates abnormally, the temporary file might not be removed.

- The location and attributes (directory name, file name, access permission, etc.) of the file created are implementation-defined. Some implementations (including SVID) provide a macro `P_tmpdir`, which indicates the "path" of temporary files. There is no guarantee that the filename will actually "appear" in any directory listing during its existence—it may be a "hidden" file.

- You cannot find out the name of the temporary file. Even if you could, you cannot close it and reopen it since, once you close it, it is removed.

- If a temporary file cannot be created, `NULL` is returned; otherwise a `FILE` pointer is returned. ANSI C does not directly specify a minimum number of temporary files that can be created. However, it is reasonable to assume that `tmpfile` calls `tmpnam` to get a unique filename, in which case, the macro `TMP_MAX` indicates the number of unique names available to `tmpfile`. Of course, the host file system may further limit this in terms of actual concurrent files.

- The ANSI C macro `FOPEN_MAX` specifies the number of files that a program can have open concurrently. Files created by `tmpfile` are subject to this limit.

- ANSI C provides no way to indicate the reason for a failure to create the file. Refer to `fopen` failures for more information about `errno`, etc. (On error, SVID displays a message on `stderr` using `perror` as well as returning `NULL`.)

- A call to `exit` is an implied call to `fclose` for the temporary file.

The `tmpnam` Function

Calling sequence:

```
#include <stdio.h>

char *tmpnam(char *s);
```

Description: `tmpnam` generates and returns a filename that is guaranteed not be that of any existing file. A file by that name can then be opened using `fopen`.

Comments:

- The macro `TMP_MAX` defines the number of unique names that `tmpnam` can generate when called by the same program. (Some implementations do not `#define TMP_MAX`.) If you call `tmpnam` more than `TMP_MAX` times, the behavior is implementation-defined. (SVID states that the names are recycled again.) ANSI C requires `TMP_MAX` be at least 25.

- If `s` is `NULL`, `tmpnam` leaves its result in its own area and returns a pointer to that area. Subsequent calls to `tmpnam` may modify that area. If `s` is not `NULL`, it is assumed to be a pointer to an array of at least `L_tmpnam` characters; `tmpnam` puts the result in that array and returns the address of that array. `tmpnam` has no way to communicate an error so if you give it a non-`NULL` address that points to an area smaller than `L_tmpnam` characters, the behavior is undefined.

- While the filename is guaranteed to be unique at the time `tmpnam` was called, a file by that name may have been created before you get a chance to use it. If this is likely to be a problem, use `tmpfile` instead. And then if you need to open the file in a mode other than `"wb+"`, use `setvbuf` or `setbuf` to change it.

- The filename may include directory information. If it does, the name and attributes of the directory are implementation-defined. Some implementations provide a macro `P_tmpdir`, which indicates the "path" of temporary files.

- SVID also provides the `tempnam` function, which creates a temporary file in a user-specified directory. It also permits the user to specify a 0--5 character prefix for the filename to be generated. Another SVID function is `mktemp`, which also provides a special formatted unique filename. Neither `tempnam` nor `mktemp` are defined by ANSI C.

◆ File Access Functions ◆

The `fclose` Function

Calling sequence:

```
#include <stdio.h>

int fclose(FILE *stream);
```

Description: `fclose` causes the stream pointed to by stream to be flushed and the corresponding file to be closed.

Comments:

- If the file was being written to, the output buffer is flushed. If it was being read from, the remaining contents (if any) of the input buffer are discarded.

- On some implementations, when a file is opened, the I/O buffer for that file is dynamically allocated using `malloc` (or similar). If that is the case, then `fclose` causes that buffer space to be freed.

- If `fclose` successfully closed the stream, it returns a zero. If the stream was already closed or an error occurs, `EOF` is returned.

- If a program terminates abnormally, there is no guarantee that streams open for output will have their buffers flushed.

- `fclose` should not be confused with `close` (specified in SVID), which deals with file descriptors rather than `FILE` pointers. The two are NOT interchangeable. (An error with `close` causes `errno` to be set.)

- A call to `exit` is an implied call to `fclose` for each currently open stream.

- It is permissible to close the "special" files `stdin`, `stdout`, and `stderr`.

- Some implementations (but not ANSI C) provide a function `fcloseall`, which closes all currently open streams, except for the special ones names named `std*`. `fcloseall` returns the number of streams closed or an `EOF` on error.

- On some implementations it may not be possible to close an empty file successfully and have it retained by the file system—you may first have to write something to it.

The `fflush` Function

Calling sequence:

```
#include <stdio.h>

int fflush(FILE *stream);
```

Description: `fflush` is used to flush an open stream's I/O buffer. If the stream were being written, any unwritten data in the output buffer is written. `fflush` should only be used with streams open for output or, open for update and currently in output mode.

Comments:

- If the stream was not open for output, or it was open for update with the immediately previous operation being other than output, the behavior is undefined. However, some implementations permit input streams to be `fflush`ed reliably.

- A zero value is returned on success; an `EOF`, if a write error occurs.

- If a program terminates abnormally, there is no guarantee that streams open for output will have their buffers flushed.

- It is permissible to flush the "special" files `stdout` and `stderr`. While ANSI C states that flushing input files (including `stdin`) produces undefined behavior, some implementations permit it.

- Some implementations (but not ANSI C) provide a function `flushall` that flushes all currently open streams. `flushall` returns the number of streams currently open. No error code is possible. ANSI C provides this capability be calling `fflush` with a `NULL` argument.

- ANSI C requires that `stderr` initially be made available in other than fully buffered mode. That is, it should be either unbuffered or line buffered. In either case, you won't normally need to use `fflush` with `stderr` unless the output you write has no (or too few) new-line characters and `stderr` is line buffered. Non-ANSI implementations may make `stderr` fully buffered.

The `fopen` Function

Calling sequence:

```
#include <stdio.h>

FILE *fopen(const char *filename, const char *mode);
```

Description: `fopen` opens the file whose name is pointed to by `filename`, in the mode specified by `mode`.

Comments:

- `mode` points to a string whose initial character contents must be one of the following sequences: `"r"`, `"w"`, `"a"`, `"rb"`, `"wb"`, `"ab"`, `"r+"`, `"w+"`, `"a+"`, `"rb+"`, `"wb+"`, `"ab+"`, `"r+b"`, `"w+b"`, or `"a+b"`. Mode `'r'` signifies read mode, `'w'` signifies write (or create if the file does not already exist), and `'a'` signifies append mode. In the absence of mode `'b'`, the file is deemed to be a text file, while `'b'` signifies a binary file. (Note that under UNIX, text and binary files are the same so the `'b'` mode will be ignored. However, you may still want to use it if your code is to open binary files in non-UNIX environments.) The `'+'` mode indicates that the file is to be open for update. The set of modes `"r?+"` is equivalent to the set `"r+?"`.

- Some implementations may have difficulty seeking within text files; in which case, specifying mode `'+'` may also imply mode `'b'`.

- Some file systems permit only one version of a file by any given name; in which case, opening in `'w'` mode will cause that file to be overwritten. On other systems, a new version of the file may be created.

- The set, and meaning, of mode characters following any of the sequences specified above is implementation-defined. Other mode characters might be provided by your implementation to specify file attributes such as block length, buffer sizes, and access modes. (VAX C provides this information via optional arguments following `mode`.) Some DOS C implementations also permit a `'t'` mode to indicate a text file explicitly. And if neither `'t'` nor `'b'` is specified, the type of the file is deduced from a global variable `_fmode` declared in `stdlib.h`. The possible values of `_fmode` are `O_TEXT` and `O_BINARY` (which are defined in `fcntl.h`). The value of this approach is to use `fopen` without a `'b'` or `'t'` and to be able to change the default from `'t'` (as required by ANSI C) to `'b'` and vice versa, at will.

- Some file systems append trailing `'\0'` characters to the end of a binary file when it is closed. Subsequently, when you open such files for append, you may be positioned beyond the end of the last character you wrote.

- When you open a file in append mode, you should not immediately call `fseek` to reposition within the file since any writes you do will be written at the end of the file.

- In update mode, you must explicitly call `fflush` before changing from write to read mode. Alternatively, you may call `fseek`, `fsetpos`, or `rewind` to flush the file's buffer. Likewise, to change from input to output you must call `fseek`, `fsetpos`, or `rewind`, unless the input returned end of file, in which case you may begin writing immediately.

- A file is opened with full buffering only if the implementation can determine that it is not an interactive device.

- If `fopen` succeeds, it returns a `FILE` pointer to the opened stream. On failure, it returns `NULL`. Note that an implementation may limit the number of currently open files—`FOPEN_MAX` specifies the number permitted—in which case `fopen` will fail if you attempt to exceed this number. ANSI C does not specify whether `errno` is set. SVID specifies that `errno` may be set to one of the following values: `ENOTDIR`, `ENOENT`, `EACCESS`, `EISDIR`, `EROFS`, `ETXTBSY`, or `EINTR`.

- SVID also defines three other open functions: `create`, `open`, and `fdopen`. These are not part of ANSI C. `create` and `open` return a file descriptor while `fdopen` associates a `FILE` pointer with a file descriptor.

The `freopen` Function

Calling sequence:

```
#include <stdio.h>

FILE *freopen(const char *filename,
        const char *mode, FILE *stream);
```

Description: `freopen` is almost identical to `fopen` except that `freopen` recycles an existing `FILE` pointer, that points to a currently open file.

Comments:

- The arguments `filename` and `mode` are the same as for `fopen`.

- `freopen` attempts to first close that file. If the close fails, the error is ignored.

- If `freopen` succeeds, it returns the value of `stream`; otherwise it returns `NULL`. ANSI C does not specify if `errno` is set. SVID specifies that `errno` may be set to one of the following values: `ENOTDIR`, `ENOENT`, `EACCESS`, `EISDIR`, `EROFS`, `ETXTBSY`, or `EINTR`.

- A primary use of `freopen` is to redirect `stdin`, `stdout`, or `stderr` to a file. Since these special `FILE` pointers need not be modifiable lvalues, it is not possible to use something like `stdout = fopen(...)` to redirect them. Once you redirect these pointers you might not be able to point them back to their original "files."

The setbuf Function

Calling sequence:

```
#include <stdio.h>

void setbuf(FILE *stream, char *buf);
```

Description: setbuf is equivalent to a specific invocation of setvbuf. That is, calling setvbuf with mode equal to _IOFBF and size equal to BUFSIZ or, with buf being NULL and mode being _IONBF, is the same as calling set-buf.

Comments:

- Refer to setvbuf for a general discussion on setting file buffering.

- setbuf returns no value. The responsibility is on the programmer to make sure stream points to an open file and that buf is either NULL or a pointer to a sufficiently large buffer.

- ANSI C does not require an implementation to be able to implement each of these types of buffering. And so, an implementation is at liberty to treat one or more of these buffering types to be equivalent. Therefore, there is not guarantee that setbuf will be able to honor your request, even though no error code can be returned.

The setvbuf Function

Calling sequence:

```
#include <stdio.h>

int setvbuf(FILE *stream, char *buf, int mode,
        size_t size);
```

Description: setvbuf permits the type of buffering for a newly opened file to be changed. It also permits users to supply their own buffer for that file.

Comments:

- setvbuf must be called before any reading or writing takes place on the newly opened stream.

- mode may be one of the following: _IOFBF (fully buffered), _IOLBF (line buffered), or _IONBF (no buffering). ANSI C requires that setvbuf accept these modes, although the underlying implementation need not be able to implement each of these types of buffering. And so, an implementation is at liberty to treat one or more of these buffering types to be equivalent.

- If `buf` is `NULL`, `setvbuf` uses its own internal buffer; otherwise, it uses that pointed to by `buf`, in which case, `size` should be at least as big as the array pointed to by `buf`.

- When the programmer supplies the buffer its contents are indeterminate at any particular time. (ANSI C does not actually require an implementation to use the programmer's buffer if one is supplied.) The user-supplied buffer must remain in existence as long as the stream is open so take care if you use a buffer of class `auto`.

- If `mode` equals `_IOFBF` and `size` equals `BUFSIZ`, `setbuf` can be used instead. The same is true if `buf` is `NULL` and `mode` is `_IONBF`.

- `setvbuf` returns zero on success and nonzero on failure. A failure could result from an invalid value for `mode` or for some other reason. ANSI C does not specify that `errno` is set on error.

- At program startup, ANSI C requires `stdin` and `stdout` to be fully buffered if it can be determined they are not directed to interactive devices. `stderr` is not fully buffered. This differs slightly from SVID. Buffering of the DOS-specific special `FILE` pointers `stdprn` and `stdaux` is implementation-defined.

- The size of buffers allocated by `setvbuf` is implementation-defined although some implementations of `setvbuf` use `size` to determine the size of the internal buffer used as well.

- Allocating very large buffers may not be possible if memory is limited, particularly if you allocate it dynamically from the heap.

- Some implementations define related functions called `setbuffer` and `setbufline`. These are not defined by ANSI C.

◆ Formatted Input/Output Functions ◆

The `fprintf` Function

Calling sequence:

```
#include <stdio.h>

int fprintf(FILE *stream, const char *format, ...);
```

Description: fprintf writes formatted output to the file specified by stream in a format specified by format. It is a more general version of printf.

Comments:

- Almost all aspects of fprintf are identical to those of printf, which is defined elsewhere.

- Since the prototype for fprintf includes an ellipsis, you must always #include <stdio.h> (or explicitly declare fprintf yourself) if you wish the call to be maximally portable. This is required since, in the absence of a prototype indicating a variable length argument length, an implementation is free to assume the number of arguments is fixed and to perform argument handling optimizations as it sees fit. Therefore, calling such a function without having the appropriate prototype produces undefined behavior.

- A call to printf is equivalent to a call to fprintf using a stream of stdout.

The **fscanf** Function

Calling sequence:

```
#include <stdio.h>

int fscanf(FILE *stream, const char *format, ...);
```

Description: fscanf reads formatted output from the file specified by stream in a format specified by format. It is a more general version of scanf.

Comments:

- Almost all aspects of fscanf are identical to those of scanf, which is defined elsewhere.

- Since the prototype for fscanf includes an ellipsis you must always include stdio.h (or explicitly declare fscanf yourself) if you wish the call to be maximally portable. This is required since, in the absence of a prototype indicating a variable length argument length, an implementation is free to assume the number of arguments is fixed and to perform argument handling optimizations as it sees fit. Therefore, calling such a function without having the appropriate prototype produces undefined behavior.

- A call to scanf is equivalent to a call to fscanf using a stream of stdin.

The `printf` Function

Calling sequence:

```
#include <stdio.h>

int printf(const char *format, ...);
```

Description: `printf` writes formatted output to `stdout` as specified by `format`.

Comments:

- If there are insufficient arguments for the format, the behavior is undefined. If excess arguments are provided, they are evaluated but are otherwise ignored by `printf`. `printf` returns when the end of the format is reached.

- Since ANSI C supports multibyte characters, `format` may contain such characters. Characters in `format` other than `%` and those specifying a particular edit mask are output verbatim. To output a `%` character, use `%%`.

- An edit mask consists of an `%` followed (eventually) by a character specifying the type of conversion. The character may be any one of the following: `d`, `i`, `o`, `u`, `x`, `X`, `f`, `e`, `E`, `g`, `G`, `c`, `s`, `p`, or `n`. You are referred to the ANSI C Standard for a complete discussion on edit masks. Here, we will simply discuss issues relevant to portability. Except for clarifying a few dark corners and adding a little functionality, ANSI C has adopted existing practice.

- Between the `%` and the conversion characters, the following may optionally appear, in the order specified: flags that modify the meaning of the conversion (these include `-`, `+`, `#`, `0`, and the space character); a decimal integer specifying the minimum field width; a precision value including a leading period; an `h`, `l` or `L`, which modifies the conversion character.

- The flag `#` is defined only for the conversion characters `o`, `x`, `X`, `e`, `E`, `f`, `g`, and `G`.

- The flag `0` is defined only for the conversion characters `d`, `i`, `o`, `x`, `X`, `e`, `E`, `f`, `g`, and `G`.

- If either (or both) the field width or precision is an `*`, the integer value is taken from a corresponding `int` value in the argument list. Although not invented by ANSI C, this is a relatively new capability and may not be widely supported by non-ANSI implementations.

- The `h` modifier can be used with the conversion characters `d`, `i`, `o`, `u`, `x`, and `X`. The `l` modifier can be used with the conversion characters `d`, `i`, `o`, `u`, `x`, `X`, and `n`. (Note that using the `h` modifier may seem superfluous since declaring the argument as `short` when it must have been widened when `printf` was called. However, using it, you will get the value of the `int` argument after it has been cast to a `short int` or `unsigned short int`.) The `L` modifier can be used with the conversion characters e, E, f, g, and G to signify a `long double` argument. (The type `long double` is an ANSI C invention.) If the h, l, or L modifiers are used with any other conversion specifier, the behavior is undefined. (Note that `L` CANNOT be used in place of l with the integral types and that l cannot be used in place of L with floating-point types, even though such behavior has been suggested and, even sanctioned, in various non-ANSI C implementations.) Some older implementations supported conversion characters D, O, X, and U which meant ld, lo, lx, and lu, respectively. ANSI C does not support D, O, and U, and uses X for a different purpose. DOS C implementations may support the N and F modifiers so they can specify `near` and `far` pointers, respectively, for p, s, and n conversion characters.

- The conversion character i is new and is synonymous with d.

- Historically, it was implementation-defined whether you got upper- or lower-case alphabetic characters when using x. However, now you can specify casing using x or X as appropriate.

- The casing of the exponent's e in floating-point numbers can be controlled using e or E and g or G.

- With the g conversion character, some implementations convert from f (or F) to e (or E) at an exponent of −3 while ANSI C requires them to change at −4.

- The IEEE floating-point standard provides for representations for positive and negative infinity, indefinite, and NaN (not a number) among others. Some implementations produce text for floating-point arguments having these values; however, ANSI C provides no particular support for this standard.

- The c character expects an `int` argument, which is converted to `unsigned char` before being printed.

- The s character requires only its argument to be `'\0'`-terminated if the precision exceeds the length of the string or the precision is omitted.

- The p conversion character is new. It expects an argument of type pointer to `void`, and it displays the value of that pointer using an implementation-defined format. Be sure to cast the argument to `void *` if it isn't of that type already.

- The n character is also new, and it expects an argument of type pointer to `int`. If the l modifier is used with n, a pointer to `long int` is expected. This conversion causes the count of characters written out thus far to be stored in the integer pointed to by the corresponding argument. This is the only conversion character that writes into the argument list.

- If a conversion specification is invalid, the behavior is undefined. (Note that K&R stated that any specification not recognized was treated as text and passed through to stdout. For example, %@ produced @.) ANSI C has reserved all unused lower-case conversion specifiers for its own use in future versions.

- The behavior is undefined if any argument is, or points to, a union, a structure, or an array except for arrays with %s and void pointers with %p.

- printf returns the number of characters it transmitted. Note that this is the number printf output, not the number actually written to the output file/device. For example, '\n' may result in a CR or a CR/LF being written, yet the number output, as reported by printf, is 1. Also, '\t' may be expanded to spaces and '\v' or '\f' to multiple '\n' characters. If an output error occurred, a negative value is returned. (Some implementations specifically state that they return a −1 [or EOF] on error.) ANSI C makes no mention of errno being set.

- printf maintains an internal buffer into which it builds the formatted string, and this buffer has a finite length. Historically, this length has been implementation-defined and not always documented, and implementations have varied widely. ANSI C requires that an implementation be able to handle any single conversion of at least 509 characters. It is almost certain that existing implementations cannot support conversions of this size (some are limited to 128). Be careful with large character strings, particularly where you are attempting to output very large, or multiple, lines or perhaps even a screen full of text. In these cases, it is probably better to use puts (or fputs) or something similar.

- Since the prototype for printf includes an ellipsis you must always include stdio.h (or explicitly declare printf yourself) if you wish the call to be maximally portable. This is required since, in the absence of a prototype indicating a variable length argument length, an implementation is free to assume the number of arguments is fixed and to perform argument-handling optimizations as it sees fit. Therefore, calling such a function without having the appropriate prototype produces undefined behavior.

- A call to printf is equivalent to a call to fprintf using a stream of stdout.

- Some implementations define a function cprintf, which is printf with very minor changes. This is not defined by ANSI C.

The scanf Function

Calling sequence:

```
#include <stdio.h>

int scanf(const char *format, ...);
```

Description: `scanf` reads formatted input from `stdin` as specified by `format`.

Comments:

- If there are insufficient arguments for the format, the behavior is undefined. If excess arguments are provided, they are evaluated but are otherwise ignored by `scanf`. `scanf` returns when the end of the format is reached or a conversion error occurs.

- Since ANSI C supports multibyte characters, `format` may contain such characters. Characters in `format` other than white space and those specifying a particular edit mask are expected to appear in the input as written. `%%` matches a single `%`.

- An arbitrary amount of consecutive white space in the format causes white space on input to be skipped. When `scanf` completes its conversion, any white space left in the input buffer immediately following the last converted field is left there.

- An edit mask consists of an `%` followed (eventually) by a character specifying the type of conversion. The character may be any one of the following: `d`, `i`, `o`, `u`, `x`, `f`, `e`, `g`, `[`, `c`, `s`, `p`, or `n`. Upper-case versions of `e`, `g`, and `x` are treated identically as their lower-case counterparts, unlike with `printf`. Refer to the ANSI C Standard for a complete discussion on edit masks. Here, we will simply discuss issues relevant to portability. Except for clarifying a few dark corners and adding a little functionality, ANSI C has adopted existing practice.

- Between the `%` and the conversion characters, the following may optionally appear in the order specified: the assignment-suppression character `*`; a decimal integer specifying the maximum field width; and an `h`, `l`, or `L`, which modifies the conversion character.

- The assignment-suppression character causes the corresponding input field to be read and then discarded; it is not stored.

- The `h` modifier can be used with the conversion characters `d`, `i`, `o`, `n`, `u`, and `x`. The `l` modifier can be used with the conversion characters `d`, `i`, `o`, `n`, `u`, and `x`. `l` may also be used with `e`, `f`, and `g` to indicate the argument is a pointer to `double` instead of a pointer to `float`. The `L` modifier can be used with the conversion characters `e`, `f`, and `g` to signify a pointer to a `long double`. (The type `long double` is an ANSI C invention.) If the `h`, `l`, or `L` modifiers are used with any other conversion specifier, the behavior is undefined. (Note that `L` CANNOT be used in place of `l` with the integral types and that `l` cannot be used in place of `L` with floating-point types, even though such behavior has been suggested, and even sanctioned, in various non-ANSI C documentation.) Some older implementations supported conversion characters `D`, `O`, `X`, and `U`, which meant `ld`, `lo`, `lx`, and `lu`, respectively. ANSI C does not support `D`, `O`, and `U` and uses `X` for a different purpose. DOS C implementations may support the `N` and `F` modifiers so they can specify `near` and `far` pointers, respectively, for `p`, `s`, and `n` conversion characters.

- The conversion character `i` is new and is similar to `d` except that `d` handles decimal input only while `i` can handle other bases as well.

- The `p` conversion character is new—it expects an argument of type pointer to `void`, and it expects the input value to be a pointer specified in an implementation-defined format. (Be sure to cast the argument to `void *` if it isn't of that type already.)

- The `n` character is also new and expects an argument of type pointer to `int`. (If the `l` modifier is used with `n`, a pointer to `long int` is expected.) This conversion causes the count of characters read in thus far to be stored in the integer pointed to by the corresponding argument.

- If a conversion specification is invalid, the behavior is undefined. ANSI C has reserved all unused lower-case conversion specifiers for its own use in future versions.

- You should ensure the types of object pointed to by `scanf`'s arguments are large enough to store the values being entered. For example, you may need `long` rather than `int`.

- `scanf` returns the number of input items assigned. This does not include items skipped using the assignment-suppression character or fields written that corresponded to `n` conversion characters. Note that if an attempted conversion fails, `scanf` returns, and the unconverted input remains in the input buffer. If an error occurred, `EOF` is returned. ANSI C makes no mention of `errno` being set.

- Since the prototype for `scanf` includes an ellipsis you must always include `stdio.h` (or explicitly declare `scanf` yourself) if you wish the call to be maximally portable. This is required since, in the absence of a prototype indicating a variable length argument length, an implementation is free to assume that the number of arguments is fixed and to perform argument-handling optimizations as it sees fit. Therefore, calling such a function without having the appropriate prototype produces undefined behavior.

- A call to `scanf` is equivalent to a call to `fscanf` using a stream of `stdin`.

- Some implementations define a function `cscanf`, which is `scanf` with very minor changes. This is not defined by ANSI C.

The sprintf Function

Calling sequence:

```
#include <stdio.h>

int sprintf(char *s, const char *format, ...);
```

Description: sprintf writes formatted output to the string pointed to by s in a format specified by format.

Comments:

- Almost all aspects of sprintf are identical to those of scanf, which is defined elsewhere.

- The value returned is the number of characters written to the string. It does not include the '\0' character appended to the string. On error, a negative value is returned just as for scanf and fprintf.

- You must ensure that s points to an array large enough to hold the formatted string. Also, s should not overlap with any of the input arguments.

- Since the prototype for sprintf includes an ellipsis you must always include stdio.h (or explicitly declare sprintf yourself) if you wish the call to be maximally portable. This is required since, in the absence of a prototype indicating a variable length argument length, an implementation is free to assume that the number of arguments is fixed and to perform argument-handling optimizations as it sees fit. Therefore, calling such a function without having the appropriate prototype produces undefined behavior.

- Older implementations provide functions called ecvt, fcvt, and gcvt which provide some of the capabilities of sprintf. These functions are not defined by ANSI C.

The sscanf Function

Calling sequence:

```
#include <stdio.h>

int sscanf(const char *s, const char *format, ...);
```

Description: sscanf reads formatted input from the string specified by s in a format specified by format.

Comments:

- Almost all aspects of sscanf are identical to those of scanf, which is defined elsewhere.

- Since the prototype for sscanf includes an ellipsis you must always include stdio.h (or explicitly declare sscanf yourself) if you wish the call to be maximally portable. This is required since, in the absence of a prototype indicating a variable length argument length, an implementation is free to assume that the number of arguments is fixed and to perform argument handling-optimizations as it sees fit. Therefore, calling such a function without having the appropriate prototype produces undefined behavior.

The **vfprintf** Function

Calling sequence:

```
#include <stdio.h>

int vfprintf(FILE *stream, const char *format,
        va_list arg);
```

Description: vfprintf is equivalent to fprintf, except that the variable argument list has been replaced by arg, which has been initialized by the va_start macro (and possibly subsequent va_arg calls.)

Comments:

- vfprintf does not use the va_end macro.

- The return value is the number of characters transmitted or a negative value on error. ANSI C does not specify whether errno is set.

- Each ANSI C header is supposed to be self-sufficient. However, you may need to include stdarg.h (or varargs.h) explicitly to get the necessary va_list stuff defined.

The **vprintf** Function

Calling sequence:

```
#include <stdio.h>

int vprintf(const char *format, va_list arg);
```

Description: vprintf is equivalent to printf, except that the variable argument list has been replaced by arg, which has been initialized by the va_start macro (and possibly subsequent va_arg calls).

Comments:

- vprintf does not use the va_end macro.

- The return value is the number of characters transmitted or a negative value on error. ANSI C does not specify whether errno is set.

- Each ANSI C header is supposed to be self-sufficient. However, you may need to include stdarg.h (or varargs.h) explicitly to get the necessary va_list stuff defined.

The **vsprintf** Function

Calling sequence:

```
#include <stdio.h>

int vsprintf(char *s, const char *format, va_list arg);
```

Description: vsprintf is equivalent to sprintf, except that the variable argument list has been replaced by arg, which has been initialized by the va_start macro (and possibly subsequent va_arg calls).

Comments:

- vsprintf does not use the va_end macro.

- The return value is the number of characters written to the string s (not including the trailing '\0') or a negative value on error. ANSI C does not specify whether errno is set.

- Each ANSI C header is supposed to be self-sufficient. However, you may need to include stdarg.h (or varargs.h) explicitly to get the necessary va_list stuff defined.

◆ Character Input/Output Functions ◆

The **fgetc** Function

Calling sequence:

```
#include <stdio.h>

int fgetc(FILE *stream);
```

Description: `fgetc` gets the next character (if any) from the file pointed to by `stream`.

Comments:

- If a file position indicator is defined for the stream, it is advanced.

- The character is read as an `unsigned char` and returned as an `int`. If end-of-file is detected, `fgetc` returns `EOF`, and the end-of-file indicator is set for that stream. (`feof` can be used to test this indicator.) If a read error occurs, `EOF` is also returned, and the error indicator is set for that stream. (`ferror` can be used to test this indicator.)

- ANSI C requires `fgetc` to be a function; it cannot be a macro.

The **fgets** Function

Calling sequence:

```
#include <stdio.h>

char *fgets(char *s, int n, FILE *stream);
```

Description: `fgets` reads at most `n-1` characters from the file pointed to by `stream` into the array pointed to by `s`. A `'\0'` is appended after the last read character in `array`.

Comments:

- If a new-line is encountered, or end-of-file occurs, no more characters are read. If seen, a new-line is included in the array (unlike `gets`).

- If `fgets` succeeds it returns `s`. If an end-of-file condition is encountered and no characters have yet been read, `NULL` is returned and the contents of the array pointed to by `s` are unchanged. `NULL` is also returned on a read error; however, the contents of the array are then indeterminate.

The **fputc** Function

Calling sequence:

```
#include <stdio.h>

int fputc(int c, FILE *stream);
```

Description: `fputc` writes the character specified by `c` (converted to `unsigned char`) to the file pointed to by `stream`.

Comments:

- If a file position indicator is defined for the stream, it is advanced after the character has been written at that location.

- If the stream was open for append, or the file cannot support positioning requests, the character is appended to the output stream.

- The character written is returned. If a write error occurs, EOF is returned, and the error indicator is set for that stream. (ferror can be used to test this indicator.)

- ANSI C requires fputc to be a function; it cannot be a macro.

The **fputs** Function

Calling sequence:

```
#include <stdio.h>

int fputs(const char *s, FILE *stream);
```

Description: fputs writes the string pointed to by s to the file pointed to by stream.

Comments:

- The ' \0 ' terminating the string is not written.

- Unlike puts, fputs does not append a new-line to the output.

- fputs returns EOF if an error occurs; otherwise, it returns a nonnegative value.

The **getc** Function

Calling sequence:

```
#include <stdio.h>

int getc(FILE *stream);
```

Description: getc gets the next character (if any) from the file pointed to by stream.

Comments:

- getc is equivalent to fgetc except that getc is permitted to be an unsafe macro.

The `getchar` Function

Calling sequence:

```
#include <stdio.h>

int getchar(void);
```

Description: `getchar` gets the next character (if any) from `stdin`.

Comments:

- `getchar` is equivalent to `getc` from `stdin`. Therefore, `getchar` could be implemented as an unsafe macro.

The `gets` Function

Calling sequence:

```
#include <stdio.h>

char *gets(char *s);
```

Description: `gets` reads characters from `stdin` into the array pointed to by `s` until a new-line or end-of-file is encountered. A `'\0'` is appended after the last-read character in `array`.

Comments:

- If a new-line is encountered it is not included in the array (unlike `fgets`).
- If `gets` succeeds, it returns `s`. If an end-of-file condition is encountered, and no characters have yet been read, `NULL` is returned, and the contents of the array pointed to by `s` are unchanged. `NULL` is also returned on a read error; however, the contents of the array are then indeterminate.

The `putc` Function

Calling sequence:

```
#include <stdio.h>

int putc(int c, FILE *stream);
```

Description: `putc` writes the character specified by `c` (converted to `unsigned char`) to the file pointed to by `stream`.

Comments:

- putc is equivalent to fputc except that putc is permitted to be an unsafe macro.

The putchar Function

Calling sequence:

```
#include <stdio.h>

int putchar(int c);
```

Description: putchar writes the character specified by c (converted to unsigned char) to stdout.

Comments:

- putchar is equivalent to putc to stdout. Therefore, putchar could be implemented as an unsafe macro.

The puts Function

Calling sequence:

```
#include <stdio.h>

int puts(const char *s);
```

Description: puts writes the string pointed to by s, followed by a new-line, to stdout.

Comments:

- The '\0' terminating the string is not written.
- Unlike fputs, puts does append a new-line to the output.
- puts returns EOF if an error occurs; otherwise, it returns a nonnegative value.

The ungetc Function

Calling sequence:

```
#include <stdio.h>

int ungetc(int c, FILE *stream);
```

Description: ungetc pushes the character specified by c (after converting it to unsigned char) back into the input file pointed to by stream.

Comments:

- Characters pushed back can be gotten (in the reverse order of which they were pushed back) with subsequent reads from that stream.

- If you call rewind, fseek, or fsetpos, any unread pushed back characters are discarded. Some implementations include fflush in this list, but ANSI C does not since fflush is not a file-positioning function.

- ANSI C guarantees only one character of pushback. If more characters are pushed back than can be handled, an error is returned.

- An attempt to push back the character with value EOF causes an error.

- If ungetc is successful, the end-of-file indicator for that stream is cleared.

- The file position indicator shall be restored to its initial value after all pushed-back characters have been read or discarded.

- An implementation is not obliged to actually push the character back into the file—it may provide a place for such characters "off to the side." Subsequently, once at least one character has been pushed back, the file position indicator can be in a state of limbo until all pushed-back characters have been reread or discarded. For text files, the state of the file position indicator during this time is unspecified. For binary files, the indicator is decremented for each character pushed back, except that if the indicator is zero, a subsequent successful call to ungetc will leave the indicator in an indeterminate state.

- If ungetc is successful, it returns c; otherwise, it returns EOF.

- ungetc was the subject of significant and heated debate by the ANSI C committee, and the ANSI C version almost certainly varies from most non-ANSI C implementations.

◆ Direct Input/Output Functions ◆

The fread Function

Calling sequence:

```
#include <stdio.h>

size_t fread(void *ptr, size_t size,
        size_t nmemb, FILE *stream);
```

Description: `fread` reads up to `nmemb` fields each of size `size` into the array pointed to by `ptr` from the file pointed to by `stream`.

Comments:

- If a file position indicator is defined for the stream, it is advanced by the number of characters successfully read.

- If an error occurs, the file position indicator's value is indeterminate.

- If a partial field is read, its value is indeterminate.

- The value returned is the number of fields successfully read. This number may be less than `nmemb` if end-of-file is detected, or an error occurs.

- If either `size` or `nmemb` is 0, a zero is returned, and the contents of the array pointed to by `ptr` remains intact.

- You must use `feof` and `ferror` to test for end-of-file or an error condition, respectively, since `fread` has no way to communicate this information.

- Use a `sizeof` expression for the `size` argument wherever possible to avoid hard-coding implementation-specific size information.

- ANSI C makes no statement about the possible translation of CR/LF pairs to new-lines on input, although some implementations do so for text files.

The **fwrite** Function

Calling sequence:

```
#include <stdio.h>

size_t fwrite(const void *ptr, size_t size,
        size_t nmemb, FILE *stream);
```

Description: `fwrite` writes up to `nmemb` fields each of size `size` from the array pointed to by `ptr` to the file pointed to by `stream`.

Comments:

- If a file position indicator is defined for the stream, it is advanced by the number of characters successfully written.

- If an error occurs, the file position indicator's value is indeterminate.

- The value returned is the number of fields successfully written. This number may be less than `nmemb` if an error occurs.

- You must use `ferror` to test for an error condition since `fwrite` has no way to communicate this information.

- Use a `sizeof` expression for the `size` argument wherever possible to avoid hard-coding implementation-specific size information.

- ANSI C makes no statement about the possible translation of new-lines to CR/LF pairs on output, although some implementations do so for text files.

◆ File Positioning Functions ◆

The `fgetpos` Function

Calling sequence:

```
#include <stdio.h>

int fgetpos(FILE *stream, fpos_t *pos);
```

Description: `fgetpos` stores the current value of the stream's file position indicator in the object pointed to by `pos`.

Comments:

- `fgetpos` was invented by ANSI C to handle very large files whose file position indicator cannot be represented in a `long int` (as required by `ftell`). Is was deemed preferable to invent a new function rather than to modify `ftell` extensively.

- The object stored in `pos` is suitable for use by `fsetpos` to restore the file to that previous position. The actual type of `pos` is implementation-defined, and its internal representation at any time is unspecified. You should never attempt to modify `pos` yourself—it is merely a vehicle for communicating information between `fgetpos` and `fsetpos`.

- `fgetpos` returns zero on success. On failure, a nonzero value is returned, and `errno` is set to an implementation-defined positive value. (Some implementations use `EINVAL` and `EBADF`.)

The `fseek` Function

Calling sequence:

```
#include <stdio.h>

int fseek(FILE *stream, long int offset, int whence);
```

Description: fseek sets the current value of the stream's file position indicator to an offset based on the value of whence.

Comments:

- whence may be any one of the three macros SEEK_SET, SEEK_CUR, or SEEK_END which represent, the start of the file, the current file position, and the end of the file, respectively. (Some implementations document these as having values 0, 1, and 2, respectively, however, this is not guaranteed by ANSI C.)

- If the stream points to a binary file, the new position is the sum of offset and whence. ANSI C does not require binary files to handle SEEK_END.

- For a text file, offset must be 0, or the value returned from a call to ftell on the same file, in which case whence must be SEEK_SET.

- On success, fseek clears the end-of-file indicator, discards any pushed back characters for that stream and returns zero. On failure, it returns a nonzero value.

- For very large files whose file position indicator cannot be represented in a long int (as required by fseek) use fsetpos.

- Make sure that offset has type long int, rather than int. This is an easy mistake to make on implementations where int and long int have the same representation.

- Some implementations define a function lseek, which is used to position a file specified using a file descriptor. This function is not defined by ANSI C.

The fsetpos Function

Calling sequence:

```
#include <stdio.h>

int fsetpos(FILE *stream, const fpos_t *pos);
```

Description: fsetpos sets the file position indicator for the file pointed to by stream to the value of the object pointed to by pos.

Comments:

- fsetpos was invented by ANSI C to handle very large files whose file position indicator cannot be represented in a long int (as required by fseek). Is was deemed preferable to invent a new function rather than to modify fseek extensively.

- The object stored in `pos` is suitable for use by `fsetpos` to restore the file to that previous position. The actual type of `pos` is implementation-defined, and its internal representation at any time is unspecified. You should never attempt to modify `pos` yourself—it is merely a vehicle for communicating information between `fsetpos` and `fgetpos`.

- On success, `fsetpos` returns zero, clears the end-of-file indicator, and discards characters pushed back via `ungetc`. On failure, a nonzero value is returned, and `errno` is set to an implementation-defined positive value. (Some implementations use `EINVAL` and `EBADF`.)

- Since `fsetpos` effectively flushes the stream's buffer, it can be followed by either an input or an output request.

The `ftell` Function

Calling sequence:

```
#include <stdio.h>

long int ftell(FILE *stream);
```

Description: `ftell` returns the current value of the stream's file position indicator.

Comments:

- If the stream points to a binary file, the value returned is the number of characters from the beginning of the file. For a text file, the value contains unspecified information; however, it can be used with `fseek` to restore the file position indicator to that position.

- On failure, `-1L` is returned, and `errno` is set to an implementation-defined positive value.

- For very large files whose file position indicator cannot be represented in a `long int` (as required by `ftell`) use `fgetpos`.

- Make sure that your declare `ftell` properly and that you assign its value into a variable of type `long int` rather than `int`. This is an easy mistake to make on implementations where `int` and `long int` have the same representation.

The `rewind` Function

Calling sequence:

```
#include <stdio.h>

void rewind(FILE *stream);
```

Description: rewind sets the file's file position indicator to the start of the file.

Comments:

- A call to rewind is identical to a call to fseek with offset 0L and whence SEEK_SET. However, rewind also clears the error indicator as well. (Note that SVID does not require the error indicator to be cleared.)

◆ Error-Handling Functions ◆

The clearerr Function

Calling sequence:

```
#include <stdio.h>

void clearerr(FILE *stream);
```

Description: clearerr clears both the end-of-file and error indicators for the file pointed to by stream.

Comments:

- clearerr typically is implemented as a macro that directly manipulates the FILE object pointed to by stream.

The feof Function

Calling sequence:

```
#include <stdio.h>

int feof(FILE *stream);
```

Description: feof tests the end-of-file indicator for the file pointed to by stream.

Comments:

- feof typically is implemented as a macro that directly manipulates the FILE object pointed to by stream.

- Zero is returned if the end-of-file indicator is clear; nonzero if it is set.

The `ferror` Function

Calling sequence:

```
#include <stdio.h>

int ferror(FILE *stream);
```

Description: `ferror` tests the error indicator for the file pointed to by stream.

Comments:

- `ferror` typically is implemented as a macro that directly manipulates the `FILE` object pointed to by `stream`.

- Zero is returned if the error indicator is clear; nonzero if it is set.

The `perror` Function

Calling sequence:

```
#include <stdio.h>

void perror(const char *s);
```

Description: `perror` writes a message to `stderr` that corresponds to the current value of `errno`. The message includes the user-supplied string pointed to by `s`.

Comments:

- The message output is prefixed with the string pointed to by `s` followed by a colon and a space, provided `s` is not `NULL`, and it doesn't point to an empty string.

- The contents and format of the message are implementation-defined and are the same as those returned by the `strerror` function with argument `errno`.

- The message is followed by a new-line.

◆ ◆ ◆ ◆ ◆ ◆
22

`stdlib.h` — General Utilities

This header contains definitions for four types and five macros and declarations for numerous functions.

The types `size_t` and `wchar_t`, and the macro `NULL`, are defined under the header `stddef.h` and will not be discussed here.

`div_t` is a structure type used as the return type of the `div` function; `ldiv_t` is a structure type used as the return type of the `ldiv` function. The likely definitions for `div_t` and `ldiv_t` are:

```
typedef struct {
        int quot;
        int rem;
} div_t;

typedef struct {
        long int quot;
        long int rem;
} ldiv_t;
```

The ordering of the members is not specified by ANSI C.

The macros `EXIT_SUCCESS` and `EXIT_FAILURE` are ANSI C inventions and are used as the implementation-defined success and failure exit code values used with `exit`. They expand to integral expressions (that are not necessarily constant).

`RAND_MAX` is an integral constant expression representing the maximum value possible from `rand`. ANSI C requires `RAND_MAX` to be at least 32767. Its integral type is not specified so use an explicit cast (or a prototype) when passing it as an argument.

`MB_CUR_MAX` expands to a positive integral expression whose value is the maximum number of bytes in a multibyte character for the extended character set specified by the current locale (category `LC_CTYPE`) and whose value is never greater than `MB_LEN_MAX` (defined in `limits.h`).

◆ String Conversion Functions ◆

ANSI C does not require `atof`, `atoi` and `atol` to set `errno` if an error occurs. If an error does occur, the behavior is undefined. SVID, on the other hand, returns plus or minus HUGE (depending on the sign of the argument) if overflow is detected. On underflow, zero is returned. In both cases, SVID sets `errno` to ERANGE.

SVID does not declare these functions in any header so these must be declared explicitly. In this case, be careful to declare `atol` explicitly even if `int`s and `long`s are the same size since this may not be true with your other targets. It is possible that the `long int` returned by `labs` will subsequently be (incorrectly) interpreted as an `int`.

The `atof` Function

Calling sequence:

```
#include <stdlib.h>

double atof(const char *nptr);
```

Description: `atof` converts the leading part of the string pointed to by `nptr`, to a `double` value.

Comments:

- A call to `atof` is identical to

    ```
    strtod(nptr, (char **)NULL)
    ```

    except that `strtod` can handle errors.
- Note that the format of a valid floating-point value is locale-dependent.
- Use `strtod` instead of `atof` since the former provides more control over the conversion and error detection and handling.

The `atoi` Function

Calling sequence:

```
#include <stdlib.h>

int atoi(const char *nptr);
```

Description: `atoi` converts the leading part of the string pointed to by `nptr` to an `int` value.

Comments:

- A call to `atoi` is identical to

    ```
    (int) strtol(nptr, (char **)NULL, 10)
    ```

    except that `strtol` can handle errors.

- Use `strtol` instead of `atoi` since the former provides more control over the conversion and error detection and handling.

The `atol` Function

Calling sequence:

```
#include <stdlib.h>

long int atol(const char *nptr);
```

Description: `atol` converts the leading part of the string pointed to by `nptr` to a `long int` value.

Comments:

- A call to `atol` is identical to

    ```
    strtol(nptr, (char **)NULL, 10)
    ```

    except that `strtol` can handle errors.

- Use `strtol` instead of `atol` since the former provides more control over the conversion and error detection and handling.

The `strtod` Function

Calling sequence:

```
#include <stdlib.h>

double strtod(const char *nptr, char **endptr);
```

Description: `strtod` converts the leading part of the string pointed to by `nptr` to a `double` value.

Comments:

- Leading white space is ignored.

- The floating-point constant is terminated by any character not permissible in such a constant (including the `'\0'` that terminates the input string).

- A leading sign character is permitted as is a (possibly signed) exponent using either `'e'` or `'E'`. A floating-point suffix of `'f'` (or `'F'`) or `'l'` (or `'L'`) is not permitted.

- If no exponent or decimal point appears, a decimal point is assumed to be at the end of the number.

- The format of the floating-point number is locale-specific.

- If the input contains all white space, is empty, or contains no convertible characters, no conversion occurs, and `nptr` is stored in `*endptr` (provided `endptr` is not `NULL`). A zero value is returned.

- If the converted value causes overflow, plus or minus `HUGE_VAL` is returned (according to the sign of the value), and `errno` is set to `ERANGE`. On underflow, zero is returned, and `errno` is set to `ERANGE`.

- `strtod` is a superset of `atof` and is recommended over it.

The **strtol** Function

Calling sequence:

```
#include <stdlib.h>

long int strtol(const char *nptr, char **endptr,
        int base);
```

Description: `strtol` converts the leading part of the string pointed to by `nptr` to a `long int` value.

Comments:

- Leading white space is ignored.

- The integral constant is terminated by any character not permissible in such a constant (including the `'\0'` that terminates the input string).

- A leading sign character is permitted, but the suffixes `'u'` (or `'U'`) or `'l'` (or `'L'`) are not.

- The integral value is interpreted using radix `base`. If `base` is 0, the radix will be determined based on the presence or absence of a leading `0` or `0x` (or `0X`). Otherwise, `base` may be between 2 and 36.

- The format of the integral value is locale-specific.

- If the input contains all white space, is empty, or contains no convertible characters, no conversion occurs, and `nptr` is stored in `*endptr` (provided `endptr` is not `NULL`). A zero value is returned.

- If the converted value causes overflow, either `LONG_MAX` or `LONG_MIN` is returned (depending on the sign of the value), and `errno` is set to `ERANGE`.

- `strtol` is a superset of `atol` and `atoi` and is recommended over them.

The `strtoul` Function

Calling sequence:

```
#include <stdlib.h>

unsigned long int strtoul(const char *nptr,
        char **endptr, int base);
```

Description: `strtoul` converts the leading part of the string pointed to by `nptr` to an `unsigned long int` value.

Comments:

- This function is an ANSI C invention.

- Leading white space is ignored.

- The integral constant is terminated by any character not permissible in such a constant (including the `'\0'` that terminates the input string).

- A leading sign character is permitted, but the suffixes `'u'` (or `'U'`) or `'l'` (or `'L'`) are not.

- The integral value is interpreted using radix `base`. If `base` is 0, the radix will be determined based on the presence or absence of a leading `0` or `0x` (or `0X`). Otherwise, base may be between 2 and 36.

- The format of the integral value is locale-specific.

- If the input contains all white space, is empty, or contains no convertible characters, no conversion occurs and `nptr` is stored in `*endptr` (provided `endptr` is not `NULL`). A 0 value is returned.

- If the converted value causes overflow, `ULONG_MAX` is returned, and `errno` is set to `ERANGE`.

◆ Pseudo-Random Sequence Generation Functions ◆

The `rand` Function

Calling sequence:

```
#include <stdlib.h>

int rand(void);
```

Description: `rand` computes a sequence of pseudo-random integers in the range 0 to RAND_MAX.

Comments:

- ANSI C requires RAND_MAX to be at least 32767, while SVID requires the value returned to be from 0 through 32767, inclusive. (SVID does not define RAND_MAX.) Therefore, if your code requires a value in this range, and you are using ANSI C, you will need to ignore, or otherwise handle, numbers returned from `rand` that are greater than 32767.

The `srand` Function

Calling sequence:

```
#include <stdlib.h>

void srand(unsigned int seed);
```

Description: `srand` uses its argument as a seed for a new sequence of pseudo-random numbers to be returned by subsequent calls to `rand`.

Comments:

- If `srand` has never been called, `rand` behaves as if `srand` had been called with a seed of 1.
- Identical seeds generate identical pseudo-random number sequences.

◆ Memory Management Functions ◆

Each block of storage allocated by calls to `calloc`, `malloc`, and `realloc` can exist anywhere in the program's address space. The order and contiguity of these blocks is unspecified by ANSI C.

The space allocated is suitably aligned such that a pointer to that space can be assigned to a pointer of any type.

All concurrently allocated blocks must begin at different addresses.

NULL is returned if the space requested cannot be allocated. NEVER, EVER assume an allocation request succeeds without checking for a NULL return value.

If a zero amount of space is requested, the behavior is implementation-defined, and either NULL or a unique pointer is returned. That is, it is possible to allocate zero bytes and get a non-NULL return value.

ANSI C now has these functions dealing with void * and size_t types, as appropriate, rather than char * and int. Historically, it has been either desirable or necessary to cast the return value of the allocator routines explicitly since they returned char *. However, ANSI C has them returning void pointers, and these are assignment-compatible with all other data pointer types so no cast is necessary (although one is permitted and may be useful in documenting the default behavior).

SVID declares these function in malloc.h, rather than stdlib.h. Other implementations use alloc.h.

The size of the heap available and the details of its management and manipulation are implementation-defined. On some implementations, the amount of heap available for dynamic allocation is quite limited. It may also share the same address space with the stack, the user's code or data, or all three. If your programs use more than a small amount of heap, you MUST perform an extensive investigation to ensure that each of your implementations supports your requirements. If not, you may find a that major design change is required. Allocating heap space may also be an expensive operation, in which case you may wish to allocate one or more larger blocks and to manage them with your own allocator. The order in which you allocate and free objects may also significantly impact performance.

ANSI C does not define the mallopt and mallinfo functions and structure mallinfo present in SVID. Other allocation functions in general use, such as cfree, clalloc, mlalloc, relalloc, brk, and sbrk, are also missing from ANSI C.

ANSI C provides no way to find how much heap space is available for allocation, although some implementations do.

Allocating space for very large objects on segmented memory machines (such as Intel's) may require a set of allocation functions other than those specified by ANSI C.

The calloc Function

Calling sequence:

```
#include <stdlib.h>

void *calloc(size_t nmemb, size_t size);
```

Description: calloc allocates contiguous space for nmemb objects, each of whose size is size.

Comments:

- The space allocated is initialized to "all-bits-zero." Note that this is not guaranteed to be the same representation as floating-point zero or NULL. For example, whether the output of the two values in the following example is identical is implementation-defined.

```
#include <stdio.h>
#include <stdlib.h>

main()
{
        double *pd;

        pd = calloc(1, sizeof(double));

        if (pd != NULL)
                printf("%10.8f %10.8f\n", *pd, 0.0);
}
```

The **free** Function

Calling sequence:

```
#include <stdlib.h>

void free(void *ptr);
```

Description: free causes the space (previously allocated by calloc, malloc, or realloc) pointed to by ptr to be freed.

Comments:

- If ptr is NULL, free does nothing. Otherwise, if ptr is not a value previously returned by one of these three allocation functions, the behavior is undefined.

- The value of a pointer that refers to space that has been freed is indeterminate, and such pointers should not be dereferenced.

- Note that free has no way to communicate an error if one is detected.

The `malloc` Function

Calling sequence:

```
#include <stdlib.h>

void *malloc(size_t size);
```

Description: `malloc` allocates contiguous space for `size` bytes.

Comments:

- The space allocated has no guaranteed initial value.
- By giving `realloc` a `NULL` first argument, `malloc` can be used to produce the same effect as `malloc` with the same size.

The `realloc` Function

Calling sequence:

```
#include <stdlib.h>

void *realloc(void *ptr, size_t size);
```

Description: `realloc` changes the size of the space pointed to by `ptr` to size `size`.

Comments:

- If `ptr` is `NULL`, `realloc` behaves like `malloc`. Otherwise, if `ptr` is not a value previously returned by `calloc`, `malloc`, or `realloc`, the behavior is undefined. The same is true if `ptr` points to space that has been `freed`.
- `size` is absolute, not relative. If `size` is larger than the size of the existing space, new uninitialized contiguous space is allocated at the end; the previous contents of the space are preserved. If `size` is smaller, the excess space is `freed`; however, the contents of the retained space are preserved.
- If `realloc` cannot allocate the requested space, the contents of the space pointed to by `ptr` remain intact.
- If `ptr` is non-`NULL` and `size` is 0, `realloc` acts like `free`.
- Whenever the size of space is changed by `realloc`, the new space may begin at an address different to that given it, EVEN when `realloc` is truncating. Therefore, if you use `realloc` in this manner, you must beware of pointers that point into this possibly moved space. For example, if you

build a linked list there and use realloc to allocate more (or less) space for the chain, it is possible that the space will be "moved," in which case, the pointers now point to where successive links used to be, not where they are now. You should ALWAYS use realloc as follows:

```
ptr = realloc(ptr, new_size);
```

This way, you never care whether the object has been relocated since you always update ptr each call, to point to the (possibly new) location.

♦ Communication with the Environment ♦

Some implementations declare some or all of these function in a header called process.h, as well as, or instead of, stdlib.h. ANSI C requires them to be declared in stdlib.h.

The abort Function

Calling sequence:

```
#include <stdlib.h>

void abort(void);
```

Description: abort causes the program to terminate abnormally unless the signal SIGABRT is being caught and the signal handler does not return.

Comments:

- It is implementation-defined as to whether or not output streams are flushed, open streams are closed, or temporary files are removed.

- The exit code of the program is some implementation-defined value that represents "failure." It is generated by a call to raise using the argument SIGABRT.

- SVID declares abort to return an int. Also, it does not declare it within a header.

- Refer to exit for a discussion about normal program termination.

The atexit Function

Calling sequence:

```
#include <stdlib.h>

int atexit(void (*func)(void));
```

Description: `atexit` permits a function to be registered such that it is called automatically by the implementation during normal program termination.

Comments:

- The function being registered must take no arguments and have no return value.

- ANSI C requires that at least 32 functions can be registered. However, to get around any limitations in this regard, you can always register just one function and have it call the others directly. This way, the other functions can also have argument lists and return values.

- ANSI C does not prohibit the same function from being registered more than once, although it is hard to conceive why you would want to do so.

- If the registration fails, a nonzero value is returned; otherwise, zero is returned.

- In early drafts of ANSI C, this function was called `onexit`, the name of its parent routine as defined in the Whitesmiths library. That function returned a value of type `onexit_t`. The results of registering the same function more than once with `onexit` were undefined.

- SVID does not define `atexit`.

The `exit` Function

Calling sequence:

```
#include <stdlib.h>

void exit(int status);
```

Description: `exit` causes normal program termination to occur.

Comments:

- The functions registered by `atexit` are called in the reverse order of their registration. These functions can reliably manipulate all global objects they know about. They should not attempt to access automatic objects defined in other functions even though they may be able to access variables that pointed to those objects.

- All open output files are flushed, open files are closed, and temporary files created by `tmpfile` are removed.

- Control is then returned to the host environment, to which is given the exit code status. An exit code of zero or `EXIT_SUCCESS` signifies "success," while `EXIT_FAILURE` signifies "failure." The value or meaning of any other exit code is implementation-defined. Note that on some systems, most noticeably VAX/VMS, a value of 0 does not mean "success."

- The method used to invoke `main` during program startup can vary. ANSI C requires that it be done using

```
exit(main(argc,argv));
```

in which case, any value returned explicitly or implicitly from `main` will be passed on as the exit code. However, it is a common misconception that dropping through the closing } of `main` is the same as leaving via `exit(0);`, and this is not true, although a number of implementations have made it so. They invoke `main` as follows:

```
main(argc,argv);
exit(0);
```

in which case, any garbage value returned by `return;` or by falling through the closing } will be ignored, and an exit code of zero will be used. This is fine unless `return (n);` is used to terminate `main`. In this case, the explicit return value is discarded, and 0 is used instead, unbeknown to the user. Because of this problem, if a programmer requires an exit code of *n*, then `exit` should be used to terminate `main` rather than `return` with value *n*.

- Not all environments allow access to exit codes returned by programs. Also, some environments may truncate the `int` returned to a `signed` (or perhaps even `unsigned`) `char`. Others (such as VAX/VMS) define an exit code format such that the code returned can trigger certain events at the command-language level.

- Define exit codes using macro names. While using an enumerated type might seem attractive, you may be required to initialize explicitly some or all of the enumerations constants if you can't have a continuous range of values.

- Some implementations define a function `_exit`, which bypasses certain "cleanup" activities. This is not defined by ANSI C.

- SVID does not declare `exit` within a header.

- Versions of VAX C prior to 2.3 permitted `exit` to be called without an argument.

- Refer to `abort` for a discussion about abnormal program termination.

The `getenv` Function

Calling sequence:

```
#include <stdlib.h>

char *getenv(const char *name);
```

Description: `getenv` searches an environment list for a string that matches the string pointed to by `name`.

Comments:

- The environment list is maintained by the host environment, and the set of names available is implementation-defined.

- A function, called `putenv`, is often provided to define and/or change environment strings. However, this is not part of ANSI C. It is possible that an implementation does not even support environment strings, in which case, `getenv` could always fail.

- The value returned is a pointer to a string that "matches" the string pointed to by `name`. If no match is found, `NULL` is returned.

- The behavior is undefined if you attempt to modify the contents of the string pointed to by the return value.

- Some implementations supply a third argument to `main`, called `envp`. `envp` is an array of pointers to `char` (just like `argv`) with each pointer pointing to an environment string.

- SVID does not declare `getenv` in any header.

The `system` Function

Calling sequence:

```
#include <stdlib.h>

int system(const char *string);
```

Description: `system` passes off the string pointed to by `string` to the host environment command-line processor.

Comments:

- ANSI C does not require that a command-line processor (or equivalent) exist, in which case an implementation-defined value is returned. To ascertain whether such an environment exists, call `system` with a `NULL` argument; if a nonzero value is returned, a command-line processor is available.

- The format of the string passed is implementation-defined.

- SVID declares system in `stdio.h`.

- Numerous implementations provide a family of functions called `exec*` to spawn command-lines and programs. These are not defined by ANSI C.

♦ Searching and Sorting Utilities ♦

The **bsearch** Function

Calling sequence:

```
#include <stdlib.h>

void *bsearch(const void *key, const void *base,
        size_t nmemb, size_t size,
        int (*compar)(const void *, const void *));
```

Description: `bsearch` searches an array of `nmemb` objects, the initial member of which is pointed to by `base`, for a member that matches the object pointed to by `key`.

Comments:

- `size` specifies the size of each member in the array.

- The members of the array are sorted in an ascending order corresponding to that expected by the comparison function pointed to by `compar`. `compar` is passed two arguments; the first pointing to the key object and, the second pointing to the array member.

- Based on the comparison, a negative, zero, or positive value is returned from `compar`.

- If no match is found, NULL is returned; otherwise, a pointer to the matching member in the array is returned.

- If two members compare as equal, it is unspecified as to which member is matched.

- SVID declares `bsearch` in the header `search.h`.

The **qsort** Function

Calling sequence:

```
#include <stdlib.h>

void qsort(void *base, size_t nmemb, size_t size,
        int (*compar)(const void *, const void *));
```

Description: qsort sorts an array of nmemb objects, the initial member of which is pointed to by base.

Comments:

- size specifies the size of each member in the array.
- The members of the array are sorted in an ascending order corresponding to that expected by the comparison function pointed to by compar. compar is passed two arguments that point to the objects being compared.
- Based on the comparison, a negative, zero, or positive value is returned by compar.
- If two members compare as equal, it is unspecified as to their order in the array.
- SVID does not declare qsort in any header.

◆ Integer Arithmetic Functions ◆

The abs Function

Calling sequence:

```
#include <stdlib.h>
int abs(int j);
```

Description: abs computes the absolute value of the int j.

Comments:

- The behavior is undefined if the result cannot be represented (such as abs(-32768) on a twos-complement 16-bit machine).
- Some implementations declare abs in math.h.
- SVID does not declare abs in any header.
- abs could be implemented as a macro.

The div Function

Calling sequence:

```
#include <stdlib.h>

div_t div(int numer, int denom);
```

Description: `div` computes the quotient and remainder of `numer/denom`.

Comments:

- If the division is inexact, the sign of the resulting quotient is that of the algebraic quotient, and the magnitude of the resulting quotient is the largest integer less than the magnitude of the algebraic quotient.
- If the result cannot be represented, the behavior is undefined.
- The value returned has a structure type `div_t`, which contains the two `int` members, `quot` and `rem`, in either order.
- `div` is an ANSI C invention.

The **labs** Function

Calling sequence:

```
#include <stdlib.h>

long int labs(long int j);
```

Description: `labs` computes the absolute value of the `long int j`.

Comments:

- The behavior is undefined if the result cannot be represented.
- Some implementations declare `labs` in `math.h`.
- SVID does not define `labs`.
- `labs` could be implemented as a macro.

The **ldiv** Function

Calling sequence:

```
#include <stdlib.h>

ldiv_t ldiv(long int numer, long int denom);
```

Description: `ldiv` computes the quotient and remainder of `numer/denom`.

Comments:

- If the division is inexact, the sign of the resulting quotient is that of the algebraic quotient, and the magnitude of the resulting quotient is the largest integer less than the magnitude of the algebraic quotient.

- If the result cannot be represented, the behavior is undefined.

- The value returned has a structure type `ldiv_t`, which contains the two `long int` members, `quot` and `rem`, in either order.

- `ldiv` is an ANSI C invention.

♦ Multibyte Character Functions ♦

The behavior of these functions is subject to the current locale, in particular, to the `LC_CTYPE` category.

Multibyte character processing was a very late ANSI C invention; refer to the Standard for a complete explanation of these functions.

The `mblen` Function

Calling sequence:

```
#include <stdlib.h>

int mblen(const char *s, size_t n);
```

Description: `mblen` computes the number of bytes in the multibyte character pointed to by `s`.

The `mbtowc` Function

Calling sequence:

```
#include <stdlib.h>

int mbtowc(wchar_t *pwc, const char *s, size_t n);
```

Description: `mbtowc` computes the number of bytes in the multibyte character pointed to by `s`. It then determines the code for a value of type `wchar_t` that corresponds to that multibyte character.

The `wctomb` Function

Calling sequence:

```
#include <stdlib.h>

int wctomb(char *s, wchar_t wchar);
```

Description: `wctomb` determines the number of bytes needed to represent the multibyte character corresponding to the code whose value is `wchar`.

◆ Multibyte String Functions ◆

The behavior of these functions is subject to the current locale, in particular, to the LC_CTYPE category.

Multibyte string processing was a very late ANSI C invention; refer to the Standard for a complete explanation of these functions.

The **mbstowcs** Function

Calling sequence:

```
#include <stdlib.h>

int mbstowcs(wchar_t *pwcs, const char *s, size_t n);
```

Description: mbstowcs converts a sequence of multibyte characters into a sequence of corresponding codes.

The **wcstombs** Function

Calling sequence:

```
#include <stdlib.h>

int wcstombs(char *s, wchar_t *pwcs, size_t n);
```

Description: wcstombs converts a sequence of codes that represent multibyte characters into the array pointed to by pwcs.

23

`string.h` — String Handling

This header was invented by ANSI C as a place to declare the family of library functions with names of the form `str*` and `mem*`. Previously, some of these functions (usually the `mem*` routines) were declared in a header called `memory.h` (and sometimes `mem.h`).

As well as providing a permanent and reliable home for these declarations, ANSI C also enhanced them to take advantage of new types and ideas. For example, the `mem*` functions really deal with generic pointers, not with pointers to `char`, and since ANSI C has a generic pointer type, `void *`, this has been used throughout `string.h` as appropriate. Also, historically the size of anything has been specified as type `int`, even though it makes no sense to have a negative size. Now the ANSI C unsigned integral type `size_t` is used instead.

A number of the functions here can either take a null pointer argument or return a null pointer value. To ensure that `string.h` is self-contained, it has a definition for the macro `NULL` so that it is not necessary to `#include` another header just for that definition.

◆ Copying Functions ◆

The `memcpy` Function

Calling sequence:

```
#include <string.h>

void *memcpy(void *s1, const void *s2, size_t n);
```

Description: `memcpy` copies n characters from the location pointed to by s2 to the location pointed to by s1.

Comments:

- The value of s1 is returned.

- If the objects located at s1 and s2 overlap, the behavior of `memcpy` is undefined. To copy overlapping objects, use `memmove` instead. (Some implementations of `memcpy` may also correctly handle overlapping objects, although they are not required to by ANSI C.)

- If you are using `memcpy` to copy aggregates such as arrays or structures, or to copy unions, make sure you use a `sizeof` expression for n so that structure holes and object size considerations are automatically taken care of.

- An implementation is at liberty to place certain alignment considerations on any of C's data types, and it may do this during compile-time or run-time storage allocation. Presumably, any copy you make in memory of such an aligned object should itself also be aligned appropriately. If this is not the case, it is possible that the created copy might not be accessible, or it may be misinterpreted. It is the programmer's responsibility to ensure the resultant object copy is in a format and memory location suitable for further and meaningful use.

The **memmove** Function

Calling sequence:

```
#include <string.h>

void *memmove(void *s1, const void *s2, size_t n);
```

Description: `memmove` copies n characters from the location pointed to by s2 to the location pointed to by s1.

Comments:

- The value of s1 is returned.

- `memcpy` works correctly even if the objects located at s1 and s2 overlap. If the objects are known not to overlap, it may be more efficient to use `memcpy` instead.

The `strcpy` Function

Calling sequence:

```
#include <string.h>

char *strcpy(char *s1, const char *s2);
```

Description: `strcpy` copies the string pointed to by `s2` to the location pointed to by `s1`. The destination string is `'\0'`-terminated.

Comments:

- The value of `s1` is returned.
- If the strings located at `s1` and `s2` overlap, the behavior of `strcpy` is undefined. To copy overlapping objects, use `memmove` instead.

The `strncpy` Function

Calling sequence:

```
#include <string.h>

char *strncpy(char *s1, const char *s2, size_t n);
```

Description: `strncpy` copies, at most, the first `n` characters from the string pointed to by `s2` to the location pointed to by `s1`. The destination string is `'\0'`-terminated.

Comments:

- The value of `s1` is returned.
- If a `'\0'` is not found in the first `n` characters of `s2`, the string pointed to by `s1` will not be `'\0'`-terminated. If a `'\0'` is found, it is copied to `s1`. If there are less than `n` characters in the string pointed to by `s1`, extra `'\0'` characters are appended to the end of the string pointed to by `s1` such that `n` characters are actually copied there.
- If the strings located at `s1` and `s2` overlap, the behavior of `strncpy` is undefined. To copy overlapping objects, use `memmove` instead.

◆ Concatenation Functions ◆

The strcat Function

Calling sequence:

```
#include <string.h>

char *strcat(char *s1, const char *s2);
```

Description: strcat copies the string pointed to by s2 to the end of the string pointed to by s1. In the process, the trailing '\0' of s1 is overwritten by the first character of the string pointed to by s2. The destination string is '\0'-terminated.

Comments:

- The value of s1 is returned.
- If the strings located at s1 and s2 overlap, the behavior of strcat is undefined.

The strncat Function

Calling sequence:

```
#include <string.h>

char *strncat(char *s1, const char *s2, size_t n);
```

Description: strncat copies, at most, the first n characters from the string pointed to by s2 to the end of the string pointed to by s1. The destination string is '\0'-terminated.

Comments:

- The value of s1 is returned.
- If a '\0' is not found in the first n characters of s2, n characters will be copied followed by a '\0'. If a '\0' is found, it is copied to s1, and the copy is terminated.
- If the strings located at s1 and s2 overlap, the behavior of strncat is undefined.

◆ Comparison Functions ◆

Recommendation: All the comparison functions return an integer indicating less than, greater than, or equal to zero. Do not assume the positive or negative values indicating greater than and less than, respectively, have any predictable value. Always compare the return value against zero, never against a specific nonzero value.

The memcmp Function

Calling sequence:

```
#include <string.h>

int memcmp(const void *s1, const void *s2, size_t n);
```

Description: memcmp compares n characters at the location pointed to by s2 to the location pointed to by s1.

Comments:

- An integer less than, equal to, or greater than zero is returned to indicate whether s1 is less than, equal to, or greater than s2, respectively.

- Take care when comparing structures that may contain holes since the contents of the holes may be indeterminate. C does not guarantee that the holes in static and global structures have the value 0; only named members have that default initial value.

- A problem can also occur when comparing a particular member in two unions of the same type. For example,

```
#include <string.h>
#include <stdio.h>

union tag {
        int i;
        double d;
};

main()
{
        union tag u1, u2;

        u1.i = 6;
        u2.i = 6;
```

```
        if (memcmp(&u1, &u2, sizeof(u1)) == 0)
                printf("unions are equal\n");
        else
                printf("unions are not equal\n");

        memset(&u1, 0, sizeof(u1));
        memset(&u2, 0, sizeof(u2));

        u1.i = 6;
        u2.i = 6;

        if (memcmp(&u1, &u2, sizeof(u1)) == 0)
                printf("unions are equal\n");
        else
                printf("unions are not equal\n");
}
```

```
unions are not equal
unions are equal
```

- The unions u1 and u2 are large enough to hold the double member. Since the int member almost certainly takes up less than the total allocated space, comparing the unions byte-for-byte will also involve the comparisons of the (currently) unused part of the union. And since the unions have class auto, the initial value of the whole union is undefined, and, not surprisingly, the comparison is unequal. However, once the whole of the union storage area is initialized with zeros (using memset), the equality test works.

- A similar situation can occur when comparing objects residing in space allocated by malloc or realloc since with these, the initial contents of the allocated space is undefined. Using calloc instead causes the space to be initialized to all-bits-zero.

The strcmp Function

Calling sequence:

```
#include <string.h>

int strcmp(const char *s1, const char *s2);
```

Description: strcmp compares a string at the location pointed to by s2 to a string at the location pointed to by s1.

Comments:

- An integer less than, equal to, or greater than zero is returned to indicate whether s1 is less than, equal to, or greater than s2, respectively.

The `strcoll` Function

Calling sequence:

```
#include <string.h>

int strcoll(const char *s1, const char *s2);
```

Description: strcoll compares a string at the location pointed to by s2 to a string at the location pointed to by s1.

Comments:

- An integer less than, equal to, or greater than zero is returned to indicate whether s1 is less than, equal to, or greater than s2, respectively.
- The comparison is locale-specific and, therefore, permits any arbitrary collation sequence to be used provided that sequence is provided by the implementation as a locale. The sequence can include non-English letters and characters.
- In the "C" locale, strcoll should give the same result as strcmp.
- This function is an ANSI C invention.

The `strncmp` Function

Calling sequence:

```
#include <string.h>

int strncmp(const char *s1, const char *s2, size_t n);
```

Description: strncmp compares no more than n characters from a string at the location pointed to by s2 to a string at the location pointed to by s1. If a '\0' is seen in the first n characters, the comparison is terminated.

Comments:

- An integer less than, equal to, or greater than zero is returned to indicate whether s1 is less than, equal to, or greater than s2, respectively.

The **strxfrm** Function

Calling sequence:

```
#include <string.h>

size_t strxfrm(char *s1, const char *s2, size_t n);
```

Description: `strxfrm` transforms the string pointed to by `s2` into another string pointed to by `s1`. The transformation is locale-specific.

Comments:

- If two strings are transformed, and the resultant strings are compared using `strcmp`, the same result should be obtained as if the original two strings had been compared using `strcoll`.

- No more than `n` transformed characters are to be written into `s1`. If the transformed string is bigger than n, only `n` are copied to `s1`, and the function returns the total number needed to hold the whole transformed string. Normally, `n` is large enough and the return value is the number of characters actually used in `s1` (excluding the `'\0'`).

- If `s1` and `s2` designate strings that overlap, the results are undefined.

- This function is an ANSI C invention.

◆ Search Functions ◆

The **memchr** Function

Calling sequence:

```
#include <string.h>

void *memchr(const void *s, int c, size_t n);
```

Description: `memchr` searches the first `n` characters of a string `s` for a character `c`.

Comments:

- If `c` is found, `memchr` returns a pointer to that location within `s`, else it returns `NULL`.

- c is converted to `unsigned char` before the search begins.

The **strchr** Function

Calling sequence:

```
#include <string.h>

char *strchr(const char *s, int c);
```

Description: `strchr` searches the string `s` for a character `c`.

Comments:

- If `c` is found, `strchr` returns a pointer to that location within `s`, else it returns `NULL`.
- c is converted to `char` before the search begins.
- The `'\0'` terminating `s` is included in the search. Therefore, `strchr` can be used to locate the trailing `'\0'` as well as any embedded character.
- Some implementations provide a version of `strchr` called `index`.

The **strcspn** Function

Calling sequence:

```
#include <string.h>

size_t strcspn(const char *s1, const char *s2);
```

Description: `strcspn` finds the longest string starting at the location pointed to by `s1` such that is does not contain any of the characters in the string at the location pointed to by `s2`. Alternatively, it could be viewed that `strcspn` locates the first character in the string pointed to by `s1` that is present in the string pointed to by `s2`.

Comments:

- The return value indicates the length of the nonmatching string found at `s1` (which is the same as the subscript of the first matching character in `s1`). For example,

```
#include <stdio.h>
#include <string.h>

main()
{
        int i;

        i = strcspn("abcdefg", "xyz");
        printf("i = %d\n", i);

        i = strcspn("abcdefg", "xyzd");
        printf("i = %d\n", i);

        i = strcspn("abcdefg", "");
        printf("i = %d\n", i);
}


i = 7
i = 3
i = 7
```

The strpbrk Function

Calling sequence:

```
#include <string.h>

char *strpbrk(const char *s1, const char *s2);
```

Description: strpbrk search the string pointed to by s1 for the first of any one of the characters in the string pointed to by s2.

Comments:

- The return value is a pointer to the character found in s1 or NULL if no match was found.

The strrchr Function

Calling sequence:

```
#include <string.h>

char *strrchr(const char *s, int c);
```

Description: strrchr searches the string s from its end backwards for a character c.

Comments:

- If c is found, strrchr returns a pointer to that location within s, else it returns NULL.

- c is converted to char before the search begins.

- The '\0' terminating s is included in the search. Therefore, strrchr can be used to locate the trailing '\0' as well as any embedded character.

- Some implementations provide a version of strrchr called rindex.

The **strspn** Function

Calling sequence:

```
#include <string.h>

size_t strspn(const char *s1, const char *s2);
```

Description: strspn finds the longest string starting at the location pointed to by s1 such that it contains only those characters in the string at the location pointed to by s2. Alternatively, it could be viewed that strspn locates the first character in the string pointed to by s1 that is not present in the string pointed to by s2.

Comments:

- The return value indicates the length of the matching string found at s1 (which is the same as the subscript of the first nonmatching character in s1). For example,

```
#include <stdio.h>
#include <string.h>

main()
{
        int i;

        i = strspn("abcdefg", "xyzabdc");
        printf("i = %d\n", i);

        i = strspn("abcdefg", "xyza");
        printf("i = %d\n", i);

        i = strspn("abcdefg", "");
        printf("i = %d\n", i);
}
```

```
i = 4
i = 1
i = 0
```

The **strstr** Function

Calling sequence:

```
#include <string.h>

char *strstr(const char *s1, const char *s2);
```

Description: strstr searches the string pointed to by s1 for the substring pointed to by s2.

Comments:

- The return value represents the location of the substring s2 within the string s1, if any, else NULL.
- By definition, the null string is always found at the beginning of any string, including a null string.
- This function is an ANSI C invention.

The **strtok** Function

Calling sequence:

```
#include <string.h>

char *strtok(char *s1, const char *s2);
```

Description: Successive calls to strtok can be used to break a string pointed to by s1 into a series of '\0'-terminated tokens using the token terminator characters specified by the string pointed to by s2.

Comments:

- The value returned is either a pointer to the token found or NULL if no token was found. For example,

```
#include <stdio.h>
#include <string.h>

main()
{
        static char c[] = "efg,hij kl,m.";
        char *pc;

        pc = strtok(c, " ,.");
        if (pc == NULL) {
                printf("No tokens found\n");
                exit(1);
        }


        while (1) {
                printf("Token: >%s<\n", pc);
                pc = strtok(NULL, " ,.");
                if (pc == NULL) {
                        printf("No more tokens\n");
                        break;
                }
        }
}
```

```
Token: >efg<
Token: >hij<
Token: >kl<
Token: >m<
No more tokens
```

♦ Miscellaneous Functions ♦

The memset Function

Calling sequence:

```
#include <string.h>

void *memset(void *s, int c, size_t n);
```

Description: memset sets the first n characters of the object pointed to by s to the value c.

Comments:

- c is converted to an unsigned char before the copying begins.
- The return value is s.
- This function can be used to initialize two unions (or structures containing holes) such that the unions (or structures) could later be compared using memcmp.

The strerror Function

Calling sequence:

```
#include <string.h>

char *strerror(int errnum);
```

Description: strerror returns the address of a string containing a message corresponding to the message code used as the argument.

Comments:

- strerror is similar in capability to perror in that it is designed for use with errno. However, whereas perror writes the message directly to stderr along with the user-supplied text, strerror returns a pointer to the message allowing the programmer to process it as they wish. For example,

```
#include <string.h>
#include <stdio.h>
#include <errno.h>

main()
{
        double d;

        errno = 0;
        d = sqrt(-1.234);
        printf("%s\n", strerror(errno));

        perror("Error");
}


Math argument

Error: Math argument
```

- The contents of the text of the message returned is implement-defined. In fact, the string could be empty or might contain a message such as "Unknown error."

- The programmer should not attempt to write to the location pointed to by the returned value.

The `strlen` Function

Calling sequence:

```
#include <string.h>

size_t strlen(const char *s);
```

Description: `strlen` returns the length of the string (excluding the trailing `'\0'`) pointed to by `s`.

Comments:

- An empty string has length zero.

♦ Non-Standard Functions ♦

Numerous other library functions (mostly with names of the form `str*` and `mem*`) are or have been provided with various implementations. However, none of these is part of the ANSI C Standard Library. Some of these functions are: `bcmp`, `bcopy`, `bzero`, `instr`, `memccpy`, `memccpy`, `memicmp`, `notstr`, `scnstr`, `strcmpi`, `strdup`, `stricmp`, `strlwr`, `strnicmp`, `strnset`, `strpos`, `strrev`, `strrpbrk`, `strrpos`, `strset`, and `strupr`.

24

`time.h` — Date and Time

✦ Components of Time ✦

The header `time.h` defines several macros and types and declares functions that manipulate time information.

The macros are `NULL` (discussed under `stddef.h`) and `CLK_TCK`, which is the number of `clock_t` intervals in a second. (`clock_t` is an implementation-defined type discussed below.) For example, if `clock_t` is measured in milliseconds, `CLK_TCK` will be 1000.

The types defined are `size_t` (discussed under `stddef.h`), `clock_t`, `time_t`, and `struct tm`. `clock_t` and `time_t` are arithmetic times (not necessarily integral) capable of representing times. Many implementations define both of these to be `long int` or `unsigned long int`. (The only other likely types are `float`, `double`, or `long double`.) Objects of type `clock_t` and `time_t` are expected, and/or returned, by several of the functions declared in `time.h`.

The structure type `tm` contains the individual components of a calendar time. Collectively, they are known as the broken-down time. The following members must be present in the structure, in any order. Other implementation-defined members may also be present.

```
struct   tm {
         int tm_sec;          /* seconds after midnight */
         int tm_min;          /* minutes after the hour */
         int tm_hour;         /* hours since midnight */
         int tm_mday;         /* day of the month */
         int tm_mon;          /* months since January */
         int tm_year;         /* years since 1900 */
         int tm_wday;         /* days since Sunday */
         int tm_yday;         /* days since January 1 */
         int tm_isdst;        /* daylight saving time flag */
};


/*
tm_isdst          >  0 - daylight savings in effect
                  == 0 - daylight savings not in effect
                  <  0 - information not available
*/
```

◆ Time Manipulation Functions ◆

The clock Function

Calling sequence:

```
#include <time.h>

clock_t clock(void);
```

Description: clock determines the amount of processor time used from the beginning of an implementation-defined era.

Comments:

- The era is related to the time at which the program was started running and may be an approximation. The intent here is that clock gives the CPU time from the start of the program to the time clock is called.

- The value returned has type clock_t, whose units are implementation-defined. However, by definition, when this value is divided by CLK_TCK, the result is in seconds. SVID declares that clock returns type long int and that the units of this type are microseconds.

- If the processor time cannot be determined, or if the time cannot be represented in the return type, the value returned is (clock_t)-1. Note that, in theory, this could cause a problem if clock_t is an unsigned type since `(unsigned long)-1` produces the same value as a time that can legitimately be returned from `clock`. However, in practice, it is very unlikely the actual time returned has exactly the same value as `(unsigned long)-1`.

- Some implementations (including SVID) provide a version of `clock` called `times`. This is not defined by ANSI C.

The `difftime` Function

Calling sequence:

```
#include <time.h>

double difftime(time_t time1, time_t time0);
```

Description: `difftime` computes the difference between two calendar times using `time1 - time0`.

Comments:

- The return value indicates the number of seconds separating the two times.

- This function was an ANSI C invention.

The `mktime` Function

Calling sequence:

```
#include <time.h>

time_t mktime(struct tm *timeptr);
```

Description: `mktime` converts a broken-down time, in the structure pointed to by `timeptr`, into a calendar time.

Comments:

- The value returned is the calendar time resulting from the conversion. If this time cannot be represented, the value returned is `(time_t)-1`.

- All the members required to be in the `tm` structure (except `tm_wday` and `tm_yday`) must be initialized. When `mktime` completes successfully, these two members have been filled in.

- This function was an ANSI C invention and is not defined by SVID.

The time Function

Calling sequence:

```
#include <time.h>

time_t time(time_t *timer);
```

Description: time determines the current calendar time.

Comments:

- The encoding of the type time_t is unspecified.

- The returned value is an approximation of the current calendar time. If this time is not available, (time_t)-1 is returned. If timer is not NULL, the return value is also assigned to object pointed to by timer.

- SVID declares time to return a long int, which represents the number of seconds since 00:00:00 GMT, January 1, 1970. It also declares the argument as having type long int.

◆ Time Conversion Functions ◆

All these functions (except strftime) return values in one of two static objects. When any of these functions is executed, they may overwrite these objects.

The asctime Function

Calling sequence:

```
#include <time.h>

char *asctime(const struct tm *timeptr);
```

Description: asctime converts the broken-down time stored in the structure pointed to by timeptr into a string.

Comments:

- The pointer returned points to a string containing the time in the form Day Mon dd hh:mm:ss yyyy\n\0.

- This function is not affected by changes in locale. For locale-specific times use strftime.

The ctime Function

Calling sequence:

```
#include <time.h>

char *ctime(const time_t *timer);
```

Description: ctime converts the calendar time pointed to by timer to a local time in the form of a string.

Comments:

- A call to ctime is equivalent to asctime(localtime(timer)), so the return value points to a string of the form identical to that returned by asctime.

  SVID declares ctime as having a long int argument, which represents the number of seconds since 00:00:00 GMT, January 1, 1970.

The gmtime Function

Calling sequence:

```
#include <time.h>

struct tm *gmtime(const time_t *timer);
```

Description: gmtime converts the calendar time pointed to by timer into a broken-down time, expressed as Greenwich Mean Time (GMT).

Comments:

- Nowadays, GMT is called Universal Time Coordinated (UTC).

- The value returned is a pointer to the converted object or NULL if GMT is not available.

- SVID declares the argument of gmtime to be of type long int.

The localtime Function

Calling sequence:

```
#include <time.h>

struct tm *localtime(const time_t *timer);
```

Description: localtime converts the calendar time pointed to by timer into a broken-down time, expressed as local time.

Comments:

- The value returned points to the broken-down time object.

- SVID declares the argument of localtime to be of type long int.

The **strftime** Function

Calling sequence:

```
#include <time.h>

size_t strftime(char *s, size_t maxsize, const char *format,
                const struct tm *timeptr);
```

Description: strftime constructs a date and time string by putting characters into the array pointed to by s according to the controlling format specified by format.

Comments:

- This is an ANSI C invention that provides a locale-specific way of generating date and time strings. Refer to the ANSI C Standard for specific details of the controlling format edit masks.

◆ **Miscellaneous Functions** ◆

The **tzset** Function

Calling sequence:

```
#include <time.h>

/* The following are declared
in the SVID version of time.h */

extern long timezone;
extern int daylight;
extern char *tzname[];

void tzset(void);
```

Description: `tzset` initializes the external variables `timezone` and `daylight` according to the contents of the environment variable `TZ`.

Comments:

- `tzset`, `timezone`, and `daylight` are defined by SVID but are not part of ANSI C.

- `tzset` is called by `asctime`, and it may also be called directly by the programmer.

- If the environment variable `TZ` is defined, it is used to override the default time zone used by `asctime`. The format of this variable is `AAA[-]99[BBB]`, where `[]` identify optional parts. `AAA` represents a three-letter time zone name (such as PST for Pacific Standard Time); `BBB` is a daylight savings time zone; and `99` is the difference, in hours, between local time and GMT, a negative value indicating the zone is east of Greenwich.

- `tzname` is an array of two pointers to strings, each of which points to the strings `AAA` and `BBB` above. For example, in the Pacific Standard Time zone, `tzname[0] = "PST"` and `tzname[1] = "PDT"`.

P A R T

4

Appendices

A

Keywords and Reserved Identifiers

Most of the information in this appendix is taken from the proposed ANSI Standard draft, dated May 1988. While most of the headers will likely remain the same in the final Standard, they are subject to change. New headers and/or identifiers may be added (and, therefore, will become reserved), and identifiers may be removed or have their names changed. Note that the identifier lists include macro, function, `typedef`, and structure tag names.

Refered to the official ANSI C Standard documents for a precise definition of the standard header contents.

◆ C Keywords ◆

The following tokens are defined as keywords by ANSI C: `auto`, `break`, `case`, `char`, `const`, `continue`, `default`, `do`, `double`, `else`, `entry`, `enum`, `extern`, `float`, `for`, `goto`, `if`, `int`, `long`, `register`, `return`, `short`, `signed`, `sizeof`, `static`, `struct`, `switch`, `typedef`, `union`, `unsigned`, `void`, `volatile`, and `while`.

◆ C++ Keywords ◆

The following tokens are defined as keywords in the C++ language but not by ANSI C: `asm`, `class`, `delete`, `friend`, `inline`, `new`, `operator`, `overload`, `public`, `this`, and `virtual`. Avoid using these identifiers if you intend to move C programs to a C++ environment.

C++ implementations provide a header called stream.h, which defines and declares numerous identifiers. These identifiers are included in the alphabetical list at the end of this chapter. Note that at this writing the published definition of C++ (see Appendix B) is not a strict superset of ANSI C so problems may be encountered when porting ANSI-conforming C code to C++. For example, in C++, structure, union, and enumeration tags share the same name space as ordinary identifiers.

◆ The ANSI Standard Headers ◆

The proposed Standard headers and their purposes follow.

Header	Purpose
assert.h	Program diagnostic purposes
ctype.h	Character testing & conversion
errno.h	Various error checking facilities
float.h	Floating type characteristics
limits.h	Integral type sizes
locale.h	Internationalization support
math.h	Math functions
setjmp.h	Nonlocal jump facility
signal.h	Signal handling
stdarg.h	Variable argument support
stddef.h	Miscellaneous
stdio.h	Input/output functions
stdlib.h	General utilities
string.h	String functions
time.h	Date and time functions

◆ Identifiers Alphabetically by Header ◆

The following list contains the identifiers in alphabetical order within header. (Those in <math.h> marked with a † are not required to be present in an ANSI-conforming implementation. They have a suffix of f or l and represent float and long double versions, respectively, of the math library. If an implementation chooses to provide functions with this capability, they must use the names as shown.)

Header	Identifier		
`<assert.h>`	`assert`		
`<ctype.h>`	`isalnum`	`islower`	`isxdigit`
	`isalpha`	`isprint`	`tolower`
	`iscntrl`	`ispunct`	`toupper`
	`isdigit`	`isspace`	
	`isgraph`	`isupper`	
`<errno.h>`	`EDOM`	`ERANGE`	`errno`
`<float.h>`	`DBL_DIG`	`FLT_EPSILON`	`LDBL_DIG`
	`DBL_EPSILON`	`FLT_MANT_DIG`	`LDBL_EPSILON`
	`DBL_MANT_DIG`	`FLT_MAX`	`LDBL_MANT_DIG`
	`DBL_MAX`	`FLT_MAX_10_EXP`	`LDBL_MAX`
	`DBL_MAX_10_EXP`	`FLT_MAX_EXP`	`LDBL_MAX_10_EXP`
	`DBL_MAX_EXP`	`FLT_MIN`	`LDBL_MAX_EXP`
	`DBL_MIN`	`FLT_MIN_10_EXP`	`LDBL_MIN`
	`DBL_MIN_10_EXP`	`FLT_MIN_EXP`	`LDBL_MIN_10_EXP`
	`DBL_MIN_EXP`	`FLT_RADIX`	`LDBL_MIN_EXP`
	`FLT_DIG`	`FLT_ROUNDS`	
`<limits.h>`	`CHAR_BIT`	`LONG_MIN`	`UCHAR_MAX`
	`CHAR_MAX`	`MB_LEN_MAX`	`UINT_MAX`
	`CHAR_MIN`	`SCHAR_MAX`	`ULONG_MAX`
	`INT_MAX`	`SCHAR_MIN`	`USHRT_MAX`
	`INT_MIN`	`SHRT_MAX`	
	`LONG_MAX`	`SHRT_MIN`	
`<locale.h>`	`lconv`	`LC_MONETARY`	`NULL`
	`LC_ALL`	`LC_NUMERIC`	`setlocale`
	`LC_COLLATE`	`LC_TIME`	
	`LC_CTYPE`	`localeconv`	
`<math.h>`	`acos`	`ceill`[†]	`floorf`[†]
	`acosf`[†]	`cos`	`floorl`[†]
	`acosl`[†]	`cosf`[†]	`fmod`
	`asin`	`cosh`	`fmodf`[†]
	`asinf`[†]	`coshf`[†]	`fmodl`[†]
	`asinl`[†]	`coshl`[†]	`frexp`
	`atan`	`cosl`[†]	`frexpf`[†]
	`atan2`	`exp`	`frexpl`[†]
	`atan2f`[†]	`expf`[†]	`HUGE_VAL`
	`atan2l`[†]	`expl`[†]	`ldexp`
	`atanf`[†]	`fabs`	`ldexpf`[†]
	`atanl`[†]	`fabsf`[†]	`ldexpl`[†]
	`ceil`	`fabsl`[†]	`log`
	`ceilf`[†]	`floor`	`log10`

Header	*Identifier*		
`<math.h>` (cont'd)	log10f[†]	powl[†]	sqrtl[†]
	log10l[†]	sin	tan
	logf[†]	sinf[†]	tanf[†]
	logl[†]	sinh	tanh
	modf	sinhf[†]	tanhf[†]
	modff[†]	sinhl[†]	tanhl[†]
	modfl[†]	sinl[†]	tanl[†]
	pow	sqrt	
	powf[†]	sqrtf[†]	
`<setjmp.h>`	jmp_buf	longjmp	setjmp
`<signal.h>`	raise	SIGINT	sig_atomic_t
	SIGABRT	signal	SIG_DFL
	SIGFPE	SIGSEGV	SIG_ERR
	SIGILL	SIGTERM	SIG_IGN
`<stdarg.h>`	va_arg	va_list	
	va_end	va_start	
`<stddef.h>`	NULL	ptrdiff_t	wchar_t
	offsetof	size_t	
`<stdio.h>`	_IOFBF	fputs	rewind
	_IOLBF	fread	scanf
	_IONBF	freopen	SEEK_CUR
	BUFSIZ	fscanf	SEEK_END
	clearerr	fseek	SEEK_SET
	EOF	fsetpos	setbuf
	fclose	ftell	setvbuf
	feof	fwrite	size_t
	ferror	getc	sprintf
	fflush	getchar	sscanf
	fgetc	gets	stderr
	fgetpos	L_tmpnam	stdin
	fgets	NULL	stdout
	FILE	perror	tmpfile
	FILENAME_MAX	printf	tmpnam
	fopen	putc	TMP_MAX
	FOPEN_MAX	putchar	ungetc
	fpos_t	puts	vfprintf
	fprintf	remove	vprintf
	fputc	rename	vsprintf
`<stdlib.h>`	abort	atof	bsearch
	abs	atoi	calloc
	atexit	atol	div

Header	Identifier		
`<stdlib.h>`	`div_t`	`MB_CUR_MAX`	`srand`
(cont'd)	`exit`	`mblen`	`strtod`
	`EXIT_FAILURE`	`mbstowcs`	`strtol`
	`EXIT_SUCCESS`	`mbtowc`	`strtoul`
	`free`	`NULL`	`system`
	`getenv`	`qsort`	`wchar_t`
	`labs`	`rand`	`wcstombs`
	`ldiv`	`RAND_MAX`	`wctomb`
	`ldiv_t`	`realloc`	
	`malloc`	`size_t`	
`<string.h>`	`memchr`	`strchr`	`strncmp`
	`memcmp`	`strcmp`	`strncpy`
	`memcpy`	`strcoll`	`strpbrk`
	`memmove`	`strcpy`	`strrchr`
	`memset`	`strcspn`	`strspn`
	`NULL`	`strerror`	`strstr`
	`size_t`	`strlen`	`strtok`
	`strcat`	`strncat`	`strxfrm`
`<time.h>`	`asctime`	`difftime`	`size_t`
	`CLK_TCK`	`gmtime`	`strftime`
	`clock`	`localtime`	`time`
	`clock_t`	`mktime`	`time_t`
	`ctime`	`NULL`	`tm`
Predefined macros	`__DATE__`	`__LINE__`	`__TIME__`
	`__FILE__`	`__STDC__`	

◆ Identifiers in Alphabetical Order ◆

The following list contains all identifiers in alphabetical order. This list may be used as the basis for a project's reserved identifier list. (Those in `<math.h>` marked with a † are not required to be present in an ANSI-conforming implementation. They have a suffix of `f` or `l` and represent `float` and `long double` versions, respectively, of the math library. If an implementation chooses to provide functions with this capability, they must use the names as shown.)

Identifier	Header	Identifier	Header
abort	<stdlib.h>	cos	<math.h>
abs	<stdlib.h>	cosf†	<math.h>
acos	<math.h>	cosl†	<math.h>
acosf†	<math.h>	cosh	<math.h>
acosl†	<math.h>	coshf†	<math.h>
asctime	<time.h>	coshl†	<math.h>
asin	<math.h>	cout	C++ identifier
asinf†	<math.h>	ctime	<time.h>
asinl†	<math.h>	__DATE__	Predefined macro
asm	C++ keyword	DBL_DIG	<float.h>
assert	<assert.h>	DBL_EPSILON	<float.h>
atan	<math.h>	DBL_MANT_DIG	<float.h>
atanf†	<math.h>	DBL_MAX	<float.h>
atanl†	<math.h>	DBL_MAX_10_EXP	<float.h>
atan2	<math.h>	DBL_MAX_EXP	<float.h>
atan2f†	<math.h>	DBL_MIN	<float.h>
atan2l†	<math.h>	DBL_MIN_10_EXP	<float.h>
atexit	<stdlib.h>	DBL_MIN_EXP	<float.h>
atof	<stdlib.h>	declare	C++ identifier
atoi	<stdlib.h>	default	C keyword
atol	<stdlib.h>	delete	C++ keyword
auto	C keyword	difftime	<time.h>
break	C keyword	div	<stdlib.h>
bsearch	<stdlib.h>	div_t	<stdlib.h>
BUFSIZ	<stdio.h>	do	C keyword
calloc	<stdlib.h>	double	C keyword
case	C keyword	EDOM	<errno.h>
ceil	<math.h>	else	C keyword
ceilf†	<math.h>	entry	C keyword
ceill†	<math.h>	enum	C keyword
cerr	C++ identifier	EOF	<stdio.h>
char	C keyword	ERANGE	<errno.h>
CHAR_BIT	<limits.h>	errno	<errno.h>
CHAR_MAX	<limits.h>	exit	<stdlib.h>
CHAR_MIN	<limits.h>	EXIT_FAILURE	<stdlib.h>
chr	C++ identifier	EXIT_SUCCESS	<stdlib.h>
cin	C++ identifier	exp	<math.h>
class	C++ keyword	expf†	<math.h>
clearerr	<stdio.h>	expl†	<math.h>
CLK_TCK	<time.h>	extern	C keyword
clock	<time.h>	fabs	<math.h>
clock_t	<time.h>	fabsf†	<math.h>
const	C keyword	fabsl†	<math.h>
continue	C keyword	fclose	<stdio.h>

Identifier	Header	Identifier	Header
feof	<stdio.h>	fscanf	<stdio.h>
ferror	<stdio.h>	fseek	<stdio.h>
fflush	<stdio.h>	fsetpos	<stdio.h>
fgetc	<stdio.h>	ftell	<stdio.h>
fgetpos	<stdio.h>	fwrite	<stdio.h>
fgets	<stdio.h>	getc	<stdio.h>
FILE	<stdio.h>	getchar	<stdio.h>
filebuf	C++ identifier	getenv	<stdlib.h>
__FILE__	Predefined macro	gets	<stdio.h>
FILENAME_MAX	<stdio.h>	gmtime	<time.h>
float	C keyword	goto	C keyword
floor	<math.h>	hex	C++ identifier
floorf[†]	<math.h>	HUGE_VAL	<math.h>
floorl[†]	<math.h>	implement	C++ identifier
FLT_DIG	<float.h>	INT_MAX	<limits.h>
FLT_EPSILON	<float.h>	INT_MIN	<limits.h>
FLT_MANT_DIG	<float.h>	if	C keyword
FLT_MAX	<float.h>	inline	C++ keyword
FLT_MAX_10_EXP	<float.h>	int	C keyword
FLT_MAX_EXP	<float.h>	_IOFBF	<stdio.h>
FLT_MIN	<float.h>	_IOLBF	<stdio.h>
FLT_MIN_10_EXP	<float.h>	_IONBF	<stdio.h>
FLT_MIN_EXP	<float.h>	isalnum	<ctype.h>
FLT_RADIX	<float.h>	isalpha	<ctype.h>
FLT_ROUNDS	<float.h>	iscntrl	<ctype.h>
fmod	<math.h>	isdigit	<ctype.h>
fmodf[†]	<math.h>	isgraph	<ctype.h>
fmodl[†]	<math.h>	islower	<ctype.h>
fopen	<stdio.h>	isprint	<ctype.h>
FOPEN_MAX	<stdio.h>	ispunct	<ctype.h>
for	C keyword	isspace	<ctype.h>
form	C++ identifier	istream	C++ identifier
fortran	Extended keyword	isupper	<ctype.h>
fpos_t	<stdio.h>	isxdigit	<ctype.h>
fprintf	<stdio.h>	jmp_buf	<setjmp.h>
fputc	<stdio.h>	labs	<stdlib.h>
fputs	<stdio.h>	lconv	<locale.h>
fread	<stdio.h>	LC_ALL	<locale.h>
free	<stdlib.h>	LC_COLLATE	<locale.h>
freopen	<stdio.h>	LC_CTYPE	<locale.h>
frexp	<math.h>	LC_MONETARY	<locale.h>
frexpf[†]	<math.h>	LC_NUMERIC	<locale.h>
frexpl[†]	<math.h>	LC_TIME	<locale.h>
friend	C++ keyword	LDBL_DIG	<float.h>

Identifier	Header	Identifier	Header
LDBL_EPSILON	<float.h>	NULL	<locale.h>
LDBL_MANT_DIG	<float.h>	NULL	<stddef.h>
LDBL_MAX	<float.h>	NULL	<stdio.h>
LDBL_MAX_10_EXP	<float.h>	NULL	<stdlib.h>
LDBL_MAX_EXP	<float.h>	NULL	<string.h>
LDBL_MIN	<float.h>	NULL	<time.h>
LDBL_MIN_10_EXP	<float.h>	oct	C++ identifier
LDBL_MIN_EXP	<float.h>	offsetof	<stddef.h>
ldexp†	<math.h>	operator	C++ keyword
ldexpf†	<math.h>	ostream	C++ identifier
ldexpl†	<math.h>	overload	C++ keyword
ldiv	<stdlib.h>	perror	<stdio.h>
ldiv_t	<stdlib.h>	pow	<math.h>
__LINE__	Predefined macro	powf†	<math.h>
localeconv	<locale.h>	powl†	<math.h>
localtime	<time.h>	printf	<stdio.h>
log	<math.h>	ptrdiff_t	<stddef.h>
logf†	<math.h>	public	C++ keyword
logl†	<math.h>	putc	<stdio.h>
log10	<math.h>	putchar	<stdio.h>
log10f†	<math.h>	puts	<stdio.h>
log10l†	<math.h>	qsort	<stdlib.h>
long	C keyword	raise	<signal.h>
longjmp	<setjmp.h>	rand	<stdlib.h>
LONG_MAX	<limits.h>	RAND_MAX	<stdlib.h>
LONG_MIN	<limits.h>	realloc	<stdlib.h>
L_tmpnam	<stdio.h>	register	C keyword
malloc	<stdlib.h>	remove	<stdio.h>
MB_CUR_MAX	<stdlib.h>	rename	<stdio.h>
MB_LEN_MAX	<limits.h>	return	C keyword
mblen	<stdlib.h>	rewind	<stdio.h>
mbstowcs	<stdlib.h>	scanf	<stdio.h>
mbtowc	<stdlib.h>	SCHAR_MAX	<limits.h>
memchr	<string.h>	SCHAR_MIN	<limits.h>
memcmp	<string.h>	SEEK_CUR	<stdio.h>
memcpy	<string.h>	SEEK_END	<stdio.h>
memmove	<string.h>	SEEK_SET	<stdio.h>
memset	<string.h>	setbuf	<stdio.h>
mktime	<time.h>	setjmp	<setjmp.h>
modf	<math.h>	setlocale	<locale.h>
modff†	<math.h>	setvbuf	<stdio.h>
modfl†	<math.h>	short	C keyword
name2	C++ identifier	SHRT_MAX	<limits.h>
new	C++ keyword	SHRT_MIN	<limits.h>

Identifier	Header	Identifier	Header
SIGABRT	<signal.h>	strftime	<time.h>
SIGFPE	<signal.h>	strlen	<string.h>
SIGILL	<signal.h>	strncat	<string.h>
SIGINT	<signal.h>	strncmp	<string.h>
signal	<signal.h>	strncpy	<string.h>
signed	C keyword	strpbrk	<string.h>
SIGSEGV	<signal.h>	strrchr	<string.h>
SIGTERM	<signal.h>	strspn	<string.h>
sig_atomic_t	<signal.h>	strstr	<string.h>
SIG_DFL	<signal.h>	strtod	<stdlib.h>
SIG_ERR	<signal.h>	strtok	<string.h>
SIG_IGN	<signal.h>	strtol	<stdlib.h>
sin	<math.h>	strtoul	<stdlib.h>
sinf†	<math.h>	struct	C keyword
sinl†	<math.h>	strxfrm	<string.h>
sinh	<math.h>	switch	C keyword
sinhf†	<math.h>	system	<stdlib.h>
sinhl†	<math.h>	tan	<math.h>
size_t	<stddef.h>	tanf†	<math.h>
size_t	<stdio.h>	tanl†	<math.h>
size_t	<stdlib.h>	tanh	<math.h>
size_t	<string.h>	tanhf†	<math.h>
size_t	<time.h>	tanhl†	<math.h>
sizeof	C keyword	this	C++ keyword
sprintf	<stdio.h>	time	<time.h>
sqrt	<math.h>	__TIME__	Predefined macro
sqrtf†	<math.h>	time_t	<time.h>
sqrtl†	<math.h>	tm	<time.h>
srand	<stdlib.h>	tmpfile	<stdio.h>
sscanf	<stdio.h>	tmpnam	<stdio.h>
__STDC__	Predefined macro	TMP_MAX	<stdio.h>
static	C keyword	tolower	<ctype.h>
stderr	<stdio.h>	toupper	<ctype.h>
stdin	<stdio.h>	typedef	C keyword
stdout	<stdio.h>	UCHAR_MAX	<limits.h>
str	C++ identifier	UINT_MAX	<limits.h>
strcat	<string.h>	ULONG_MAX	<limits.h>
strchr	<string.h>	ungetc	<stdio.h>
strcmp	<string.h>	union	C keyword
strcoll	<string.h>	unsigned	C keyword
strcpy	<string.h>	USHRT_MAX	<limits.h>
strcspn	<string.h>	va_arg	<stdarg.h>
streambuf	C++ identifier	va_end	<stdarg.h>
strerror	<string.h>	va_list	<stdarg.h>

Identifier	Header	Identifier	Header
va_start	<stdarg.h>	vsprintf	<stdio.h>
vfprintf	<stdio.h>	wchar_t	<stddef.h>
virtual	C++ keyword	wchar_t	<stdlib.h>
void	C keyword	wcstombs	<stdlib.h>
volatile	C keyword	wctomb	<stdlib.h>
vprintf	<stdio.h>	while	C keyword

◆ Identifiers Reserved for Future Use ◆

The following families of identifiers are reserved for future use by standards-making bodies such as ANSI and ISO. In the table, $ represents an upper-case letter optionally followed by any combination of letters, digits, and underscores. # represents a lower-case letter optionally followed by any combination of letters, digits, and underscores. % represents an upper-case letter or digit optionally followed by any combination of letters, digits, and underscores.

Name	Purpose
E%	errno.h macros
is#	ctype.h macros and functions
LC_$	locale.h macros
mem#	string.h macros and functions
SIG$	signal.h macros
SIG_$	signal.h macros
str#	string.h and stdlib.h macros and functions
to#	ctype.h macros and functions
wcs#	string.h macros and functions

As indicated in the previous sections, the function names in the Standard math library together with a suffix of f or l are reserved for implementations that wish to provide float and/or long double versions as well as double.

All external identifiers that begin with an underscore are reserved. All other identifiers that begin with an underscore followed by another underscore or an upper-case letter are reserved. This name space is reserved for implementers so they may add macros and library functions to the Standard headers. Users should not use such names except to map into those provided by the implementer.

B

Recommended Reading and References

The following books and documents should prove useful in any C language port project.

- *American National Standard X3.159-198x, Programming Language C*, ANSI X3J11 Committee.

  This two-volume document comprises the ANSI C Language Standard and Rationale. It is the first formal and official definition of the C language, its preprocessor, and run-time library. It is expected that the final version of the Standard will be completed in late 1988. A copy of the Standard is available from Global Engineering Documents, Inc., in Santa Ana, California. Telephone (800) 854-7179 or (714) 540-9870, telex 692373 callback globaldoc sna. Price US $65 (US $84.50 for international orders), prepaid.

- *POSIX Standard P1003.1 – Portable Operating System Interface for Computer Environments*, Institute of Electrical and Electronics Engineers, Inc. (IEEE), New York.

  This Standard defines an operating system interface and environment based on the UNIX operating system. It is designed to support applications portability at the source level. While X3J11 ANSI C has responsibility for operating system-independent library routines, POSIX has adopted the UNIX-specific routines from the *de facto* Standard C library provided by AT&T.

- *System V Interface Definition* (SVID), AT&T, 1986. ISBN 0-932764-10-X.

  This three-volume set defines the interface mechanisms for the UNIX System V operating system. Both operating system-specific and general-purpose library routines are defined, many of which are included (possibly in a modified or expanded form) as part of either the IEEE POSIX or the ANSI C X3J11 standards.

- *The X/OPEN Portability Guide*, Elsevier Science Publishers. ISBN 0-444-70179-6. (The Guide is a five-volume set.)

X/OPEN is a consortium of computer vendors that is defining a common software interface for operating systems, languages, and access methods. Originally comprising European vendors such as Bull, ICL, Nixdorf, Philips, and Siemens, it now includes major U.S. vendors such as DEC, Hewlett-Packard, and Unisys. This standard, for the most part, is based on existing and emerging standards, such as those from ANSI C and IEEE POSIX.

- *Quick Reference Guide to Standard C*, by Plauger, P.J., and Brodie, Jim, Microsoft Press, 1988.

At the time of writing, this book was in the final stages of publication. However, this author was a technical reviewer of the mansucript and believes it will be one of the very best distillations of the ANSI C Standard. This is especially so since Plauger not only served as the Standard committee's Secretary, he was instrumental in crafting much of the new terminology. Brodie served as the Committee's Chair.

- *The C Programming Language*, by Kernighan, Brian W., and Ritchie, Dennis M., Prentice-Hall, Inc., 1978. ISBN 0-13-110163-3.

This classic text, affectionately referred to as K&R, was the definitive C reference when it was published in 1978. Since then, Appendix A has formed the basis for the grammar handled by the vast majority of C language translators. However, the language definition was incomplete, and the book contains little information regarding the C library. In April 1988, the second edition was released. This version is essentially the same book as the earlier one, with the new language and preprocessor capabilities retrofitted. In particular, function prototypes are used throughout. A summary of almost the complete library is included.

- *A C Reference Manual*, second edition, by Harbison, Samuel P., and Steele, Guy L., Prentice-Hall, Inc., 1987. ISBN 0-13-109810-1. ISBN 0-13-109802-0 (pbk.)

Although the first edition was an excellent book, the second edition added a considerable amount of information about the ANSI C Standard as well as common language extensions. It also contains one of the few complete treatments of the run-time library. Harbison is a respected member of the ANSI C Committee.

- *Notes on the Draft C Standard*, Plum, Thomas, Plum Hall, Inc., 1987. ISBN 0-911537-06-6.

  This 90-page booklet contains an overview of the differences between ANSI C and K&R C. Presumably, it is a forerunner to a full-length ANSI C text once the Standard is completed.

- *Portable C and UNIX System Programming*, by Lapin, J E., Rabbit Software. Prentice-Hall, Inc., 1987. ISBN 0-13-686494-5.

  This book is aimed specifically at those porting code between UNIX and its derivative systems. It describes a port philosophy, briefly covers C language issues, and concentrates on the operating system and library issues.

- C *Programming Guidelines*, by Plum, Thomas., Plum Hall, Inc., 1984. ISBN 0-911537-03-1.

  Programming style is most important when writing code that is to be ported and Tom Plum is one of the masters in this area. He is also the Vice-Chair of the ANSI C Standards Committee.

- *Efficient C*, by Plum, Thomas., and Brodie, Jim. Plum Hall, Inc., 1985. ISBN 0-911537-05-8.

  There is little point having code that is portable yet fails to perform in a time- and space-efficient manner on any of the target environments. This text provides considerable insight into defining and measuring efficiency. Brodie and Plum are the Chair and Vice-Chair, respectively, of the ANSI C Standards Committee. All of the source code in the book is available on DOS diskettes and is in the public domain.

- *Reliable Data Structures in C*, Plum, Thomas., Plum Hall, Inc., 1985. ISBN 0-911537-04-X.

  Plum discusses approaches to coding in a reliable manner. All the source code in the book is available on DOS diskettes and is in the public domain.

- *C Standard Library*, by Purdum, Jack, and Leslie, Timothy C., Que, 1987. ISBN 0-88022-279-4.

  This book contains a thorough definition and tutorial on almost all the library routines defined by ANSI C. It also contains discussion of numerous SVID-specific routines and indicates whether or not a particular routine is supported by ANSI C and SVID.

- *Advanced C Programming for Displays*, by Rochkind, Marc J., Prentice-Hall, Inc., 1988. ISBN 0-13-010240-7.

This book is a great aid to those writing programs that are to interact with character displays and keyboards on various UNIX and DOS systems.

- *The C Journal*, Winter 1986. Edited by Rex Jaeschke, the issue's theme was Portability.

  Specific articles include: *The Economics of Portability* by P.J. Plauger; *Portability Case Study* by Matt Bishop; *Porting (Lattice) C to the IBM 370* by Oliver Bradley; *A VAX-11 to M68000 Port* by Howard Modell; and *Portability and I/O* by Ken Pugh. *The C Journal* is now called *The C User's Journal* and is published by The C User's Group, PO Box 97, McPherson, Kansas 67460, USA. (316) 241-1065.

- *Micro/Systems Journal*, July/August 1987, *volume 3, number 4.* The column *C Forum* by Don Libes, was entitled *Byte Ordering*.

  This column discusses the possible problems encountered when communicating between systems on which the byte ordering differs. The terms *big-endian* and *little-endian* are defined and C source is provided for several conversion routines.

- *Computer Language* April 1987, *volume 4, number 4* ran a column by P.J. Plauger called *Programming on Purpose*.

  One of the topics in this column is called *The NUXI Problem* and numerous issues about byte ordering are addressed.

- *The C++ Programming Language*, by Stroustrup, Bjarne, Addison-Wesley, 1986. ISBN 0-201-12078-X.

  This definitive reference on C++ was written by that language's author. It is to C++ what K&R was (originally) to C. This book is useful should you consider moving from C to C++. Note though that C++ is evolving, and other documents have been written about its evolution. One possible source of more recent information is the *Bell Laboratories Technical Journal*.

C

Portability Software Suite

In researching and writing this book, I found myself writing lots of small experimental programs and compiling and running them on numerous compilers on several different systems. And as with many "real world" projects, we recognize the need for a more disciplined approach only after we've been working in an *ad hoc* manner for some time. It's a bit like deciding to use headers after you've been hard-coding function declarations in your source for three months.

In any case, I began methodically developing a suite of test programs that would exercise a C compiler to detect areas where the compiler differed from K&R and/or ANSI C. While the suite does test various aspects of ANSI C support, it is not intended to be an ANSI validation test suite. Rather, some source files are designed such that they may legitimately fail to compile, while others should compile and run, and demonstrate implementation-defined behavior.

♦ Test Examples ♦

The following examples give some indication to the kinds of checking done by the suite. I am continually adding to, and refining, the suite so the examples shown here may vary slightly in the final suite.

```
/***************************************************

Portability Test Suite V1.0

The C Preprocessor - Checking Phases of translation.

***************************************************/
```

```
/*
Check phases of translation - under ANSI C rules
you should get a syntax error since the /* in DBG
definition is the start of a comment that doesn't end
until the end of the printf call line, in which case,
the closing brace is left dangling, giving a syntax
error.  If this is not the case, DBG may well be set
to the token /*, which either comments out the printf
call or leaves it in - either way, no error is
produced.
*/


#undef DEBUG
#ifdef DEBUG
#define DBG
#else
#define DBG /\
*
#endif

f()
{
DBG          printf("test\n");          /*...*/
}


/*--------------------------------------------------*/

/*
See if directive names can be redefined (forbidden by
ANSI C)
*/

#define DEF define
#DEF N 100

#define INC include
#INC <stdio.h>

/*--------------------------------------------------*/

/*************************************************

Portability Test Suite V1.0.

The C Preprocessor - checkout the #undef directive

*************************************************/
```

```
#undef TEST                        /* OK */

#define MAX 10
#undef MAX
#define MAX 100


/*
The following five macros are predefined in ANSI C and
CANNOT be #undefed. Of course, if these names are not
predefined in your compiler, they can legitimately be
#undefed. If these directives work, AND you are
compiling in "standard" mode, the compiler is
deficient.


Note that while ANSI C requires __STDC__ to be 1, a
nonconforming implementation is permitted to either
predefine it with some other value or not to predefine
it at all.
*/


#undef __DATE__
#undef __TIME__
#undef __FILE__
#undef __LINE__
#undef __STDC__

/*------------------------------------------------*/


/**************************************************

Portability Test Suite V1.0

The C Library - checkout stdarg.h

**************************************************/


/* ANSI C requires va_start, va_arg, and va_end to be
macros. Also, va_list should be a typedefed type.
*/


#include <stdarg.h>
```

```
void xstdarg(int parmn, ...)
{
        va_list ap;
        int i;

        va_start(ap, parmn);
        i = va_arg(ap, int);
        va_end(ap);
}


#undef va_list
#undef va_start
#undef va_arg
#undef va_end

void ystdarg(int parmn, ...)
{
        va_list ap;
        int i;

        va_start(ap, parmn);
        i = va_arg(ap, int);
        va_end(ap);
}
```

◆ Further Information ◆

The portability suite will be available in various media formats, and, of course, all source code will be included. It is anticipated that other tools found useful in porting will be added to the distribution kit as will a file containing all of the reserved identifiers listed in Appendix A.

For further information on pricing and media availability, mail in the tear-out card enclosed in this book or call or write the following address:

Portability Software Suite
Rex Jaeschke
2051 Swans Neck Way
Reston, VA 22091
U.S.A.
(703) 860-0091

Index